GENIUS DESSERTS

FOOD52

GENIUS
DESSERTS

100 RECIPES THAT WILL CHANGE
THE WAY YOU BAKE

KRISTEN MIGLORE

PHOTOGRAPHY BY JAMES RANSOM

TEN SPEED PRESS
California | New York

Contents

FOREWORD

Genius Desserts is—let's be clear—the book that every person needs. When you're not a baker, but you need *the* birthday cake. When you've tried every chocolate mousse but haven't found one that sticks. When you're short on time and want your efforts in the kitchen to count. We knew Kristen was the one to create the ultimate desserts resource.

We've been working with Kristen for more than eight years, since the beginning of Food52. One of the things we bonded over in those early days was our appreciation for desserts, especially unassuming yet wonderful ones like cream cheese cookies, lemon sponge cups (lemon, milk, eggs, flour, and sugar baked in a cup, basically), and *pouding chômeur*, a sticky toffee pudding made with Canada's go-to maple syrup.

Kristen considered marshmallows and sweetened condensed milk as staples that should live alongside buckwheat flour and cacao nibs—a detail that showed her values, her lack of pretension, her ability to discern greatness in a sea of good. It has been no surprise to us that her column, Genius Recipes, became a hit and that the book that followed was a *New York Times* best seller. Kristen knows how to root out the best, most memorable recipes and to captivate us with her take on what qualifies a recipe as a standout genius.

We've suffered through her meticulous testing and vetting process. As baking sheets and pie plates filled with sweets were paraded through our office over the past year, we gritted our teeth and dutifully tasted and assessed as many as possible. There were mountains of ice cream and armies of cookies. It is not easy to impress Kristen or for her to get comfortable calling something a genius recipe. We've decided that the best cookbook writers (many of whose recipes are celebrated in this book) possess a mix of intense curiosity and perpetual dissatisfaction. Kristen has another advantage—she's funny and sly, willing to challenge your predispositions.

Only Kristen would include Rose Levy Beranbaum's All-Occasion Downy Yellow Butter Cake with Neoclassic Buttercream (page 118) and J. Kenji López-Alt's Ten-Minute Lime Cracker Pie (page 159) in the same book. Her world of sweets is a meritocracy.

From the canon of the justifiably famous, Kristen has made some carefully considered selections—including Nancy Silverton and Dahlia Narvaez's iconic Butterscotch Budino (page 160), Maida Heatter's freshly tart East 62nd Street Lemon Cake (page 89), and David Leibovitz's silken Chocolate Sorbet (page 175). You'll also find Pierre Hermé and Dorie Greenspan's World Peace Cookies (page 18), which Kristen first introduced us to several years ago. The recipe yields a deeply refined, crumbly mouthful of chocolate and, as we've learned firsthand, they keep beautifully in the freezer in log form for unexpected VIP guests. For every legendary dessert, Kristen has ferreted out an equally appealing upstart like Parsnip Cake with Blood Orange Buttercream (page 132), Thin & Crispy Black Sesame Oatmeal Cookies (page 50), Fried Stuffed Dates (page 257), and Charlotte Druckman's Cacio e Pepe Shortbread (page 54), a sweet-savory hybrid baked in a cast iron skillet that defies expectations and keeps you murmuring contentedly well into your third and fourth wedge.

Perhaps most importantly, Kristen deeply understands the human needs to aspire and to relate—we are happiest when these qualities coexist. Which is why you, too, will feel like a genius with recipes like Bill Smith's Atlantic Beach Pie (with its saltine cracker crust, page 199) and the three-ingredient Coconut Fudge (page 70) and Weird & Wonderful Banana Cake (page 98) at your side.

—Amanda Hesser & Merrill Stubbs,
  cofounders of Food52

INTRODUCTION

The Genius Recipes column on Food52 started in June 2011 as a weekly showcase of recipes from legendary cookbook authors and chefs that we claimed—boldly! shamelessly!—would change the way you cook. You'd never truss another chicken, or simmer tomato sauce for hours, or feel intimidated by baking bread or making piecrust again.

And we learned nothing from our hubris, because the recipes indeed took hold and found new life, virtually on their own. The conversations around them grew, with readers exchanging pointers in the comments sections and on social media. Tips for more genius recipes kept pouring in. In 2015, *Genius Recipes* became a cookbook, which then became a *New York Times* best seller. The world of Genius Recipes had become a force unto itself, one of the internet's most generous water coolers. I have been the lucky one who gets to keep showing up and filling the cooler.

Quite naturally, while people will always appreciate a quicker roast chicken or the very best guacamole, what they really go wild for are desserts. If you want to give the people what they want, it's gloriously chewy cookies (page 30), the flakiest-ever piecrust (page 204), and chocolate cakes of all kinds. (We included three, and yes, we needed them all, pages 105, 109, and 127).

So as we started mulling the next Genius cookbook that the world needed, we knew it was the sweet stuff— for the birthday parties, potlucks, bake sales, Friday afternoon meetings, kid-distracting weekends, late-night snacks, and everything in between. Not *too* sweet, of course—our tastes have evolved toward fuller-flavored, less sugary desserts—but we still want them to be just sweet enough. It took all of five minutes to settle on the subject matter, and the title and subtitle took another five. Dreaming up a cookbook should always be this easy!

But the research and testing phases went on a good deal longer—every recipe was made many, many times as we adapted them to fit this book. While close to half of this book is made up of best-loved hits from the column that we couldn't leave out—Maialino's Olive Oil Cake

(page 93), Rose Levy Beranbaum's Chocolate Oblivion Truffle Torte (page 105), and Nigella Lawson's One-Step, No-Churn Coffee Ice Cream (page 172) chief among them—I had a whole lot of help unearthing the remaining gems.

This time around, I asked the Food52 community for their lifelong favorites and reached out to home bakers, food editors, test-kitchen directors, and pastry chefs I thought might have strong opinions on the matter. I've thanked the ones whose recipe tips landed in the book on page 267, but many more generously shared their wisdom and time, enhancing the collection in ways big and small. I spent more than a year testing, retesting, and gathering feedback from opinionated tasters at Food52 HQ. (Want to know what their favorite was? It's almost too obvious; see page 41.) In the process, we whittled this book down to a complete set of iconic baking recipes that will reliably turn you into a local legend. I'm proud to say that it's a caliber of recipes that none of us would have ever been able to find without the collective experience of crowdsourcing, hundreds of bakers strong.

Here are the criteria I kept in mind and what you can expect to find in this book—right before you find yourself surrounded by Almond Crackle Cookies (page 66) and Greek Yogurt Chocolate Mousse (page 151).

What are Genius Desserts? Most importantly, they must taste very, very good.

Dessert is—arguably—not an essential part of any meal, nor to our survival. It is only about joy and celebration. So as I was testing recipes for this book, no matter how clever or quick or surprising a recipe was, if it didn't taste great and make the people hovering nearby smile and come back for more, it didn't make the cut.

They solve problems.

Maybe you want to make candies for more personal (and budget-friendly) holiday gifts or churn ice cream with your kids on a sticky summer day, but you don't have a candy thermometer or an ice cream maker.

Never fear! You will find many ways to do all those things and more, without any fancy tools (pages 69 and 172). And for those moments you need to come up with a dessert that's gluten-free or vegan, using only ingredients you can find at your corner store? This book is full of delicious solutions with easy-to-find, easy-to-pronounce ingredients—check out the index on page 268 for more help finding them.

Most are super easy. A few aren't, but they're worth it.

The majority of this book is full of the utterly simple: the one-bowl, no-churn, and three-ingredient wonders. We're all busy, so baking generally needs to fall in line. But sometimes it doesn't, and there are a handful of recipes that are a little more trouble, quite fun to make, and abundantly worth the extra effort—especially in the Show Cakes (page 105) and Fancy Tarts (page 227) sections. There you'll find Claudia Fleming's Chocolate Caramel Tart (page 237), which she served at her own wedding—it was one of the most widely copied desserts in New York City in the early 2000s. You'll have to make a few components, but when you cut a slice and the caramel spills out, your dinner guests will turn into feral dogs. There's a theme here: chef Suzanne Goin served the Hazelnut–Brown Butter Cake with Sautéed Pears on page 110 at her wedding—luckily, you won't need 150 eggs to make it for your next dinner party.

They surprise us.

Genius Desserts teach us to throw our old assumptions out the window. To wit: the most important tool for making Marcella Hazan's brittle, bittersweet Italian candy Croccante (page 79) is not a candy thermometer (you won't need one) but a potato. The best chocolate sauces have no dairy in them—in fact, there are two different, equally compelling recipes in this book, and you can make them both for a (suddenly very fun) ice cream party in all of 10 minutes (page 182). You will be shocked, and maybe even a little disturbed, by what makes the fluffiest, most otherworldly banana cake (page 98). You can make a piecrust out of saltine crackers with your bare hands (page 199)—and it will go even better with a sweet-tart lemony filling than the more predictable graham cracker route would. Not to mention there's a whipped cream frosting that holds up for a week in the refrigerator (how?!) with no suspicious ingredients (page 124). These shockers and more await.

They innovate and move our baking forward.

We tend to think of cooking as creative, but baking as immutable: cake and custard recipes are chemistry at work, mysteriously and alchemically coming together, so we don't want to go off-script and disrupt the fine balance. But that can also mean that dessert techniques start to feel quite static. How many recipes have you read that call for the exact same method that's on the back of the chocolate chip bag? And how many do we really need?

Thank goodness we have smart people who've made it their life's work to tinker—either by having a goal and driving toward it, like Alice Medrich, who took chocolate completely out of her brownie recipe to rebuild it precisely as she wanted (the chocolate never came back, though cocoa powder did, page 22). Or by knowing enough about the existing culinary canon to realize when they've stumbled onto something remarkable, like Stella Parks and the forgotten pan of roasting sugar on page 42.

Genius Desserts is about honoring those innovations, the recipes and discoveries and the people behind them who keep pushing our baking forward, saving us from making the same chocolate chip cookie over and over.

And as it turns out, there's more room to play in baking than we thought. Throughout the book, I've pointed out places that are perfect for riffing and mixing and matching. There are Magic Potions (page 42) that you can toss in at will to deepen flavors and make your desserts even better, and Saucy and Crunchy Toppers (page 194) to take a perfectly nice cake or bowl of ice cream, and spangle and bedazzle it with Candied Sesame Seeds or Double-Chocolate Cookie Crumbles. And the three recipes marked Wonder Dough offer a single base recipe that can spin off in a million ways, give or take.

Best of all, the more you bake, the more making desserts can become a continuum. If there's leftover lemon cream (page 241), you should definitely smear it between cookies and freeze it for a treat the next time you get home from work in a funk. Stale cake and cookies make amazing trifles, icebox cakes, and something chef Alex Raij calls *migas dulces* (page 147). Pie dough scraps turn into all sorts of brand-new treats (page 209)—never throw them out. And I promise you this: every dessert in this book also makes an excellent breakfast the next morning.

BAKING RULES & ASSUMPTIONS

These are the baking rules that have become self-evident at Food52; they tell us what to pay attention to and what not to worry about. Memorize them: they will help you as you read this book, shop for recipes, and bake them (or any other dessert recipe, for that matter). Welcome to baking, Food52-style.

Measuring flour—this is important!

If you're using measuring cups and not a scale for measuring flour and other powdery substances (like cocoa powder), use the Spoon and Sweep Method: stir the flour or other dry ingredient in the container a couple of times, then spoon it into the measuring cup and sweep the back of a knife or a bench scraper across the top. (This corresponds to how we tested recipes for the book; dipping the cup directly into the flour without stirring will result in much more compacted and heavier cupsful, and denser desserts.) Unless otherwise noted, these recipes were all tested with a variety of unbleached flours; bleached flours should also work, despite being a bit lower in gluten.

Measuring salt—this is slightly less important.

You'll see that some recipes call for fine sea salt and others for kosher salt—typically based on what the original author used—and some have different finishing salts sprinkled on top, too. That doesn't mean that you need to stock every type of salt listed here—whatever you use as your everyday seasoning salt will work in the small amounts used in these baking recipes. Just bear in mind that fine sea salt or iodized table salt will be about twice as salty per teaspoon as Diamond Crystal kosher salt (Morton's kosher is somewhere in between), so if you're substituting a different salt, you may want to round up or down accordingly.

For sprinkling on top of brownies, chocolate chip cookies, or the Chocolate Caramel Tart on page 237, just a little bit of Maldon, fleur de sel, or other flaky, crunchy, fancy salt will make a big difference in texture, looks, and pops of flavor.

The difference between bittersweet and semisweet chocolate. (A trick question.)

Most chocolate in this book is listed as bittersweet for simplicity's sake, but chocolates labeled bittersweet, semisweet, and dark are interchangeable, and there's no regulated standard for any of them. What's more important is that you use good-quality stuff where it counts. Some recipes where the flavor of the chocolate will be extra prominent have a recommended cacao percentage, but just get as close to that percentage as you can.

Why don't we say preheat the oven?

Since Food52 was founded, we've always said to *heat* the oven rather than *preheat*, because we're George Carlin fans, and the words *heat* and *preheat* really mean the same thing: turn on the oven in enough time to get up to the temperature specified for baking. To be even more sure, get a $5 oven thermometer.

When you should scrape down your bowls.

I've included a few cues, but you should scrape bowls down anytime they start to look globby and the undermixed parts creep up the sides. Also be sure to scrape the bottom of the bowl, even when you think you're done—pockets of dry ingredients can get hidden down there.

Storage recommendations, not deadlines.

I've included storage instructions but not "eat by" dates unless they're extreme outliers, like a cookie that keeps forever, or a pie you should say goodbye to after a day. I don't believe that a cookie will last only three days, and then poof, stop being good—it's a continuum, which will vary depending on your environment and storing conditions. And even quite stale cookies and cakes can be great for other things (see page 2).

On keeping it together.

Most importantly, don't panic! We all make mistakes and have off days. Melty pie doughs can go back in the refrigerator to firm up. Burnt cakes get the outer layer scraped off and become a trifle or *Migas Dulces* (page 147). Cookies that don't look quite right become *very* exciting once you turn them into an ice cream sandwich. And if something is truly not salvageable, that's why we have desserts you can make from a loaf of bread (page 83) and Cookies, Now! (page 66).

silicone spatula

wide-mouthed storage jars

bench scraper

bowl scraper

butter warmer

pastry brush

digital scale

GENIUS BAKING TOOLS

Don't think of these tools as essential, per se. You can get by with little more than a mixing bowl and some measuring spoons if you really need to. (That said, investing in a good stand mixer and food processor will open a new world of baking to you—but you knew that.) These are the baking tools you might not have thought you needed—the unexpected companions that make baking feel more calm and effortless and that I would attach as my go-go gadget arms if I could.

Basic digital scale If you love to bake, please get one—you'll have more predictably genius cakes and cookies and fewer bowls and measuring cups to clean. My OXO scale cost $25 and has lasted me a decade already.

Bench scraper (stiff, metal, with a straight edge) This is for scraping flour and stuck-on bits from the counter, scooping up piles of chopped fruit, cleaving doughs into even portions, and delicately removing rolled-out cookies and crusts that have stuck to the counter without a tear.

Bowl scraper (bendy, plastic, with a curved edge) Somewhat similar to the stiff and straight version, this curves to cleanly hug the inside surface of bowls and pots. It also doubles as a dish scraper that won't scratch sensitive surfaces.

If you have a stand mixer, this same principle is at work in the paddle attachment with the built-in bowl scraper (also called a flex edge). San Francisco pastry chef Emily Luchetti swears by this attachment for more evenly mixed doughs that you don't have to scrape down by hand.

Butter warmer So many baking recipes call for a stick of melted butter or a tiny amount of boiling water or hot coffee. This little guy lets you heat small amounts quickly while keeping a close eye—and ear—on things on the stovetop. You'll never have a bowlful of melting butter explode in the microwave again.

Old-fashioned pastry brush The paintbrush-style type will help you apply glazes and egg washes and brush off excess flour from dough more effectively than the silicone-tentacled versions.

Wide-mouthed storage jars You'll bake more quickly (and more often) if you can get into sundries such as flour and sugar easily. Be sure there's plenty of room for your scooping hand to get in and out.

Sturdy, one-piece silicone spatula This all-purpose utensil can be used for anything from stirring curds and compotes to scraping down bowls to folding ingredients together. I prefer mine to be strong and a bit stiff, with handles that don't detach. (Wooden handles can't go in the dishwasher, and water and other sketchy materials can get trapped in the gap that holds the handle.)

Spring-loaded cookie scooper (or disher)
A cookie scooper makes scooping dough both easier and more uniform, which is the best way to get the consistently chewy/crispy/doughy texture you're after. For a good all-purpose size, choose a 1- to 2-tablespoon scooper, unless you like to show off with giant, bakery-style cookies.

Bundt pan (for more than cakes) Set one into an ice bath and you have the quickest, most conductive way to cool down ice cream bases and puddings fast. Oh, you want to use it for cakes? Get one with a light-colored interior. The black-coated nonstick versions are prone to overbaking (burning).

Offset spatula Just try smoothing batter or icing evenly into a tight corner with anything else. The thin, blunt edge is also handy for lifting delicate cookies off a baking sheet, or prying a sticky tart or upside-down cake off the bottom of the pan without damaging your sharp knives or accidentally poking through the bottom.

Ruler (or tape measurer) Not every pan has its measurements printed on the bottom, and if you are like me, you don't really know what ¼ inch (6mm) looks like when it counts. This will come in handy more often than you think.

Pastry roller Serial bar and tart makers, this tool is for you. It smooths out doughs quickly and evenly in the pan (even corners)—a constant companion of Mindy Segal and Kate Leahy's when they were writing *Cookie Love*.

Your hands! There's no better tool for separating eggs, wiping the last of the batter off the mixer's paddle attachment, poking a cake to see if it's springy and done, or making a pie dough when there's no other equipment in sight. Use them with joy.

ruler

bundt pan

pastry roller

cookie scooper

offset spatula

your hands!

ROAD MAP TO ALL
OF THE GENIUS TIPS

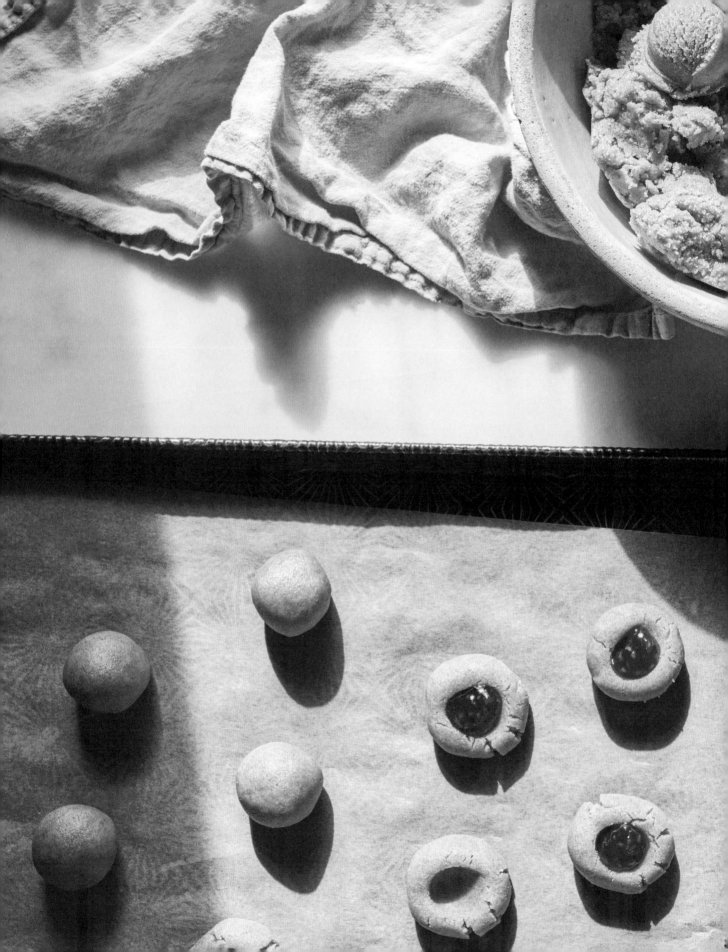

Cookies & Candy

Flourless Chocolate-Walnut Cookies

FROM FRANÇOIS PAYARD

This is a recipe that defies all logic: it looks and acts like a rich, chewy chocolate cookie, but lacks many of the ingredients we think of as nonnegotiable (butter, flour, egg yolks). This also means that it's gluten-free, dairy-free, and Passover-friendly.

But none of these abstentions, as strategic as they seem, were by design. When French pastry chef François Payard opened his first patisserie in Manhattan in 1997, he didn't want to compete with iconic American cookies, so he based this one off a French macaron, a featherlight confection with a chewy middle and a thin, crisp outer shell that's made from little more than egg whites, ground almonds, and sugar.

Ironically, the cookie that he came up with feels quintessentially American. The middles are fudgy and studded with toasted walnuts; the surface is fetchingly crackled and shiny. It's essentially a (yes, lighter and more delicately chewy) good, old-fashioned brownie.

MAKES ABOUT 12 (4-INCH/10CM) COOKIES

2¾ cups (275g) walnut halves

3 cups (350g) confectioners' sugar

½ cup plus 3 tablespoons (70g) Dutch-processed cocoa powder (see page 5)

¼ teaspoon kosher salt

4 large egg whites, at room temperature

1 tablespoon pure vanilla extract

1 Heat the oven to 350°F (175°C), with racks in the upper and lower thirds. Spread the walnut halves on a large rimmed baking sheet and toast in the oven until they turn golden and smell toasty, about 9 minutes.

2 Let the walnuts cool to the touch, then transfer them to a cutting board and coarsely chop them. Line two large rimmed baking sheets with parchment paper or silicone baking mats.

3 Combine the confectioners' sugar, cocoa powder, salt, and walnuts in the bowl of a stand mixer fitted with the paddle attachment. Mix on low speed until well combined. With the mixer running, slowly add the egg whites and vanilla. Mix on medium speed until the mixture has just slightly thickened, about 3 minutes.

4 Using a 2-ounce (60ml) cookie scoop or a large spoon, scoop the batter onto the baking sheets in 12 mounds, spacing them 3 inches (7.5cm) apart. Put the baking sheets in the oven, immediately lower the temperature to 325°F (165°C), and bake until the tops are glossy and lightly cracked, 14 to 16 minutes, rotating the baking sheets from front to back and top to bottom halfway through baking. Slide the parchment paper (with the cookies) onto two racks to let the cookies cool completely before removing the cookies from the parchment. They shouldn't stick, but if they do, check out the tip for releasing them on page 30. Store in an airtight container at room temperature.

World Peace Cookies

FROM DORIE GREENSPAN & PIERRE HERMÉ

A little bit French chocolate sablé and a little bit American chocolate chip, World Peace Cookies are a force of their own: fine and sandy, but with a friendly, soft chew and generous pockets and wisps of chocolate. As the story goes, Dorie Greenspan's neighbor told her that a daily dose of these cookies would ensure lasting world peace, and so they became—naturally, ambitiously—World Peace Cookies. (The internet responded well to that.)

Greenspan has always credited Pierre Hermé for the original recipe, which he created in the early 2000s for a then-cutting edge restaurant in Paris called Korova. (She points out that the restaurant launched the lobster roll trend in Paris. "It was called Le Hot Dog Chic," she says.) But Greenspan was the one to test and translate the recipe for American kitchens, then popularize the cookies with their lovable new name.

So what was it about these cookies that made them so memorable? According to Greenspan, Hermé had American chocolate chip cookies in mind when he first made these. "I think it was the addition of brown sugar, not a very commonly used ingredient in France, that made it most like our cookie. But, of course, it was the salt, the fleur de sel, that made the cookie such a standout."

Even though these little cookies are the stuff of legend, they're as simple as any other slice-and-bake recipe and perfect for anytime baking. Keep a few logs of this dough in your freezer at all times.

> "I've seen World Peace Cookies made with peanut butter chips, with cinnamon, with icing, and with gluten-free flours. I've seen them huge and small. Happily, there's little you can do to ruin them."
> —Dorie Greenspan

MAKES ABOUT 3 DOZEN COOKIES

1¼ cups (170g) all-purpose flour (see page 5)

⅓ cup (30g) unsweetened cocoa powder (see page 5)

½ teaspoon baking soda

½ cup plus 3 tablespoons (155g) unsalted butter, at room temperature

⅔ cup (135g) lightly packed light brown sugar

¼ cup (50g) sugar

½ teaspoon fleur del sel or ¼ teaspoon fine sea salt

1 teaspoon pure vanilla extract

5 ounces (140g) bittersweet chocolate, chopped into irregularly-sized pieces smaller than ⅓ inch/8mm

1   Sift together the flour, cocoa powder, and baking soda into a bowl or onto a sheet of waxed paper. In a stand mixer fitted with the paddle attachment, or using a handheld mixer in a large bowl, beat the butter and the sugars on medium speed until soft and creamy, about 3 minutes. Add the salt and vanilla extract and beat until incorporated.

2   Turn off the mixer and pour in the dry ingredients. For the best texture, mix the dough as little as possible once the dry ingredients are added. Drape a kitchen towel over the mixer to contain any flying flour and pulse at low speed about five times. Take a peek: if there's still a lot of flour on the surface of the dough, pulse a couple more times; if not, remove the towel. Mix on low speed just until the flour disappears and the dough starts to come together in large clumps, 30 seconds to 1 minute more. Add the chocolate pieces and mix just to incorporate.

3   Dump the dough out onto a work surface, gather it together, and divide it in half. Working with one half at a time, roll the dough into logs that are 1½ inches (4cm) in diameter. Bundle the logs in plastic wrap, twisting the ends tightly to help even out the shape, and refrigerate for at least 3 hours. To help maintain their round shape, refrigerate the logs in empty paper-towel rolls or tall drinking glasses. (The dough can be refrigerated for up to 3 days or frozen for up to 2 months. If you've frozen the dough, no need

CONTINUED

World Peace Cookies

to defrost it before baking; let it warm just enough so you can slice the logs into rounds easily and bake the cookies 1 minute longer.)

4 Heat the oven to 325°F (165°C) with a rack in the center. Line two large rimmed baking sheets with parchment or silicone baking mats.

5 Using a serrated or other sharp, thin knife, start to slice one of the logs into ½-inch (1.3cm) rounds. (The rounds may crack as you're cutting them—don't be concerned, just squeeze the bits back together.) Arrange the rounds on the baking sheets, spacing them about 2 inches (5cm) apart. Keep any remaining dough chilled until you are ready to bake.

6 Bake the cookies one sheet at a time for 12 minutes. They won't look done or feel firm to the touch, but that's exactly how they should be. Let the cookies cool on the baking sheets on racks until they are just warm. Serve warm or let cool completely. Store in an airtight container at room temperature.

GENIUS TIP: SMART STORAGE FOR CRUNCHIER (AND CHEWIER) COOKIES

According to Dorie Greenspan, you should never store crunchy cookies and soft, chewy ones in the same container. The crunchy cookies will inherit moisture from the softer ones and lose their snap.

Best Cocoa Brownies

FROM ALICE MEDRICH

Most brownie recipes are remarkably consistent: melt chocolate with butter, then mix with sugar, eggs, and flour. They come together fast, and you are a happy clam.

But pastry chef Shuna Lydon told me about a recipe that changed her life by simply replacing the chocolate with cocoa powder. It did not surprise me to learn that the recipe belonged to Alice Medrich (you can thank her for popularizing chocolate truffles in America in the 1970s at her Berkeley shop, Cocolat).

"Alice knows chocolate. It speaks to her. We're lucky to have her as a translator," Lydon wrote to me. Not only is cocoa less expensive than chocolate— a boon to pastry chefs, or anyone who makes a lot of brownies—but the fudgy bars that result are, counterintuitively, better.

By taking out the chocolate, with its variable fat and sugar, Medrich was able to control and fine-tune the proportions of both. When she added the fat back (in the form of butter), the centers stayed softer. With just the right amount of sugar, the crusts were shinier. Commit, as Medrich does, to stirring for forty strokes in step 3—the effort will give you a satisfying jump in heart rate and build structure in the very rich batter.

MAKES 16 LARGE OR 25 SMALL BROWNIES

½ cup plus 2 tablespoons (140g) unsalted butter	½ teaspoon pure vanilla extract
1¼ cups (250g) sugar	2 large eggs, cold
¾ cup plus 2 tablespoons (80g) unsweetened cocoa powder (see note and page 5)	½ cup (65g) all-purpose flour (see page 5)
¼ teaspoon fine sea salt	⅔ cup (65g) walnut or pecan pieces (optional)
	Flaky salt, for garnish (optional)

1 Heat the oven to 325°F (165°C), with a rack in the lower third. Line an 8-inch (20cm) square baking pan with parchment paper, leaving a 1-inch (2.5cm) overhang on two opposite sides for easier lifting when the brownies are done.

2 Combine the butter, sugar, cocoa powder, and salt in a metal bowl and set the bowl directly in gently simmering water in a wide skillet. Stir occasionally with a wooden spoon or rubber spatula, until the butter is melted and the mixture is hot enough that you want to remove your finger quickly after dipping it in. (It might look gritty here but don't worry, it will smooth out later.) Remove the bowl from the skillet and let it cool briefly, until the mixture is only warm, not hot.

3 Stir in the vanilla. Beat in the eggs, one at a time, stirring vigorously after each one. When the batter looks thick, shiny, and well mixed, add the flour, stir until no streaks of flour remain, and then beat vigorously for 40 strokes. It's worth it! Fold in the nuts and scrape the batter into the pan, smoothing the top.

4 Bake until a toothpick stuck in the center comes out slightly moist with batter, 20 to 25 minutes. Let cool completely in the pan on a rack.

5 Lift up the overhanging ends of the parchment paper and transfer the brownies to a cutting board. Cut into 16 or 25 squares, then lift brownies off the parchment. (If you want really good, clean slices, freeze or refrigerate just until firm first.) Sprinkle with flaky salt just before serving. Store in an airtight container at room temperature.

Note: There are two types of unsweetened cocoa powder—natural or Dutch-processed. Either will work here, but they give you slightly different results. Natural cocoa makes brownies with a more complex flavor and, as Alice Medrich puts it, lots of tart, fruity notes. Dutch-processed cocoa powder makes a darker brownie with a mellower flavor, like old-fashioned chocolate pudding.

Blondies

FROM AMERICA'S TEST KITCHEN

As ever, the cooks at America's Test Kitchen were relentless in dissecting the perfect blondie, and all that can go wrong along the way. Their first act of genius was in de-cake-ifying (my fake word, not theirs) the recipe. Since many of the qualities we avoid in a cake—chew, heft, density—are marks of a very good blondie, they axed anything that would render it cake-like: they cut back on the butter and eggs and melted the butter rather than creaming it, all of which would have otherwise made the whole operation fluffier. For sweetness, they went the butterscotch route: all brown sugar, plus a bit of salt to keep it in check.

But the most surprising move was this: they quadrupled the vanilla extract. You might think of vanilla as a volatile ingredient, like cayenne or salt—all but impossible to correct once overdone. But it's much harder to overdo than you'd think. And once you stop putting a single teaspoon into baking recipes because it's what you've always done, you can embrace vanilla as a flavor all its own—complex, haunting, memorable. Measure out 4 teaspoons or feel free to just upend the bottle.

MAKES ABOUT 3 DOZEN BLONDIES

1 cup (100g) pecan or walnut halves

1½ cups (190g) all-purpose flour (see page 5)

1 teaspoon baking powder

½ teaspoon fine sea salt

¾ cup (170g) unsalted butter, melted and cooled

1½ cups (300g) lightly packed light brown sugar

2 large eggs, lightly beaten

4 teaspoons pure vanilla extract

1 cup (170g) white chocolate chips, or ½ cup (85g) white chocolate chips and ½ cup (85g) semisweet chocolate chips

1 Heat the oven to 350°F (175°C), with a rack in the center. Spread the nuts on a large rimmed baking sheet and toast in the oven until they turn deep golden brown and smell toasty, 10 to 15 minutes. Let the nuts cool, then transfer them to a cutting board and coarsely chop them.

2 While the nuts toast, butter and line a 9 by 13-inch (23 by 33cm) metal baking pan with parchment paper, leaving a 1-inch (2.5cm) overhang on two opposite sides for easier lifting when the blondies are done. Butter the parchment.

3 Whisk together the flour, baking powder, and salt in a medium bowl. Whisk together the melted butter and brown sugar in a separate medium bowl, add the eggs and vanilla, and mix well. Using a rubber spatula, fold the dry ingredients into the wet ingredients until just combined. Fold in the chocolate chips and nuts and scrape the batter into the pan, smoothing the top.

4 Bake until the top is shiny, cracked, and lightly golden at the edges, about 22 minutes—err on the side of underbaking, so the blondies don't dry out. Let cool in the pan on a rack.

5 Lift up the overhanging ends of the parchment paper and transfer the blondies to a cutting board. Cut into 36 bars. Store airtight at room temperature, though these also taste extraordinarily good straight from the refrigerator or the freezer.

GENIUS TIP: HOW TO MAKE MINT (OR BASIL OR TARRAGON) CHOCOLATE CHIP COOKIES

For any cookie you'd like to take on a fresh herby vibe, do as farmer–cookbook author Andrea Bemis does: infuse the butter first. The cookies won't look any different, so the pop of cool, breezy flavor will be a surprise.

How to do it: For every **½ cup (110g) of butter**, add **½ cup firmly packed fresh mint leaves**, coarsely chopped, and melt them together in a saucepan, swirling occasionally. Once the mint oils are released and smelling good (2 to 3 minutes), set pan aside to cool for 30 minutes, then strain the butter through a fine-mesh sieve, pressing to capture any lingering minty juices. You can either refrigerate the butter again and use it for creaming and so forth or proceed with it in melted form.

Secretly Vegan Chocolate Chip Cookies

FROM AGATHA KULAGA & ERIN PATINKIN OF OVENLY

This cookie isn't genius *for* being a vegan chocolate chip cookie or *despite* being one. It rests entirely on its own merits: its soft-bellied, chewy, caramelly crisp-edged, incidentally vegan merits.

Unlike other veganized recipes, which can be bogged down with odd substitutions and taste like a loose, disappointing approximation of the real thing, Ovenly's version uses standard ingredients—they simply replace the egg and butter (which are largely made up of fat and water) with oil and water (same). You might be thinking the cookie would lose its richness, but a smart technique makes up for it.

The method is nothing fancy—just a vigorous whisking of all the wet ingredients before adding the dry. But there is one important extra step: the dough should be refrigerated for 12 to 24 hours to help the flour hydrate.

This trick first made headlines in the *New York Times* in 2008, when food writer David Leite revealed that the top bakeries in Manhattan let their dough cool its heels in the fridge for a few days before baking. The flavor is richer and more developed; the texture smoother. Leite recommended at least a 36-hour rest, but because Ovenly's cookie dough has no egg or butter to slow down the hydration, it hits its peak much faster.

MAKES ABOUT 18 COOKIES

2 cups (250g) all-purpose flour (see page 5)

1 teaspoon baking powder

¾ teaspoon baking soda

½ teaspoon fine sea salt

1¼ cups (215g) bittersweet or semisweet chocolate chips (60% cacao or higher)

½ cup (100g) sugar (see Genius Tip, right)

½ cup (110g) packed dark brown sugar (see Genius Tip, right)

½ cup plus 1 tablespoon (120g) neutral oil (such as grapeseed)

5 tablespoons (75g) water

Coarse-grained or flaky sea salt like Maldon, for topping

1 Whisk together the flour, baking powder, baking soda, and fine sea salt in a large bowl. Add the chocolate chips and toss to coat. Vigorously whisk together the sugars with the oil and water in a separate large bowl until smooth and well incorporated, about 2 minutes. (If there are clumps in the brown sugar, break them up before whisking.)

2 Using a wooden spoon or rubber spatula, stir the dry flour mixture into the wet sugar mixture until just combined and no streaks of flour remain. The dough will look a bit oily—that's okay! Cover the bowl with plastic wrap. Refrigerate the dough for at least 12 hours and up to 24 hours.

3 Heat the oven to 350°F (175°C), with racks in the upper and lower thirds. Line two rimmed baking sheets with parchment paper or silicone baking mats. Remove the dough from the refrigerator. Using a cookie scoop or a spoon, scoop the dough onto the baking sheets in 2-inch (5cm) mounds, spacing them 3 inches (7.5cm) apart. To minimize spreading, freeze the balls of dough for 10 minutes before baking.

4 Remove the balls of dough from the freezer and sprinkle with coarse-grained sea salt. Bake until the edges are just golden, 12 to 13 minutes, rotating baking sheets from front to back and top to bottom halfway through baking. Do not overbake. Let cookies cool on the pan until firm enough to transfer to a rack, about 5 minutes; let finish cooling on the rack. Store in an airtight container at room temperature.

GENIUS TIP: WAIT, ISN'T SUGAR VEGAN?

If you want to make sure the cookies are all-the-way vegan, use organic sugars (nonorganic sugars often use something called bone char in processing) and double-check the ingredient list on the chocolate chips to make sure there's no dairy. My favorite version of these cookies is with Wholesome brand's exceptionally dark brown organic sugar, a muscovado that's heavy on the molasses.

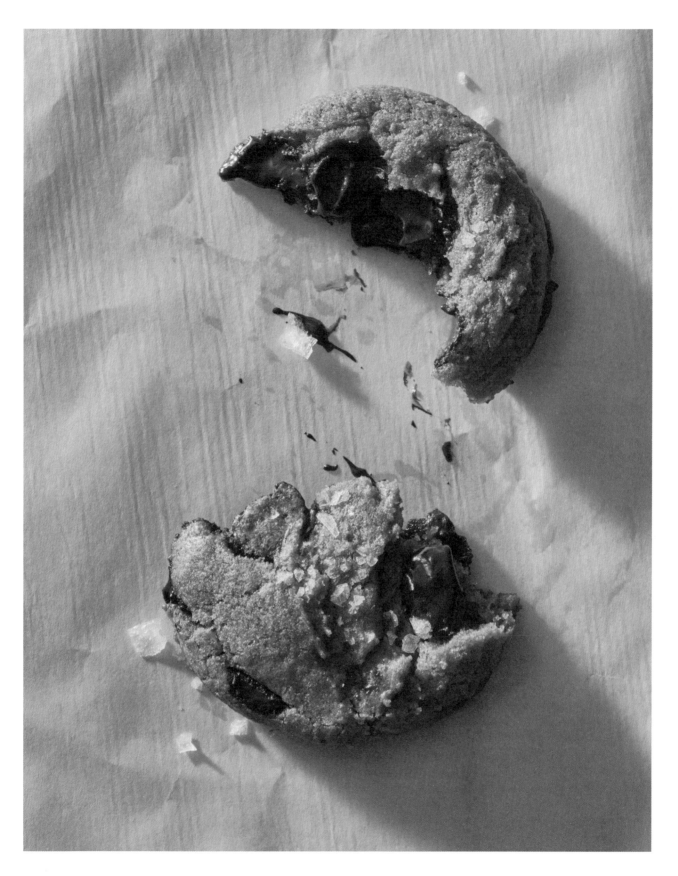

Chocolate Chip Cookie Brittle

FROM SHAUNA SEVER

This is what happens if you take out any trace of leavener in chocolate chip cookies—no eggs, no baking powder or soda, no airy creamed butter—and mash the dough into a thin layer on a baking sheet. It sounds like something curious kids would make by mistake and has all the makings of a terribly ill-fated idea.

But instead, thanks to a generous proportion of melted butter and raw sugar, this dough turns into an addictive, crunchy brittle that falls somewhere between candy and cookie. Cookbook author and blogger Shauna Sever developed this naturally sweetened version based off a recipe she found in *The American Country Inn and Bed & Breakfast Cookbook*, and after it was pinned a half million times on Pinterest, she ended up demoing it on the *Today* show to an incredulous Al Roker. The brittle packs up well in a big jar for birthdays, holidays, and sugar-fueled road trips and is friendly to swap-ins for the nuts and chocolate. Coconut? Chile? Pretzels? Set your inner curious kid free.

MAKES ABOUT 3 DOZEN (3-INCH/7.5CM) PIECES

¾ cup plus 2 tablespoons (200g) unsalted butter, cut into tablespoons

1 cup (200g) turbinado sugar

2 teaspoons pure vanilla extract

1 teaspoon fine sea salt

2 cups (250g) all-purpose flour (see page 5)

½ cup (60g) coarsely chopped pecans or walnuts

¾ cup (130g) bittersweet or semisweet chocolate chips (60% to 70% cacao—Ghirardelli bittersweet chips work very well)

1 Heat the oven to 350°F (175°C), with a rack in the center.

2 In a large microwave-safe bowl, combine the butter and sugar. Microwave in 20-second bursts, stirring between bursts, just until the butter is almost completely melted and the sugar has started to dissolve, about 2 minutes. (Alternatively, melt the butter and sugar in a saucepan over medium heat, being careful not to let the mixture come to a boil.)

3 Whisk the mixture until the butter is completely melted. Let cool for 5 minutes. Whisk continuously until the mixture is thickened and smooth and no longer looks separated, about 1 minute. Whisk in the vanilla and salt until combined. Add the flour and stir until no streaks of flour remain, then stir in half of the nuts.

4 Scrape the dough onto a rimmed 12 by 17-inch (30 by 43cm) ungreased baking sheet and pat it into a very thin, even layer with your hands. It won't look like you'll be able to fill the entire baking sheet, but you will! Just keep patting the dough to the edges. Use an offset or rubber spatula to smooth the top. Sprinkle the chocolate chips and the remaining nuts over the dough and press them down lightly with your hands.

5 Bake until light golden brown and slightly firm to the touch all over, 22 to 25 minutes, rotating the baking sheet every 7 to 8 minutes. Let the brittle cool completely in the pan on a rack.

6 Use a wide, thin spatula to loosen the edges of the brittle, then ease the whole slab of brittle onto the rack. Alternatively, if it looks as if the slab might not come out cleanly, line a second baking sheet with parchment paper. Flip the brittle slab onto the parchment and then immediately invert it right side up onto the rack, peeling off the paper. Once completely cool, break into pieces—try to avoid smudging the chocolate chips. Store in an airtight container at room temperature.

Coconut Custard Macaroons

FROM DANIELLE KARTES

Most simple coconut macaroons are made with shredded coconut and little else, bound with sweetened condensed milk or egg white. But Danielle Kartes, author of the blog and cookbook *Rustic Joyful Food*, took it upon herself to add butter, egg yolk, and an unstinting measure of good salt.

Adding more fat and salt isn't necessarily the answer to making everything better, but the difference it makes here is profound. Instead of a straightforward sweet, coconutty chew, you get a more rounded richness and a welcome savory oomph. And the butter has an amplifying effect—the cookies don't just taste better because butter inherently tastes rich and good, but because it turns to browned butter in the oven and mingles with the sugars and salt to become caramel.

At the same time, the pointy outer edges of the macaroon brown and crisp up while the inside stays soft and custardy. In fact, the cookies are so moist that they can soften and lose some of their addictive crunch over the course of a day. Don't worry; I've stress-tested them for you—a quick toast in the oven brings them back to their full crispy-chewy glory (see step 4).

This makes them as good a treat to eat now (and I do mean now—they're ready fast) as to share with your lucky coworkers and friends tomorrow.

MAKES ABOUT 5 DOZEN COOKIES

6½ cups (510g) sweetened shredded coconut

¾ cup (235g) sweetened condensed milk

½ cup (110g) unsalted butter, melted and slightly cooled

1 large egg

1 teaspoon pure vanilla extract (available kosher for Passover)

¾ teaspoon fleur de sel or other flaky sea salt

1 Heat the oven to 375°F (190°C), with racks in the upper and lower thirds. Line two large rimmed baking sheets with parchment paper or silicone baking mats. (Don't skip lining the baking sheets because the cookies will stick like glue.)

2 Combine the coconut, condensed milk, butter, egg, vanilla, and salt in a large bowl and stir until the batter is evenly mixed.

3 Using a 2-tablespoon cookie scoop or a spoon, scoop the batter onto the baking sheets, spacing them 2 inches (5cm) apart. Bake until the edges and tops of the cookies are dark golden brown, about 14 minutes, rotating the baking sheets from front to back and top to bottom halfway through baking.

4 Let the cookies cool on the baking sheet for 5 minutes, then transfer to a rack to cool completely. Make sure the macaroons are completely cool before packing them up (I recommend leaving them out to dry for as long as possible) and leave the container cracked open at room temperature to help keep them crisp and chewy. If they do become soggy and you'd like to restore them to their former crispy-chewy state, toast them on a lined baking sheet in a 350°F (175°C) oven for 5 to 10 minutes, keeping a close eye on them so they don't get too dark.

GENIUS TIP: DE-STICKING COOKIES & CAKES

Parchment paper is all but guaranteed to be nonstick, but sometimes especially gooey cookies or cakes will latch on anyway. When that happens, a trick from Scott Peacock and the late Edna Lewis will keep you from mangling their bottoms: Dip a pastry brush or paper towel in water and paint the underside of the parchment in any spot an offender is sticking. Parchment is slightly permeable, so the moisture will release whatever sugary concoction that's stuck there. Rose Levy Beranbaum has been known to use a hair dryer to warm up the goo so that it releases gently from the parchment.

Skinny Peanut Wafers

FROM MAIDA HEATTER

File these cookies emphatically under peanut, not peanut butter. They're subtler in flavor, with a delicate carnival of textures: a chewy-crisp wafer cobbled with all sizes of salted peanut and topped memorably with more peanuts, ideally honey-roasted.

Maida Heatter was fearless in experimenting with unconventional ingredients like this—another cookie was secretly sweetened with ground banana chips, a brownie layered with peppermint patties, and of course, there's the elephant omelet incident that launched her career.

The story goes like this: when the Republican convention was coming to Miami Beach in 1968, Heatter seized on the moment to grab national attention for the restaurant she owned with her husband, where she baked all the desserts. "The symbol of the Republican party is an elephant," as she recalled in *Maida Heatter's Cakes*. "If you serve an elephant meat omelet, you will get a lot of publicity." After consulting experts on cooking wild game in Kenya, she sourced canned elephant meat from Bloomingdale's and served it in a rolled omelet, flanked by sautéed bananas and topped with salted peanuts. "And it was delicious. It was like Boeuf Bourguignonne," she wrote.

Though only one person ordered the omelet, she got the publicity she was after. Craig Claiborne, the then food editor of the *New York Times* (who also kick-started the cookbook careers of Marcella Hazan and Madhur Jaffrey), flew down to Miami to interview Heatter. After tasting her desserts and seeing her files of recipes, he encouraged her to write a cookbook of her own. Over the next 23 years, she would write ten.

MAKES ABOUT 28 WAFERS

1 cup (110g) roasted salted peanuts

1 cup (200g) sugar

2 tablespoons unsalted butter

1 cup (110g) sifted all-purpose flour

½ teaspoon baking soda

1 large egg

2 tablespoons milk

1 cup (110g) honey-roasted peanuts (or more roasted salted peanuts)

1 Heat the oven to 400°F (200°C), with a rack in the center. Line two large baking sheets (if they're rimmed, turn them upside down so you can slide the finished cookies off more easily) with parchment paper or silicone baking mats.

2 In a food processor, pulse the roasted salted peanuts and ¼ cup (50g) of the sugar until the nuts are in irregular pieces—some should be powdery, some coarse, some whole.

3 Melt the butter in a small saucepan or skillet over medium heat. Stir together the flour and baking soda in a bowl.

4 In a large bowl, use a handheld mixer or rubber spatula to beat together the egg, milk, melted butter, and the remaining ¾ cup (150g) of sugar until well combined, about 2 minutes. Add the dry ingredients and the chopped peanut mixture and beat again until combined.

5 Using a 1-tablespoon cookie scoop or a tablespoon, scoop slightly rounded tablespoonfuls of the dough onto the baking sheet in mounds, spacing them 3 inches (7.5cm) apart. Try to keep the mounds neat and round. Top each cookie with a few honey-roasted peanuts.

6 Bake one sheet at a time until the cookies are barely brown, 7 to 8 minutes, rotating the baking sheet front to back after 5 minutes. The cookies will rise, spread out, and then flatten into thin wafers.

7 Let the cookies cool on the baking sheet for a minute or two, then slide the parchment paper (with the cookies) onto a rack. Let the cookies stand until they are firm enough to be removed, about 5 minutes. Store in an airtight container at room temperature.

Nonfat Gingersnaps

FROM DAVID LEBOVITZ

I made sure to keep *nonfat* in the name here, not because it's an ideal quality in cookies—not since the 1990s anyway, and besides, you're reading a dessert book. But the name of this recipe is important because it's such a shock when you taste these cookies, which aren't the snappy sort of gingersnaps, but chewy, moist, pillowy ginger cookies with lots of fiery spice—a bit like German pfeffernuesse on a very well-hydrated day. (They even stay chewy in the freezer, making them perfect for ice cream sandwiches.)

I'd argue that the lack of fat is incidental, but surprisingly, David Lebovitz (the man who wrote *The Perfect Scoop*, one of the most popular ice cream cookbooks on the market) developed this recipe after tasting a version he loved from the prepared foods section at Whole Foods. The molasses and applesauce more than make up for the stripping away of oil and egg yolks, leaving a buoyant cookie that lacks for nothing.

MAKES 20 TO 22 COOKIES

1 cup (200g) lightly packed dark brown sugar

⅓ cup (100g) molasses (preferably mild, not blackstrap)

¼ cup (75g) applesauce

2¼ cups (315g) all-purpose flour (see page 5)

1 teaspoon baking soda

2½ teaspoons ground cinnamon, plus more for rolling

1½ teaspoons ground ginger

¼ teaspoon ground cloves

½ teaspoon freshly ground black pepper

¼ teaspoon kosher salt

2 large egg whites, at room temperature

½ cup (50g) finely chopped candied ginger

About ½ cup (100g) sugar, for rolling

1 In the bowl of a stand mixer fitted with the paddle attachment, beat the brown sugar, molasses, and applesauce on medium speed for 5 minutes, until the mixture has thickened and lightened to a milky coffee color, and the sugar has mostly dissolved.

2 Meanwhile, sift together the flour, baking soda, cinnamon, ground ginger, cloves, pepper, and salt into a bowl or onto a sheet of waxed paper.

3 Stop the mixer, scrape down the sides of the bowl, and add the egg whites. Beat for 1 minute more on medium speed. Turn the mixer to its lowest speed, slowly add the dry ingredients, and mix until completely incorporated. Turn the mixer to medium speed and blend for 1 minute more, until the dough has smoothed out.

4 On low speed, stir in the candied ginger. Cover the bowl tightly with plastic wrap and refrigerate the batter until very firm, at least 1 hour. (It will keep like this for up to 1 week, or freeze for up to 2 months.)

5 When ready to bake the cookies, heat the oven to 350°F (175°C), with racks in the upper and lower thirds. Line two large rimmed baking sheets with parchment paper or silicone baking mats.

6 Stir together the sugar and a big pinch of cinnamon in a shallow dish. Using a 1-tablespoon cookie scoop or a tablespoon, scoop the dough by heaped tablespoonfuls into mounds about the size of a walnut in its shell and drop the mounds into the sugar. Use your hands to roll the mounds into generously sugar-coated balls.

7 Arrange the mounds on the baking sheets, spacing them about 3 inches (8cm) apart. Bake until the cookies feel just barely set and slightly firm in the center, about 10 minutes, rotating the baking sheets from front to back and top to bottom halfway through baking. Watch the cookies vigilantly, or they will be dry, not soft and chewy. Let cool on the baking sheets on racks or, for extra-soft cookies, transfer to a rack to cool as soon as they're firm enough to do so. Store in an airtight container at room temperature.

Peanut Butter Sandies

FROM JULIA MOSKIN & CITY BAKERY

When you're within trotting distance of New York City's Flatiron District, you go to City Bakery and get the peanut butter cookies (and a few pretzel croissants for the trot back). And when you're not, consider yourself lucky that *New York Times* staff writer Julia Moskin pilfered the recipe from the internet and fiddled with it until she came close enough to the bakery version. Pregnant at the time, she was especially committed.

The recipe starts with a similar base proportion to that perfectly acceptable three-ingredient peanut butter cookie that has circulated online (1 cup sugar, 1 cup peanut butter, 1 egg—there, now you have it). Those are just fine in a pinch, especially when still warm from the oven. But by adding a few more cookie-like ingredients (butter, brown sugar, flour), you get a more complex and lasting treat. It's everything a peanut butter cookie really should be, with a crisp-crumbly edge and the slightest chew that melts away to a softer sandy core—salty and nutty and caramelly sweet.

MAKES ABOUT 6 DOZEN COOKIES

1 cup (225g) unsalted butter, softened

2 cups (400g) sugar

2/3 cup (145g) packed light brown sugar

1 teaspoon kosher salt

2 cups (510g) peanut butter, creamy or chunky (if using natural peanut butter, stir well before measuring)

2 large eggs

2¼ cups (280g) all-purpose flour (see page 5)

Flaky salt like Maldon, for sprinkling

1 Heat the oven to 375°F (190°C) with racks in the lower and upper thirds. Line two large rimmed baking sheets with parchment paper or silicone baking mats.

2 In the bowl of a stand mixer fitted with the paddle attachment, cream the butter, sugars, and salt on medium-high speed until light and fluffy, at least 3 minutes. Scrape down the sides of the bowl, add the peanut butter and eggs, and mix on medium-high speed until well combined. Add the flour and mix on low speed until no streaks of flour remain.

3 Using a 1-tablespoon cookie scoop or a spoon, scoop the dough onto the baking sheets, spacing them 1 inch (2.5cm) apart. (They won't spread.) Sprinkle the tops with flaky salt (or bottoms—see the Genius Tip below). To speed up time in between batches, see page 61.

4 Bake until golden, 10 to 11 minutes, rotating the baking sheets from back to front and top to bottom halfway through baking. Transfer the cookies onto a rack to let cool. Serve warm, or let cool completely and store in an airtight container at room temperature. These are best the day they're made, but after that they can be rewarmed at 350°F (175°C) for about 5 minutes. (You can also freeze extra scooped cookies for later and bake them without defrosting—they'll take 1 to 2 minutes longer to bake.)

GENIUS TIP: WHERE YOU SALT MATTERS

Known for the warm sea salt–chocolate chip cookies they set out for guests in the afternoons, the Captain Fairfield Inn in Kennebunkport, Maine, is rumored to sprinkle salt on the *bottoms* of the cookies before baking, rather than the tops. I emailed them, and they couldn't confirm this (how mysterious!), but the tip is still a fun one to experiment with. Not only does this help keep the flakes of salt from bouncing off the dough, but they also hit your tongue first, leading you from savory into sweet.

Coconut Slice

FROM SARIT PACKER & ITAMAR SRULOVICH

Somewhere between a chewy, chocolate-dipped coconut macaroon and a granola bar jeweled with good fruit and nuts lies this coconut slice from Sarit Packer and Itamar Srulovich of Honey & Co. bakery and café in London. It has all the simple, stirred-together ease of either goodie and, like both, the coconut slice needs no flour to hold it together, which can come in handy during Passover or when serving the gluten-free.

But this also raises a lot of questions: why *haven't* you tucked happy surprises like dried cherries and chopped pistachios into your macaroons before? Or pressed the dough into a single slab, à la blondies and brownies, instead of scooping them into balls? Now you can—and you will!

MAKES ONE 9-INCH (23CM) SQUARE PAN, WHICH CAN BE CUT INTO LARGE OR SMALL BARS

3½ ounces (100g) bittersweet chocolate (56% cacao or higher), coarsely chopped

2½ cups (200g) unsweetened shredded dried coconut

¾ cup (150g) sugar

½ cup (60g) dried sour cherries

½ cup (70g) whole almonds, coarsely chopped

½ cup (60g) shelled pistachios, coarsely chopped

7 tablespoons (100g) unsalted butter, melted

2 large eggs, lightly beaten

1 Heat the oven to 375°F (190°C), with a rack in the center. Line a 9-inch (23cm) square baking pan with parchment paper, leaving a 2-inch (5cm) overhang on two opposite sides for easier lifting when the bars are done.

2 Melt the chocolate in a heatproof bowl set over (but not touching) gently simmering water in a saucepan, or microwave in a microwave-safe bowl in 15-second bursts, stirring between bursts. Pour the melted chocolate into the pan, spread to cover the bottom entirely, and refrigerate until the chocolate is set, about 20 minutes.

3 Stir together the coconut, sugar, cherries, and nuts in a bowl with a rubber spatula, pour in the melted butter, and stir to combine. Add the eggs and stir well. Scrape the mixture into the pan, covering the chocolate. Smooth the top of the mixture with the spatula but leave the surface a little rough, so that it will brown and crisp up nicely.

4 Bake until the coconut is golden, 16 to 18 minutes, rotating the pan from front to back after 10 minutes. Let cool in the pan on a rack for 10 to 15 minutes and then refrigerate until chilled, at least 2 hours.

5 Once fully chilled, loosen the unlined edges of the pan with a sharp knife. Lift up the overhanging ends of the parchment paper and transfer the bars to a cutting board. Run your knife under hot water, wipe it dry, and slice into whatever size bars you like, repeating the hot water trick as needed to get clean slices. Lift the bars off the parchment and transfer to an airtight container. These are deliciously chewy straight from the refrigerator but hold up well if stored at cool room temperature, too.

Salted Brown Butter Crispy Treats

FROM DEB PERELMAN

Here's the truth: the classic recipe that's been printed on the Rice Krispies box since 1940 is already a genius dessert. It's ready in 10 minutes without heating the oven, using three ingredients you can find anywhere: cereal, marshmallows, butter. In fact, it's so ubiquitous that we tend to thumb past it in our mental recipe files in favor of newer, flashier prospects. But here's another truth: most people will walk past all sorts of fancy cookies and tarts to get to the stack of crispy treats before the rest of us make off with them.

This modernized riff from Deb Perelman of *Smitten Kitchen* fame is very much like the original—the same siren crunch surrounded by sweet, soft goo—and uses virtually the same technique. The only differences are that you sizzle the butter a bit longer, until the milk solids have turned toasty and brown, and add salt to balance the sweet. (Oh, and what was 3 tablespoons became a full stick of butter—more to brown!) You might be tempted to brown the marshmallow, too, but don't: it will only turn the bars dry and stiff, and I know you're in it for the goo.

MAKES 16 TREATS

½ cup (110g) unsalted butter, plus more for the pan

1 (10-ounce/283g) bag marshmallows

6 cups (160g) Rice Krispies cereal (about half a 12-ounce/340g box)

Heaping ¼ teaspoon coarse sea salt

1 Generously butter an 8 by 8 by 2-inch (20 by 20 by 5cm) cake pan. If you want to make it extra easy to pop out the treats, line the pan with parchment paper, leaving a 1-inch (2.5cm) overhang on two opposite sides for easier lifting when the bars are done.

2 Melt the butter in a large pot over medium-low heat, stirring frequently with a silicone spatula, until it browns. The butter will melt, then foam, then turn clear golden with brown bits and start to smell nutty. Be patient and don't wander away—the bits will go from brown to black quickly, and you don't want black.

3 Turn off the heat as soon as the bits in the butter are a deep nut brown color. Immediately add the marshmallows and stir until smooth. The residual heat from the pot should be enough to fully melt the marshmallows, but if not, return the heat to low and cook until the marshmallows are completely smooth.

4 Remove the pot from the heat and pour in the cereal and salt. Stir well to make a big sticky mass, then quickly scrape the mixture into the prepared pan. Flatten the gooey mix evenly with a spatula or buttered waxed or parchment paper, pressing into the edges and corners.

5 Let cool to room temperature, about 30 minutes, and cut into squares to serve. Store in an airtight container at room temperature.

GENIUS TIP: JUST ADD MILK POWDER

A little dry milk powder, usually sold in nonfat form, has the power to make ice creams creamier and less icy, brown butter extra brown-buttery, and everything else just taste mysteriously richer and better. Momofuku Milk Bar's Christina Tosi calls it MSG for pastry chefs. As a starting point, add 2 tablespoons milk powder to your favorite chocolate chip cookie recipe "and watch your eyes pop out of your head," as Tosi says. The same trick works well in these Salted Brown Butter Crispy Treats. If you want to take it a step further, see the Toasted Milk Powder on page 42.

roasted sugar

MAGIC POTIONS

As if butter and sugar weren't magical enough, here are four secret potions you can keep in your kitchen that will give your desserts superpowers.

Roasted Sugar
From Stella Parks

Stella Parks may have discovered this by accident—she was warming up sugar in a too-cold pastry kitchen and forgot about it—but the investigation and reporting that followed earned her a James Beard Award. Here's the gist: if you heat sugar at a low temperature (about 300°F/150°C) in a container that's not superconductive (ceramic, glass, or even in a piecrust that's blind-baking, as Parks does; see page 204), it slowly caramelizes instead of liquefying. The roasted sugar can be swapped for white sugar in any recipe for a less-sweet, more caramel-like flavor, without messing with the moisture or pH.

How to make it: Heat the oven to 300°F (150°C), with a rack in the center. Pour **4 pounds (1.8kg) sugar** into a 9 by 13-inch (23 by 33cm) glass or ceramic baking dish and bake until the sugar is the color of ivory, about 1 hour. Stir well, and then continue to bake, stirring every 30 minutes (carefully—the sugar will be very hot!), until darkened to light or sandy beige (your call), 2 to 4 hours more. Beyond this point, the sugar will begin to liquefy. Let the sugar cool on a rack to room temperature, about 2 hours. Once cool, if the sugar is lumpy, pulse in a food processor until finely ground. Store airtight at room temperature.

Ground Croccante
From Marcella Hazan

Step 1: Make Marcella Hazan's crunchy, bittersweet brittle on page 79 (no candy thermometer required, though you will need a potato). Step 2: Grind in a food processor or spice grinder. Step 3: Sprinkle on ice cream, fold into cookie dough, or roll on the edges of sandwich cookies or chocolate-dipped anything.

Toasted Milk Powder
From Ideas in Food

Aki Kamozawa and H. Alexander Talbot at Ideas in Food have played around a lot with toasting dry milk powder, to bump up the intensity of brown butter and allow its flavor to go places it hadn't before. They've made brown butter stock, ice cream, pasta, even mayo. You can sizzle the powder directly in browning butter for a greater concentration of toasted milk solids, but if you want to keep a dry jar of it on hand, just microwave **1¼ cups (100g) nonfat dry milk powder** in a big bowl on high, stirring and breaking up the clumps with a fork every 30 seconds, for a good 10 minutes. The powder will turn deep caramel brown and smell otherworldly, and it will give any dessert you sprinkle it into an undercurrent of, yes, brown butter, but also dulce de leche. Store airtight at room temperature.

ground croccante

Chocolate Magic Dust
From Jami Curl

"Welcome to my favorite ingredient of all time," says Jami Curl, founder of Quin Candy and author of the cookbook *Candy Is Magic*. Use this potion anywhere you'd use sweetened cocoa powder. Curl adds it to whipped cream and butter, stirs it into cookie doughs, sprinkles it on top of banana bread and pie, and uses it to make a very fine cup of hot chocolate.

How to make it: For **3 cups (600g) chocolate magic dust**, whisk together **2 cups + 3 tablespoons (460g) sugar, 1 cup + 2 tablespoons (116g) unsweetened cocoa powder** (see page 5, Curl's favorite is Felchlin cocoa powder), **½ teaspoon kosher salt, 1 teaspoon ground cinnamon**, and **1 tablespoon + 1 teaspoon vanilla bean powder** (aka finely ground vanilla beans). Buy vanilla bean powder online or at specialty baking shops—or grind your own with the dried pods you've saved (page 152)!

toasted milk powder

chocolate magic dust

Lemon Square Cookies

FROM ANITA JAISINGHANI

When Anita Jaisinghani, founder of Pondicheri Bake Lab & Shop in Houston and New York City, devised this unconventional vegan and gluten-free cookie, she didn't simply go to an accepted blueprint. She wanted to start with inherently gluten-free ingredients and build out a cookie from there. That's how it occurred to her to whip avocado into the dough as a smooth, creamy binder. She initially used xanthan gum in the mix, but when she realized the cookies held together just fine without it, it was gone. (You will need to chill the dough for four hours to fully meld, so be sure to plan ahead.)

The cookies are genre-defying and unusually addicting: soft with a mochi-like chew, with a bit of grit from the almond flour and crunchy tiles of sliced almond on top. They're warmly spiced and loud with lemon, from lots of zest and juice in the batter plus a final squeeze of lemon juice baked into the cookies at the end. You wouldn't know the avocado is there, but the cookie wouldn't be holding together, smooth and buttery, without it.

MAKES 12 BIG SQUARES

1¼ cups plus 3 tablespoons (285g) sugar

⅔ cup (140g) well-mashed, ripe avocado (from 1 or 2 avocados)

Finely grated zest of 3 lemons (about 3 tablespoons)

⅔ cup (140g) unrefined coconut oil, melted and cooled

2 cups (220g) almond flour (see page 5)

2 cups (310g) white rice flour (see page 5)

¾ teaspoon ground turmeric

¾ teaspoon ground mace or freshly grated nutmeg

1½ teaspoons baking powder

¾ teaspoon baking soda

½ teaspoon fine sea salt

¼ cup (60g) freshly squeezed lemon juice

¾ cup (70g) toasted sliced almonds

Half of 1 large lemon, for topping

1 In the bowl of a stand mixer fitted with the whisk attachment, whip the sugar, avocado, and lemon zest on medium-high speed until fluffy, 4 to 5 minutes. Slowly pour in the coconut oil and continue mixing until well combined.

2 In a separate bowl, whisk together the flours, turmeric, mace, baking powder, baking soda, and salt. With the mixer on low, add the dry ingredients to the avocado mixture in three additions, alternating with the lemon juice in two additions, and mix only until incorporated after each addition.

3 Line a 9 by 13-inch (23 by 33cm) baking dish (or a larger pan or baking sheet) with plastic wrap and press the dough evenly into the pan. If your pan is larger, simply pat the dough into a ¾-inch (2cm) thick rectangle or square—it will stand firm. Top with the almonds, cover with plastic wrap, and refrigerate for at least 4 hours.

4 Heat the oven to 325°F (165°C), with racks in the upper and lower thirds. Line two large rimmed baking sheets with parchment paper or silicone baking mats. Slice the chilled dough into 3-inch (7.5cm) squares and arrange on the baking sheets, spacing them at least 2 inches (5cm) apart. Bake until the edges are golden brown but the insides are still a little soft, about 15 minutes, rotating the sheets front to back and top to bottom halfway through baking. Be careful not to overbake.

5 Remove the cookies from the oven and immediately squeeze the lemon half over the top. Return the baking sheets to the oven and bake for 2 minutes more. Let the squares cool in the baking sheets on racks until they're firm enough to transfer to the racks to cool completely, about 10 minutes. Store in an airtight container at room temperature.

Pistachio Millionaire's Shortbread with Coriander Butterscotch

FROM MAX FALKOWITZ

This sultry take on millionaire's shortbread was developed by Max Falkowitz, then food editor at *Serious Eats*, as part of a love letter to coriander, a spice that isn't used as often in baking as it should be. "It brightens and deepens buttery flavors," Falkowitz says, landing "halfway between lemon zest and cinnamon."

Here, coriander gives the butterscotch an unexpected buzzing warmth. The shortbread bottom is rounded with pistachio and lemon zest and baked softer than you'd think, for optimal melding. And the chocolate up top is good and dark.

MAKES ABOUT 3 DOZEN (1-INCH/2.5CM) SQUARES

SHORTBREAD
1 cup (225g) unsalted butter, softened

3/4 cup (150g) sugar

1 packed tablespoon finely grated lemon zest

1½ teaspoons kosher salt

1¼ cups (150g) shelled pistachios

1½ cups (190g) all-purpose flour (see page 5)

BUTTERSCOTCH
2 tablespoons coriander seeds

½ cup (110g) unsalted butter

1½ cups (300g) turbinado sugar

½ cup (120g) heavy cream, plus more if needed

½ cup (115g) Irish whiskey

2 teaspoons kosher salt

CHOCOLATE TOP
8 ounces (225g) bittersweet chocolate (about 70% cacao), finely chopped

2 tablespoons unsalted butter

1 To make the shortbread, heat the oven to 350°F (175°C), with a rack in the center. Line a large rimmed baking sheet with parchment paper. In the bowl of a stand mixer fitted with the paddle attachment, cream the butter, sugar, lemon zest, and salt on high speed until fluffy, about 3 minutes.

2 In a food processor, pulse the pistachios to a fine meal (some small chunks are okay). Add the ground pistachios to the butter mixture and blend on low speed until incorporated. With the mixer running on low speed, add the flour, about ½ cup (60g) at a time. When no streaks of flour remain, increase the speed to high and mix just until the mixture holds together in a thick dough, about 1 minute.

3 Scrape the dough onto the baking sheet and press with your hands into a 12 by 9-inch (30 by 23cm) rectangle that's ½ inch (1.3cm) thick. Bake until the edges brown and the top is dry but still slightly sticky, about 15 minutes. The center should look underbaked. Let the shortbread cool completely in the baking sheet on a rack.

4 To make the butterscotch, toast the coriander seeds in a medium skillet over medium heat, shaking occasionally, until they smell fragrant and have darkened slightly, then pour off into a wide bowl to cool. Once cool, grind finely in a spice grinder or a mortar and pestle. You should have 2 tablespoons, plus a bit extra to sprinkle over at the end.

5 Melt the butter in a heavy 3-quart (2.8L) saucepan over medium heat. Increase the heat to high, add the sugar, and stir to toast the sugar for about 30 seconds. Carefully pour in the cream and whiskey, then add 2 tablespoons of the coriander and the salt, stirring to dissolve the sugar. Bring to a boil, stirring constantly until the butterscotch is thick enough that a rubber spatula leaves a dry trail that quickly closes across the bottom of the pan, 5 to 10 minutes. Remove from the heat and let cool until warm and spreadable. If the butterscotch hardens, reheat it over low heat, stirring in an extra tablespoon or two of cream. It may look broken, but just whisk it back together.

6 To make the chocolate top, melt the chocolate and butter in a small saucepan over low heat, stirring often to keep the chocolate from scorching. When the chocolate is mostly melted, remove it from the heat and stir until smooth.

7 To assemble the bars, pour the butterscotch over the shortbread and spread into an even layer with an offset spatula. Refrigerate until the butterscotch is firm, about 10 minutes, then spread the chocolate on top of the butterscotch in a thin layer. Sprinkle with ground coriander and refrigerate until the chocolate is firm, about 20 minutes.

8 Cut into 1-inch (2.5cm) squares with a sharp knife and serve chilled or at room temperature. (Alternatively, cover the cookies well in plastic wrap and freeze for up to 1 month.)

Nibby Buckwheat Butter Cookies

FROM ALICE MEDRICH

Alice Medrich, ever the rebel, has always been early to embrace less-trod, more nuanced ingredients. This buttery shortbread is a good example of how we benefit from her dedication. Instead of chocolate chips or nuts or other obvious go-tos, here's a cookie shaped by the toasty, almost grassy flavor of buckwheat flour and bitter cacao nibs, which taste like chocolate unhinged. Not only do these unusual suspects give the cookies a more intriguing flavor, but better texture, too—buckwheat is gluten-free, so it acts in the same way cornstarch does to tenderize doughs ("but with flavor!" as Medrich says). Amidst all this delicate, sandy crunch, the cacao nibs gently prickle and crack.

In making my way through the glut of cookies and cakes that I had on hand while testing recipes for this book, it was these sorts of unexpected flavors that I continued to crave and never tired of. From many return trips to the cookie tin, I am able to confirm that these keep shockingly well for a month or more.

MAKES 4 DOZEN COOKIES

1¼ cups (160g) all-purpose flour (see page 5)

¾ cup (85g) buckwheat flour (see page 5)

1 cup (225g) unsalted butter, softened

⅔ cup (135g) sugar

¼ teaspoon fine sea salt

⅓ cup (45g) cacao nibs

1½ teaspoons pure vanilla extract

1 Whisk together the flours in a medium bowl. With the back of a large spoon or spatula (or with an electric mixer) in a separate large bowl, beat the butter, sugar, and salt on medium until smooth and creamy but not fluffy, about 1 minute with the mixer. Stir in the cacao nibs and vanilla. Add the flours and mix just until no streaks of flour remain. Scrape the dough together onto a work surface lined with plastic wrap, and if it still looks loose or unevenly mixed, knead it with your hands a few times, just until smooth.

2 Roll the dough into a 12 by 2-inch (30 by 5cm) log. Bundle the log in the plastic wrap, twisting the ends tightly to help even out the shape, and refrigerate for at least 2 hours or preferably overnight. To help maintain its round shape, refrigerate the log in an empty paper towel roll or tall drinking glasses.

3 Heat the oven to 350°F (175°C), with racks in the upper and lower thirds. Line two large rimmed baking sheets with parchment paper or silicone baking mats.

4 Using a sharp knife, slice the log into ¼-inch (6mm) rounds. Arrange the rounds on the baking sheets, spacing them at least 1½ inches (4cm) apart.

5 Bake the cookies until they are just beginning to turn brown at the edges, 12 to 14 minutes, rotating the baking sheets from front to back and top to bottom halfway through baking. Let the cookies cool completely on the baking sheets on a rack. The cookies improve with time and can be stored in an airtight container for at least 1 month.

GENIUS TIP: RIFFING WITH ALTERNATIVE FLOURS

If you find yourself craving new, deeper flavors in your desserts, here's some good news: Alice Medrich says that you can conservatively start by swapping out 15 to 20 percent of the all-purpose flour in any of your favorite recipes for an alternative flour, with little risk of failure. If you like, you can bump it up from there—this is true for gluten-free flours, such as corn (flour, not meal), oat, sorghum, brown rice, teff, buckwheat, and chestnut flour, as well as for wheat relatives (which do contain gluten) like whole wheat, kamut, spelt, barley, and rye.

Thin & Crispy Black Sesame Oatmeal Cookies

FROM SANDRA WU

The baking world abounds with soft, chewy oatmeal cookies, but toward the end of her years working at America's Test Kitchen, recipe developer Sandra Wu was after something very different. She was trying to create a thinner variation with a crunchy snap that tasted of butter and toasted oats instead of cinnamon and raisins, and it was proving surprisingly hard to land. Many trials in, the cookies were still too chewy, too tough, or they spread like sugary lava. Finally, she embraced what would normally be considered a baking mistake to get exactly what she wanted.

Overdoing leaveners like baking powder or baking soda can cause cakes and cookies to pouf and then collapse. But for the cookie that she wanted, that was exactly the point—so she cranked up both. The cookies deflated to a perfect all-over sandy crisp, and an extra-thorough baking time brought forward all sorts of subtle flavors that are normally swept into the background. In her updated riff here, she not only stirs in roasted black sesame seeds for more nubbly texture, but also replaces a bit of the butter with more seeds ground with sugar, pushing its savory, toasted virtues further still. (If you can only find raw black sesame seeds, toast them lightly in a dry skillet on the stovetop just until they smell nutty, then pour them into a bowl to cool down.)

MAKES ABOUT 2 DOZEN COOKIES

1 cup (125g) all-purpose flour (see page 5)

¾ teaspoon baking powder

½ teaspoon baking soda

½ teaspoon fine sea salt

½ cup (70g) roasted black sesame seeds

¾ cup (150g) sugar

¾ cup (170g) unsalted butter, at room temperature but still cool (about 65°F/18°C)

¼ cup (55g) packed light brown sugar

1 large egg

1 teaspoon pure vanilla extract

2¼ cups (205g) old-fashioned rolled oats

½ teaspoon coarse sea salt (such as Maldon or fleur de sel)

1 Heat the oven to 350°F (175°C), with a rack in the center. Line three large rimmed baking sheets with parchment paper or silicone baking mats.

2 Whisk together the flour, baking powder, baking soda, and fine sea salt in a bowl. Grind ¼ cup (35g) of the sesame seeds and ¼ cup (50g) of the sugar in a spice grinder or mini food processor until fine and sandy.

3 In the bowl of a stand mixer fitted with the paddle attachment, beat the butter, ground sesame seed mixture, the remaining ½ cup (100g) of the sugar, and the brown sugar on medium-low speed until just combined, about 20 seconds. Increase the speed to medium and continue to beat until light and fluffy, about 1 minute more.

4 Add the egg and vanilla and beat on medium-low speed until fully incorporated, about 30 seconds. With the mixer running on low speed, add the flour mixture and mix until just incorporated and smooth, about 10 seconds. Gradually add the oats and the remaining ¼ cup (35g) of sesame seeds and mix until well incorporated, about 20 seconds. Give the dough a final stir with the rubber spatula to make sure the ingredients are evenly distributed and no streaks of flour remain, especially at the bottom of the bowl.

5 Using a 2-tablespoon scoop or a spoon, scoop the dough into mounds. Use your hands to roll the mounds into balls. Arrange the cookies on the baking sheets, spacing them about 2½ inches (6.5cm) apart. Using your fingertips or the buttered bottom of a juice glass, gently press each dough ball until it's ¾ inch (2cm) thick. Lightly sprinkle coarse sea salt evenly over the flattened dough balls before baking.

6 Bake one sheet at a time until the cookies are deep golden brown, the edges are crisp, and the centers yield to slight pressure when pressed lightly with your finger, 13 to 16 minutes, rotating the baking sheet front to back halfway through baking. Let the cookies cool completely on the baking sheet on a rack. Store in an airtight container at room temperature.

Pains d'Amande

FROM FLO BRAKER

These crisp almond wafers—the signature cookie of self-taught baking expert and cookbook author Flo Braker—could not be easier to make, yet they ooze fanciness. You won't need to pull out a mixer or food processor, just a pot to gently melt together raw sugar, butter, water, and cinnamon, then stir in sliced almonds and flour.

The secret to that mod, I-am-so-not-a-drop-cookie shape is in flattening the dough into a loaf pan, then refrigerating it until it's firm enough to slice very thinly. Or if you're impatient (or planning ahead, you model entertainer), freezing it.

The cookies bake up into wands of brown butter, caramel, and almond that snap under your teeth. They're buttery-crisp without being too fragile, so they'll even ship well cross-country. Any extra dough can be squirreled away in the freezer, to slice off a few cookies whenever you see fit.

MAKES ABOUT 6 DOZEN COOKIES

2⅓ cups (325g) all-purpose flour (see page 5)	½ cup (110g) unsalted butter, cold and cut into quarters
¼ teaspoon baking soda	⅓ cup (80g) water
1⅓ cups (280g) Hawaiian washed raw sugar (see note)	½ teaspoon ground cinnamon
	1 cup (85g) sliced almonds

1 Sift together the flour and baking soda into a bowl or onto a sheet of waxed paper. Combine the sugar, butter, water, and cinnamon in a 1½-quart/1.4L (or other medium) saucepan and cook over low heat, stirring occasionally, just until the butter melts. Don't allow the mixture to boil and don't let the sugar melt completely—the crunchy bits make for wonderful texture in the cookie. Remove from the heat and stir in the almonds. Let cool at room temperature until the mixture is lukewarm (about 90°F/32°C), about 30 minutes.

2 Pour in the dry ingredients and stir until well blended. Line an 8½ by 4½-inch (22cm by 11.5cm) loaf pan (preferably straight sided, but angled is okay, too), with plastic wrap, leaving a 3-inch (7.5cm) overhang on the long sides so the plastic can cover the dough when refrigerating. Press the dough into the loaf pan, cover the top with plastic wrap, and refrigerate or freeze until firm, about 4 hours in the refrigerator (and up to 3 days) or up to 1 month in the freezer.

3 Heat the oven to 325°F (165°C), with a rack in the lower third. Line two large rimmed baking sheets with parchment paper or silicone baking mats.

4 Once the dough is firm, lift it from the pan onto a cutting board and peel away the plastic wrap. If your loaf pan is angled, the cookies, once sliced, will be barely sloping trapezoids instead of perfect rectangles. If you want straighter sides, just shave a little extra off the sides of the block to tidy it up. Using a serrated or other very sharp knife, cut the dough as thinly as you can; you want ⅛-inch (3mm) or thinner slices. Arrange the cookies ¼ inch (6mm) apart on the lined baking sheets.

5 Bake one sheet at a time until the undersides are light golden, 8 to 10 minutes. Use a thin spatula to flip the cookies and bake until crisp and dark golden, 8 to 10 minutes more. Let the cookies cool on the baking sheet on a rack till firm, then transfer to the rack to continue cooling. Store the cookies in an airtight container at room temperature— they'll last a good 10 days or more.

Note: Hawaiian washed raw sugar is available in some supermarkets in 2-pound (900g) plastic bags. If you can't find it, substitute turbinado or Demerara.

"Serve less than perfect desserts in a dimly lit room." —Flo Braker

Cacio e Pepe Shortbread

FROM CHARLOTTE DRUCKMAN

This is a shortbread cookie that doesn't quite know if it's sweet or savory, and in my experience, it doesn't matter. Every time I set wedges of it out, I explain nothing—at first. Lurkers swarm and empty the plate, without stopping to wonder what genre of snack they're eating.

The recipe comes from the mind of Charlotte Druckman, author of *Stir, Sizzle, Bake*, a cookbook full of novel ways to use your cast-iron skillet—including this borderline psychedelic one. Druckman was inspired by Blue Bottle Coffee pastry chef Caitlin Freeman's shortbread dough–whipping technique and chef Mark Ladner's feisty *cacio e pepe*; she wondered what would happen if she were to graft a pasta recipe onto a shortbread.

She worked in not only the cheeses (*cacio*) and the black pepper (*pepe*) but also dried pasta's traditional semolina flour, which gives the shortbread a hint of warm, wheaty, pasta-like flavor, as well as a softness and a tight, fine-crumb structure. She then baked in one more round of crisp outer texture and toasty flavor by pressing the dough (carefully!) into a hot cast-iron skillet, brushing the top with olive oil, and sprinkling more pepper and cheese over it. Snack on it with your afternoon coffee or aperitifs—Prosecco, Bellinis, rosé, or whatever you like to drink at cocktail hour.

MAKES 10 TO 12 WEDGES

½ cup plus 2 teaspoons (40g) finely grated Parmesan cheese, using the small holes of a box grater

½ cup plus 2 teaspoons (40g) finely grated Pecorino Romano cheese, using the small holes of a box grater

2 teaspoons coarsely ground black pepper

1 cup (225g) unsalted butter, at room temperature

½ cup (60g) confectioners' sugar

1¼ teaspoons kosher salt

1½ cups (190g) all-purpose flour

½ cup (80g) semolina flour

1 tablespoon plus 2 teaspoons extra-virgin olive oil

1 Heat the oven to 350°F (175°C), with a 10-inch (25cm) cast-iron skillet on the center rack. Stir together 2 teaspoons each of the Parmesan and Pecorino and 1 teaspoon of the pepper in a small bowl.

2 In the bowl of a stand mixer fitted with the paddle attachment, beat the butter on medium-low speed until it's smooth, creamy, and fluffy like cake frosting, about 1 minute. Add the sugar, salt, and the remaining 1 teaspoon of pepper and stir until combined. Scrape down the sides of the bowl with a silicone spatula as needed.

3 Turn the speed to medium and mix until the mixture takes on a thick, creamy, almost mayonnaise-like texture, 4 to 5 minutes more. Add the flours and stir on low speed until just incorporated. Add the remaining ½ cup (35g) Parmesan and ½ cup (35g) Pecorino and mix on low for 1 minute. Scrape the dough together to form a ball.

4 Take the hot skillet out of the oven and set it on the stovetop or other heat-safe surface. Brush the skillet with 1 teaspoon of the olive oil. Nudge the dough into the skillet and, using the spatula or your fingers (but being careful of the hot pan), flatten the dough into the skillet, pushing it out evenly to the edges. Brush with the remaining 1 tablespoon plus 1 teaspoon olive oil. Sprinkle the dough with the cheese-pepper mixture and transfer back to the oven. (Don't forget the handle will still be hot!)

5 Bake the shortbread until the edges begin to brown, 18 to 23 minutes. The middle should be cooked through but still a bit soft, as it will firm up as it cools. Set the pan on the stovetop or other heat-safe surface and let cool in the pan for 10 minutes. Using a plate, carefully invert the pan and flip the shortbread out, then flip it once more onto another plate so it's right side up. Alternately, you can serve straight from the pan. Let cool completely.

6 To serve, cut the shortbread into 10 to 12 wedges. Store in an airtight container at room temperature.

Biscottini

FROM HEIDI SWANSON

If you're not from Italy, the word *biscotti* likely conjures up the long, chocolate-dunked planks poking out of a vase by the register at your local coffee shop. It did for me, until Christmas 1995, when my aunt and uncle conspired to create a handmade cookbook of biscotti recipes for me. Transcribed from magazines and library books and decorated with felt cutouts and scraps of ribbon, their sweet gift proved the genre could be so much more—biscotti could be made with honey or olive or pistachio-fig! The technique for making stiff, crunchy cookies to soak up coffee or wine is constant (hint: *biscotti* means "twice-baked"); the flavors are yours to decide.

These tiniest biscotti, or *biscottini*, are the work of Heidi Swanson, whose recipes are loved for their wholesome ingredients and global perspective. But it's in her wild, often unheard-of ingredient matchups that I always find inspiration—sweet potatoes with dill, strawberries with caraway, and here, the fine crunch of cornmeal and whole wheat steeped with the scents of fennel, rosemary, lemon, and brown sugar.

MAKES 2½ DOZEN BISCOTTINI

¾ cup (95g) whole wheat pastry flour (see page 5)

½ cup (60g) all-purpose flour (see page 5)

Scant ¼ cup (20g) fine cornmeal

½ teaspoon baking powder

½ teaspoon fine sea salt

1 packed tablespoon finely grated lemon zest

1 tablespoon finely chopped fresh rosemary

1 teaspoon fennel seeds

¼ cup (60g) unsalted butter, softened

½ cup (100g) lightly packed light brown sugar

2 large eggs

2 teaspoons limoncello (optional)

¾ cup (105g) almonds, toasted then chopped

1 Whisk together the flours, cornmeal, baking powder, salt, lemon zest, rosemary, and fennel seeds in a bowl. In a stand mixer fitted with the paddle attachment, or using a handheld mixer in a large bowl, cream the butter and sugar on high speed until light and fluffy, about 2 minutes. Add 1 egg and the limoncello and mix until incorporated. Add the dry ingredients and mix on low speed just until the dough comes together. Gently stir in the almonds by hand. Gather the dough into a ball and cut it in quarters. Cover the dough in plastic wrap and refrigerate to firm up a bit, 10 to 15 minutes.

2 Heat the oven to 350°F (175°C), with a rack in the center. Line a large rimmed baking sheet with parchment paper or a silicone baking mat. Whisk the remaining egg with a splash of water in a small bowl to make an egg wash.

3 On a floured surface, use the palms of your hands to roll each portion of dough into a 1-inch- (2.5cm-) wide snake-like tube. Carefully transfer each tube to the baking sheet, flatten slightly, brush with the egg wash, and bake until light golden, about 20 minutes. Remove from the oven and let cool to the touch on the baking sheet.

4 Transfer to a cutting board and use a serrated knife to cut ½-inch (1.3cm) slices, either straight or on the diagonal for a fancier look. Arrange the slices on the baking sheet, cut side up, and bake until the cut sides are golden, 10 to 15 minutes more. Let cool completely on the baking sheet. Store in an airtight container at room temperature. The biscottini will stay good and crunchy for 3 weeks or so.

Douglas's Whole Wheat Jam Thumbprints

FROM FÄVIKEN

This recipe is a testament to how rustic baking can be—an all whole wheat flour, no-fear thumbprint cookie that tastes like a bite-size piece of toast with just the right amount of jam. You'll mix the dough together with your hands so you can be gentle and feel the butter working in. This way, there's less risk of overdoing it and stiffening the gluten, as whole wheat flour can be prone to do. (You also have to roll the dough into balls and poke your thumb in to make a hollow for the jam, so your hands never had a chance of staying clean anyway.)

It might seem surprising that a recipe this simple and homespun comes from Fäviken, a pricey destination restaurant, but it makes sense when you consider that the chefs famously use hyperlocal ingredients and traditional, almost anti-technology techniques. Being located in the remote woods of Sweden, this can sometimes manifest in recipes for pine bark cake and broth of forest floor. Luckily for us, this recipe was handed down from the grandmother of a former cook named Douglas and has ingredients that can be found anywhere, although the higher-quality and fresher they are all around, the better.

MAKES 4½ DOZEN COOKIES

4 cups (480g) whole wheat flour (see page 5)

1 tablespoon baking powder

1 cup plus 2 tablespoons (225g) sugar

1⅓ cups (300g) salted butter (preferably cultured), at room temperature

2 large eggs, at room temperature, lightly beaten

¾ cup (240g) good jam (preferably homemade)

1 Heat the oven to 400°F (200°C), with racks in the upper and lower thirds. Line two large rimmed baking sheets with parchment paper or silicone baking mats.

2 With your hands, knead together the flour, baking powder, and sugar with the butter in a medium bowl until well mixed, about 1 minute. Pour the eggs into the dough mixture and knead just until smooth, taking care not to overwork the dough.

3 Immediately, using a 1-tablespoon cookie scoop or a tablespoon, scoop the dough and roll into balls. Arrange on the baking sheets, spacing them 2 inches (5cm) apart. Make an indentation in the center of each cookie with your finger and fill the indentation with about ½ teaspoon of jam. If the cookies crack, you can gently press them back together.

4 Bake until golden brown, about 10 minutes, rotating the baking sheets from front to back and top to bottom halfway through baking. Transfer the cookies to a rack to cool. Eat the cookies warm or let them cool completely before serving. Store in an airtight container at room temperature.

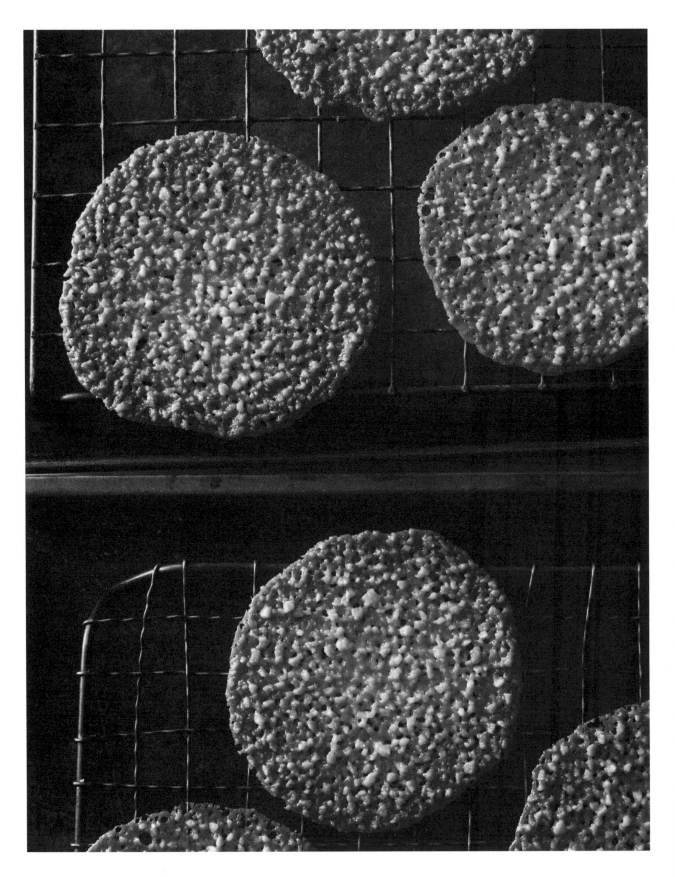

Erna's Lace Cookies

FROM MARIAN BURROS

Although these paper-thin cookies look as precious and fancy as spun sugar, they require no pastry training, no thermometer, and little time or attention. Their lacy good looks stem from the fact that the dough is bound by a mere 4 teaspoons of flour (by my calculations, that's .13 teaspoons of flour per cookie) and a good deal more ground almonds, thickened briefly with butter, milk, and sugar in a skillet on the stovetop (and no eggs or leaveners to puff them up). They spread and bubble wildly in the oven, and once cool, taste of brown butter and toasted almond, shattering politely in your mouth, and then melting away.

Marian Burros, cookbook author and longtime writer for the *New York Times*, originally credits the recipe to her friend Erna Miller, and so the name stays here. A lover of both ease and her freezer, Burros discovered that the cookies freeze beautifully. If wrapped up well, their dainty crunch doesn't suffer at all.

MAKES ABOUT 30 COOKIES

⅔ cup (85g) blanched almonds	4 teaspoons (10g) all-purpose flour
¼ cup (60g) unsalted butter	Pinch of salt
½ cup (100g) sugar	4 teaspoons (20g) low-fat or whole milk

1 Heat the oven to 350°F (175°C), with the racks in the upper and lower thirds. Line two large rimmed baking sheets with parchment paper or silicone baking mats. In a food processor or blender, pulse the almonds until they are the texture of coarse cornmeal. Don't overdo it, or you will end up with almond butter.

2 Melt the butter in a small skillet over low heat. Add sugar, flour, and salt and stir very briefly, just until the sugar is completely incorporated. Add the ground almonds and the milk. Continue to stir until well combined and the mixture thickens a little. Remove from the heat and let cool for about 1 minute.

3 Using a teaspoon, drop the batter onto the baking sheets, spacing them at least 3 inches (7.5cm) apart—they'll spread a lot. There should be 6 cookies per baking sheet. (For a tip on speeding up time between batches, see the Genius Tip below.) If the batter gets too stiff to scoop in later batches, briefly warm it over low heat on the stovetop.

4 Bake until golden brown, 6 to 8 minutes, rotating the sheets from front to back and top to bottom halfway through baking. Let the cookies cool on the baking sheets just long enough to firm up, about 5 minutes, and then use a thin knife or metal spatula to transfer them to a rack to cool completely. Store in an airtight container at room temperature. These cookies freeze beautifully if stored airtight, with waxed paper or parchment between each cookie. Thaw at room temperature before serving (or sneak them cold from the freezer).

GENIUS TIP: HOW TO MAKE A LOT OF COOKIES, FASTER

Waiting for the pans to cool between batches of cookies can be a big slowdown, especially when you need to bake a whole lot of cookies with only a couple of baking sheets—but cool pans are essential to evenly baked cookies. *Or are they?* Alice Medrich's brilliant hack is to scoop the cookies onto sheets of parchment paper and then slide them onto the still-hot baking sheet all at once and quickly stick them in the oven. (This move is *much* easier if the pans are rimless, or at least flipped upside down.) The cookies may bake a minute or two faster, but with this swift sleight of hand, no cookies will melt on a hot baking sheet while you're frantically scooping out the rest of the batch.

Back-to-School Raspberry Granola Bars

FROM KAREN DEMASCO

Sure, we can technically call these granola bars because they're made of oats and nuts and cut into rectangles, but in practice they're more like the crumbly top layer of a fruit crisp, made into a sandwich cookie. And despite their hunky granola-like ingredient list and a near absence of technique, they have the lightness of a fine, sandy shortbread cookie. I suspect this is due to the unusual addition of flour and a little more butter than usual, and because pastry chef Karen DeMasco really knows what she's doing.

The first time I made these, ostensibly for friends who were coming to town, the bars were gone before they'd even finished cooling. I had to bake them again the next day, and I was able to stir them together in 10 minutes, hardly looking at the recipe. I tell you this because it will happen to you, too, and now you know that you don't have to be too threatening when scavengers start to hover. Just pull out another jar of jam (or a mix of a few) and a hidden stash of nuts, because any combination will work, and give this delicate granola bar–ish framework new character.

MAKES 16 BARS

1 cup (115g) pecan halves, coarsely chopped

1½ cups (190g) all-purpose flour (see page 5)

1¼ cups (115g) old-fashioned rolled oats

⅓ cup (65g) sugar

⅓ cup (75g) packed dark brown sugar

1 teaspoon kosher salt

½ teaspoon baking soda

¾ cup (170g) unsalted butter, melted

1 cup (320g) raspberry jam

1 Heat the oven to 350°F (175°C), with a rack in the center. Butter an 8-inch (20cm) square baking pan. Line the bottom and sides with parchment paper, leaving a 1-inch (2.5cm) overhang on two opposite sides for easier lifting when the bars are done. Butter the parchment. Spread the pecans in a pie plate or on a rimmed baking sheet and toast in the oven until lightly browned and fragrant, about 5 minutes. Let cool.

2 Whisk together the flour, oats, sugars, salt, baking soda, and cooled pecans in large bowl. Pour in the melted butter, and using a wooden spoon or rubber spatula, stir until well combined.

3 Press two-thirds of the oat mixture (about 3 cups/470g) into an even, firmly packed layer on the bottom of the baking pan. Using an offset or rubber spatula, spread the raspberry jam evenly across the surface of the dough, leaving a ¼-inch (6mm) border uncovered at the edges (the jam will melt and spread closer to the edges). Evenly sprinkle the remaining oat mixture over the jam.

4 Bake until the top is golden brown, about 40 minutes, rotating the pan halfway through baking. Let the granola bars cool completely in the pan on a rack, about 3 hours. (Or go ahead and sneak one while they're still warm— they'll be a little crumbly but so good.) Lift up the overhanging ends of the parchment paper and transfer the granola almost-bars to a cutting board. Cut into 2-inch (5cm) squares. Store in an airtight container at room temperature.

Easy Baklava

FROM EINAT ADMONY

With its crisp, razor-thin layers of phyllo stacked and fused with syrup, baklava tends to look complicated, though it actually requires more patience than pastry skills. But Einat Admony—the chef behind Balaboosta, Taïm, and Bar Bolonat in New York City—makes hers extra easy, jelly-roll style.

As in a puff pastry pinwheel, the simple act of rolling multiplies the layers so that you don't have to do quite so much by hand. The spirals you slice off the roll also bake up crisp in half the time, since they stand free on a baking sheet instead of in a compact panful. Only after baking do you nest the spirals together tightly to drink up the rose-honey syrup. Admony's nut mixture includes the unusual addition of raw peanuts, which aren't always easy to find. You can use roasted unsalted peanuts and the baklava will be distinctly peanutty, or substitute any combination of nuts you like.

MAKES ABOUT 30 PIECES

SYRUP
2 cups (400g) sugar

1 cup (235g) water

¼ cup (85g) honey

1 (3-inch/7.5cm) strip orange zest, cut with a vegetable peeler

1 cardamom pod

¼ teaspoon rose water

BAKLAVA
6 tablespoons (85g) unsalted butter, melted

¼ cup plus 2 tablespoons (80g) neutral oil (such as grapeseed)

8 ounces (225g) raw peanuts

8 ounces (225g) raw pistachios

8 ounces (225g) raw walnuts

½ cup (60g) confectioners' sugar

1 teaspoon rose water

⅛ teaspoon ground cardamom (preferably freshly ground from the seeds of about 2 pods)

½ teaspoon ground cinnamon

1 (1 pound/454g) package frozen phyllo dough, thawed completely

1 To make the syrup, combine the sugar, water, honey, orange zest, and cardamom in a saucepan. Simmer over low heat, stirring until the sugar dissolves, about 10 minutes.

2 Remove from the heat and stir in the rose water. Let cool, then pour the syrup into an airtight container and refrigerate until chilled, or up to 1 day in advance.

3 To make the baklava, heat the oven to 350°F (175°C), with a rack in the center. Line a baking sheet with parchment paper. Stir together the melted butter and oil in a bowl and set near where you'll be rolling the baklava.

4 In a food processor, pulse the nuts, confectioners' sugar, rose water, cardamom, and cinnamon until the nuts are very finely chopped and the mixture is almost pasty.

5 Lay 3 sheets of phyllo dough stacked on top of one another on the counter or cutting board with one of the short sides closest to you. Cover the unused sheets of phyllo with a damp kitchen towel as you work, or they'll dry out.

6 Very generously brush the top layer of phyllo dough with about ¼ cup (60ml) of the butter mixture. Spread a third (1⅓ cups/245ml) of the nut mixture on the bottom third of the phyllo dough and pack it down. Roll the phyllo away from you to form a compact log. Keep the seam side down as you work on more rolls. Repeat with the remaining phyllo dough and nut mixture to form 2 more rolls. Place the rolls on the baking sheet and freeze for 10 minutes to make them easier to slice.

7 Remove from the freezer and cut the rolls evenly into about 1-inch (2.5cm) slices. Arrange the slices, cut sides up and well spaced apart, on the same baking sheet and bake until golden brown, about 30 minutes, rotating the baking sheet halfway through baking.

8 Remove from the oven. While still warm, carefully transfer the baklava and arrange snugly, cut side up, in a 9 by 13-inch (23 by 33cm) pan or another deep serving dish. Discard the orange zest and cardamom pod from the chilled rose syrup and pour the syrup all over the baklava. Let the baklava cool completely before serving.

9 Store in an airtight container at room temperature, refrigerate for up to 1 week, or freeze for up to 1 month.

COOKIES, NOW!

One of the many beautiful things about cookies—and why most bakers start out with them—is how quickly they can be yours. But these little wonders win the prize for immediacy.

Cinnamon Toast Cookies
From Molly Wizenberg

Molly Wizenberg discovered this recipe when she inherited her grandmother Elaine's enamel recipe tin. They look like little melba toasts but eat like a cookie, with a loud, buttery crunch and a gloss of caramelized cinnamon sugar on top.

How to make them: Heat the oven to 325°F (165°C). Melt **½ cup (110g) unsalted butter** in a pie pan in the oven—keep an eye on it till it melts completely. Cut **6 slices of white sandwich bread** (nothing too squishy) diagonally into quarters. Mix together about **½ cup (100g) sugar** and **2 teaspoons ground cinnamon** in a shallow dish. Brush the butter generously onto both sides of each triangle of bread—make sure that no spot is left uncoated—then dip both sides into the cinnamon sugar. Bake the toasts on a parchment paper–lined baking sheet until lightly browned, about 25 minutes. Transfer to a rack to let cool and crisp up. When cooled, store airtight. These taste even better on days two and beyond, but in desperate times, eat right away. Makes 24 cookies.

Almond Crackle Cookies
From Dorie Greenspan

When you call Dorie Greenspan to say you're coming over, this is what she bakes. "It takes longer to preheat the oven than to put these cookies together," she wrote to me, "I love them for a million reasons, but chiefly because they're a simple pleasure that can be shared on the spur of the moment."

How to make them: Heat the oven to 325°F (165°C) and line two large baking sheets with parchment paper. Whisk together **¼ cup plus 2 tablespoons (75g) sugar** and **1 large egg** in a bowl until thickened a bit, about a minute. Stir in **1¼ cups (125g) sliced almonds** and immediately scoop the batter onto the baking sheets in 2-teaspoon mounds spaced at least 2 inches (5cm) apart. Stir the batter as you're scooping to keep it from settling. Flatten each mound with the back of a fork or your fingers. Bake until the cookies are tan in color and dry and crackly on top, about 20 minutes, rotating the baking sheets from front to back and top to bottom halfway through baking. Let the cookies cool for about 10 minutes before carefully lifting off with a thin spatula. Eat soon or store airtight. Makes 20 cookies.

almond crackle cookies

cinnamon toast cookies

The World's Easiest Cookies
From Elizabeth Barbone

Make no mistake: these four-ingredient vegan and gluten-free cookies taste healthy, in a good way. Make them quite literally anytime, especially when coming down from a period with too many sweets.

How to make them: Heat the oven to 350°F (175°C) and line two large baking sheets with parchment paper. Whisk together **2 cups (225g) almond flour** (see page 5) and **½ teaspoon baking powder** in a medium bowl. Stir in **⅓ cup (100g) dark maple syrup** and **2 teaspoons pure vanilla extract** until a sticky dough holds together. For chewier cookies, drop rounded tablespoons of dough onto the baking sheets, spacing them about 1 inch (2.5cm) apart. For crispier cookies, press each dough scoop down lightly with the bottom of a measuring cup (dip the cup in water to prevent sticking). Bake until the cookies' edges are golden brown, about 12 minutes, rotating the baking sheets from front to back and top to bottom halfway through baking. Let the cookies cool on the baking sheet for about 3 minutes, then transfer to a rack to cool completely. Makes 16 cookies.

the world's easiest cookies

Easiest Peppermint Patties

FROM THE JOY KITCHEN

Making your own peppermint patties is a wonderfully unfussy project, a matter of stirring three ingredients together, shaping, and dunking in chocolate. It will be a little messy and very hands-on—excellent for children and anyone who wants to experience glee like a child for a little while. The recipe comes from *The Joy Kitchen*—the blog wing of the *Joy of Cooking* family, run by its fourth-generation stewards, Megan Scott and John Becker.

The filling is a faux fondant, the rollable, shapeable sweet putty you often see smoothed over towering wedding cakes. The real deal is a bit of a science experiment to make and is more for looks than taste; this version is simply sweetened condensed milk stiffened up with confectioners' sugar and cooled with peppermint extract, and it's quite delicious. On its own, this not-fondant would be too sweet, but that's what the shell of dark, bittersweet chocolate is there for.

If you want to store these at room temperature, you'd probably want to temper the chocolate to keep it snappy and shiny, but then they wouldn't be the easiest peppermint patties anymore. Plus, I think they taste best served cold: a crunch of chocolate, an icy rush of mint, all melting as it hits your tongue.

MAKES ABOUT 5 DOZEN PEPPERMINT PATTIES

5 to 6 cups (625 to 750g) confectioners' sugar

1 (14-ounce/396g) can sweetened condensed milk

2 teaspoons peppermint extract

2 pounds (900g) best-quality bittersweet chocolate, finely chopped

1 In a stand mixer fitted with the paddle attachment, mix 5 cups (625g) of the confectioners' sugar, the condensed milk, and peppermint extract on low speed until well combined and very thick and stiff, adding more confectioners' sugar as needed, until a patty will hold its shape without oozing flat. Cover and refrigerate until firm, at least 1 hour and up to 1 week.

2 When ready to shape the patties, line two large rimmed baking sheets with parchment paper. Using a small cookie scoop or a teaspoon (or just eyeball it), scoop the filling into mounds. Use your hands to roll the mounds into balls, then press them into flat disks about 1½ inches (4cm) wide. Arrange the disks on the lined baking sheets, spacing them about 2 inches (5cm) apart. If the mixture warms up and becomes hard to work with, freeze it until it is thoroughly chilled and firm. (Alternatively, for more perfectly round disks, roll out the filling between two sheets of parchment paper and then cut out shapes using a small round cookie cutter.) Either way you shape them, freeze the disks until firm, about 20 minutes.

3 When ready to coat the peppermint patties, melt the chocolate in a heatproof bowl set over but not touching gently simmering water in a saucepan, or in the microwave in a microwave-safe bowl in 15-second bursts, stirring between bursts. Let cool slightly, so the chocolate is still liquid enough to dip in, but not piping hot (otherwise the patties will soften in the chocolate and be difficult to handle). Use a fork or offset spatula to dip the chilled peppermint disks into the chocolate and lift them back onto the baking sheet. Work in small batches and keep the remaining disks in the freezer until you're ready to coat them. Refrigerate the coated patties until the chocolate sets, about 20 minutes. Serve cold. Store any leftovers in an airtight container in the refrigerator.

Three-Ingredient Coconut Fudge (*Topra Pak*)

FROM MEERA SODHA

What was once a lengthy, meditative process for coconut fudge—stirring and cooking down fresh grated coconut meat and milk until they turned to sticky candy—is now one of the best last-minute desserts in this book (don't tell the Cookies, Now! section on page 66).

Much like in her frozen kulfi recipe (page 186), here London-based cookbook author Meera Sodha takes full advantage of the modern conveniences of canned milks and unsweetened dried coconut to bring this traditional Gujarati sweet within reach of anyone without time for the traditional process (or ready access to fresh coconut).

But as slapdash as this recipe may seem, the treats are quite elegant, with just enough cardamom to give the chewy, milky-sweet fudge a spritz of spicy perfume without overtaking the buttery coconut. (For her grandmother, Sodha makes a special Mounds bar–inspired chocolate variation by melting good-quality chocolate and dipping the fudge in it, using a skewer, then refrigerating them until hard.) For the next time you forget to pick up a housewarming/birthday/thank you/I'm sorry gift, be sure to mark this recipe with a big neon bookmark.

MAKES 25 TO 30 LITTLE FUDGES

1 (14-ounce/396g) can sweetened condensed milk

2½ cups (200g) unsweetened shredded dried coconut

½ teaspoon ground cardamom (preferably freshly ground from the seeds of about 6 pods)

1 Pour the condensed milk into small saucepan (preferably nonstick) and cook over medium-low heat, stirring frequently so the milk doesn't stick to the bottom. (If it toasts a little, that's okay, but don't let it scorch.) When the milk comes to a simmer, turn the heat to low, add 2 cups (160g) of the dried coconut and the cardamom, and stir to combine. Continue to cook, stirring continuously until the mixture starts to look like a thick dough, about 4 minutes. To test for doneness, scoop out a small piece with a spoon and let cool for a minute or so, then use your hands to roll it into a ball. If the ball holds its shape, remove the pan from the heat, scrape the fudge into a bowl, and set aside until cool enough to continue rolling.

2 Meanwhile, put the remaining ½ cup (40g) dried coconut into a shallow dish. When the fudge is cool enough to handle, use a spoon to scoop it into mounds that are just smaller than a golf ball (about 1¼ inches/3cm in diameter). Use your hands to roll them into balls and then drop the balls into the dried coconut, turning to coat. Arrange the fudge pieces on a plate or in a shallow container. Serve at room temperature. Store any leftovers in an airtight container in the refrigerator.

Wonder Dough
Pistachio & Rose Water Meringues

FROM YOTAM OTTOLENGHI & SAMI TAMIMI

For the legions who know Yotam Ottolenghi and Sami Tamimi's restaurants as vegetable kingdoms, this line from their first cookbook may be a shocker: "If you ask someone if they've heard of Ottolenghi, the answer is often, 'Yes, I know, it's the place with the meringues.'"

This turned out to be a brilliant word-of-mouth marketing strategy as they were starting out. The front window of their first patisserie and deli in London displayed cascading tiers of pastries—at the top were always giant meringues, some rolled in craggy chopped pistachios, others spattered with raspberry purée. The meringues captivated passersby, perhaps because of their sheer enormity, but also their wildness of form: they weren't perfectly piped, but swooped roughly, letting their inherent billows and peaks and cracks define each one a bit differently. Ottolenghi and Tamimi led the wave of perfectly imperfect food, of larger-than-life splatters and tumbling messes, food that is immediate and the opposite of untouchable—it begs to be torn to pieces.

Remember that Ottolenghi was a pastry chef first, and as such, making the meringues is not just wild but also quite clever. Typically, to make the egg white foam stable enough to hold up at such extreme size without collapsing, heating the sugar would be fairly commonplace. But rather than cooking a sugar syrup to a precise temperature to drizzle into the stiff egg whites (as in Italian meringue) or heating the egg white and sugar together over a water bath (as in Swiss meringue), he simply warms the sugar in a thin layer on a baking sheet until the edges start to just melt, before pouring it into the foamy whites and beating for 10 minutes. After drying the big swoopy things in a low oven for a very long time, the outsides shatter delicately, breaking away to a soft, marshmallowy core.

MAKES 12 LARGE MERINGUES

3 cups (600g) superfine sugar (see Genius Tip on page 74)

1¼ cups (300g) large egg whites (about 10)

2 teaspoons rose water, or to taste

½ cup (60g) shelled pistachios, finely chopped

1 Heat the oven to 400°F (200°C), with racks in the upper and lower thirds. Line a large rimmed baking sheet with parchment, leaving a 2-inch (5cm) overhang on two opposite sides for easier lifting. Spread the sugar evenly on the baking sheet. Place the baking sheet in the oven on the lower rack and roast until the sugar is hot, 6 to 8 minutes—watch it closely. You should be able to see it beginning to melt at the edges, but it shouldn't caramelize or burn. (If you want to check with an instant-read thermometer, scrape some of the sugar into a little pile on the baking sheet with a heatproof spatula and poke the thermometer into the pile—it should be over 212°F/100°C.)

2 While the sugar is in the oven, pour the egg whites into the bowl of a stand mixer fitted with the whisk attachment. When the sugar is getting close, turn the mixer to high speed and let it run until the whites just begin to froth up, about 1 minute.

3 Carefully pour the hot sugar slowly onto the whisking whites—it can help to pick up the edges of the parchment to funnel it in. Once all the sugar has all been added, add the rose water and continue whisking on high speed until the meringue has cooled to room temperature, about 10 minutes (you can get a sense of the temperature without stopping the mixer by feeling the outside of the bowl). At this point, the meringue should look smooth and silky and hold its shape when you scoop a bit from the bowl. You can now taste the mixture and fold in a bit more rose water if you want a more assertive rose flavor. (From here, you can proceed with the meringues or check out the spin-offs on page 76.)

CONTINUED

Pistachio & Rose Water Meringues

4 Turn the oven temperature down to 225°F (110°C). If your oven runs hot, you may want the temperature to be even lower to keep the meringues bright white, rather than a tawny brown color. To shape the meringues, line 2 baking sheets with parchment paper. Blob a bit of the meringue under each corner of the parchment to help it stick.

5 Using two large kitchen spoons, scoop 12 large round tufts of meringue onto the baking sheets. To do this, use one spoon to scoop up a big dollop of meringue—the size of a small apple—then use the other spoon to scrape the meringue onto the baking sheet. Repeat to make more meringues, spacing them at least 2½ inches (6.5cm) apart—the meringues will almost double in size in the oven. Sprinkle with the chopped pistachios.

6 Slide the meringues into the oven and leave there for about 2 hours, rotating the baking sheets from front to back and top to bottom if they appear to be cooking unevenly. To check if they are done, lift them from the baking sheet and gently poke to make sure the outside is completely firm and the center is still a little soft. Let cool completely on the baking sheets on racks. Store in an airtight container at room temperature in a dry place.

GENIUS TIP: CLEANER-CRACKING EGGSHELLS

Cooks debate whether cracking eggs on a flat surface or the rim of a bowl leads to a cleaner break and fewer shell fragments. I cracked a heck of a lot of eggs while I was testing recipes for this book, and this is what I learned: (1) Regardless of surface, you must crack with conviction—timid taps are what cause the shell to shatter into tiny pieces. (2) There's no such thing as a no-shell guarantee, so it really is safest to crack your eggs into a separate bowl first before dumping them into your batter. (3) Here are two easy was to retrieve errant shell bits: wet a finger and dive in with that, or scoop them out with half of the eggshell itself. As Rachel Khong, who wrote *Lucky Peach*'s *All About Eggs*, told me, "For some reason, the shell bit just swims into the other eggshell."

GENIUS TIP: NO SUPERFINE SUGAR? NO PROBLEM

If you can't find superfine (or caster) sugar, you can make your own! Just pulse regular sugar in a food processor or coffee grinder until it's powdery, like fine sand. Be sure to remeasure before using, since it will be denser and take up less volume after grinding.

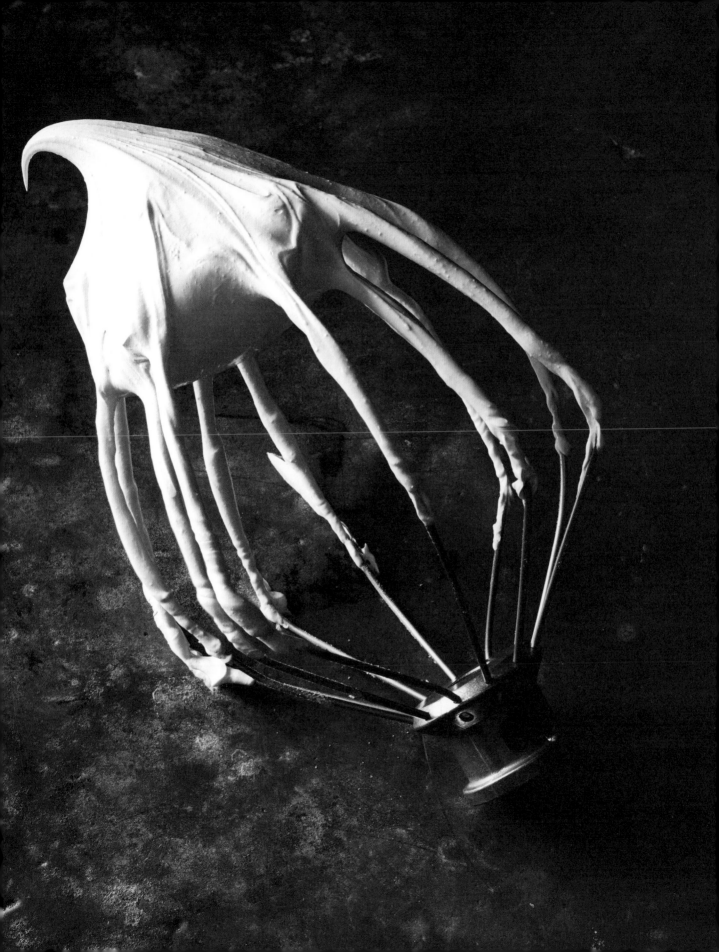

MERINGUE SPIN-OFFS

Yotam Ottolenghi and Sami Tamimi's meringue recipe (page 73) can be the diving-off point for all sorts of different delightful (and, yes, gluten-free) desserts. Here are a few:

Pavlova: Smooth the **meringue** into a large round disk, bake at 225°F (110°C) till crisp outside and mallowy inside, about 2 hours, and top with **yogurt whipped cream** (page 258) and **fresh fruit,** with optional blops of **lemon cream** (page 241) or **Marzipan Butter** (page 80) or **chocolate sauce** (pages 182 and 190). Or make mini disks for personal pavlovas.

Layered Meringue Cake: Form a few low, wide disks of the same width, either with a spatula or by piping a spiral from a resealable plastic bag with about 1 inch (2.5cm) of one lower corner snipped out. Bake at 225°F (110°C) till dry and crisp, about 2 hours. Layer with **whipped cream** and **fresh fruit.** This will meld nicely and be easier to cut without shattering the crust and squishing out the whipped cream if you let it set up in the refrigerator for a few hours before serving.

Fragilité: An especially delicious version of the Layered Meringue Cake (see left) from Danish pastry chef Johannes Steen, with **½ cup (55g) ground hazelnuts** folded into the **meringue** and **mocha buttercream** replacing the whipped cream. (Use the neoclassic buttercream on page 118, stirring in **a few teaspoons each of unsweetened cocoa powder and instant espresso,** to taste). If you've chilled the cake, be sure to bring it back to room temperature before serving or the buttercream won't be as luscious.

Eton Mess: Crush up any leftover **meringue** and serve folded into **whipped cream** with **fresh fruit** or **jams,** or especially **Slow-Roasted Strawberries** (page 258)—see the photo on page 266 for inspiration. Or work any leftover meringues into the gelato cake on page 190.

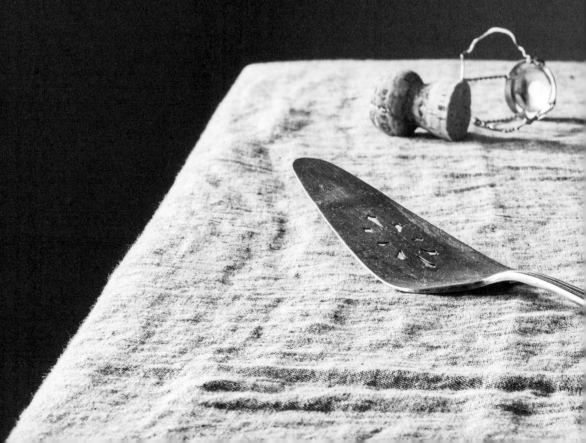

Croccante

FROM MARCELLA HAZAN

Though this looks like a snappy toffee that was made by an experienced pastry chef or at least a home candymaking enthusiast, its sole ingredients are sugar and almond and the only special equipment you need is a potato. No thermometer, no special-order invert sugars, no fancy molds. But that potato is the smartest, most effective way to smooth out hot praline to an even, glassy sheen—so, there, you should invest.

The recipe comes from the late Marcella Hazan, who we can credit, along with her husband and coauthor Victor, for introducing much of America to regional Italian cooking—mostly in savory recipes, but in plenty of memorable desserts, too. When I wrote to Victor to ask for his favorites, croccante topped the list: "I remember someone who wanted to package this praline and distribute it as a candy," Victor wrote. "It is addictively delicious, and I miss it very much."

But how did Marcella get away with fine candy-making without a drawer of special equipment? When you're not trying to land precisely on the small temperature window for the soft-crack or hard-ball stage, you don't need the precision of a candy thermometer. Any sugar that has colored this deeply and is unadulterated by cream or butter will have surpassed the hard-crack stage and wind up crunchy and brittle-like. You need only watch the color—the caramel should be deep brown, and the almonds golden (which will indicate a rich, bittersweet caramel and well-toasted, nutty flavor, respectively). And handle it with respect and care, because you definitely don't want it to splatter on anything that isn't heatproof (including *you*).

MAKES ABOUT 16 PIECES

1¼ cups (170g) whole blanched almonds (or 1½ cups/170g slivered, but not sliced)

1 teaspoon vegetable oil

1 cup plus 2 tablespoons (225g) sugar

1 large potato, washed and dried well, and cut in half crosswise

1 Using a knife, very finely chop the almonds into bits about half the size of a grain of rice. Scoop the chopped almonds into a bowl, leaving the smallest dusty particles behind.

2 Spread a large sheet of parchment paper or heavy-duty aluminum foil flat on a heat-safe counter or board and smear the parchment evenly with the vegetable oil.

3 Combine the sugar and ¼ cup (60g) water in a small saucepan with a light-colored interior (preferably lightweight) and melt the sugar over medium-high heat without stirring, but swirling and tilting the pan occasionally. When the melted sugar turns a rich tawny gold color, 8 to 10 minutes, add the chopped almonds and stir constantly with a wooden spoon or heatproof spatula, until the almond and caramelized sugar mixture turns a very dark brown, about 2 minutes more. Pour it, immediately but carefully, over the oiled parchment paper. Pick up one half of the potato and use the cut side to smooth the hot praline until it's about ⅛ inch (3mm) thick.

4 When the croccante is cool enough to touch but not fully cool, flip or slide the slab onto a cutting board and peel off the parchment. Cut the slab into roughly 2-inch (5cm) diamond shapes and let cool completely. Store in an airtight jar in a dry, cool place at room temperature. To make Ground Croccante, an excellent ice cream topping, see page 42.

Peanut Marzipans (*Mazapanes de Cacahuate*)

FROM FANY GERSON

With two ingredients and a food processor, you can make candy without caramelizing or even cooking a thing. Any nearby children who need a project (and aren't allergic to nuts) can help, because it's more like playing in the sandbox than baking. This crumbly, nutty treat is called *mazapanes*, or marzipans, and comes from Fany Gerson's cookbook *My Sweet Mexico*, based on one of her favorite candies she'd buy as a child on street corners and in bodegas in Mexico. The traditional version called for unsalted peanuts; using roasted, salted nuts calms the sugar and deepens and shapes the flavor, without tasting salty.

The marzipans are also a helpful bonus ingredient to work into other desserts when you want to fancy them up without a lot of trouble. Gerson freezes them in crumbles to mix into chocolate ice cream as it churns (try the sorbet on page 175); the same bits would also be very popular at a sundae bar. Note that if you add only half the sugar and grind longer, you'll get an entirely different, spreadable experience, in Molly Yeh's Marzipan Butter (at right).

MAKES ABOUT 10 CANDIES

2 cups (220g) roasted salted peanuts (or an equal volume of pistachios, pecans, or almonds)

1½ cups (185g) confectioners' sugar

1 In a food processor, pulse the nuts until finely ground. Add the sugar and continue to mix, scraping down the sides as needed, until the nuts release their oil and the mix holds together as a compact paste when pinched between your fingers.

2 Press some of the paste down into a 2-inch (5cm) or smaller cookie cutter, filling it about ¾ inch (2cm) high and pushing down till it's nice and compact. (If you don't have a cookie cutter the right size, wing it by using something similarly shaped, like ice cube trays, or go free-form.) Remove carefully and continue until all the paste is used. Store in an airtight container at room temperature or wrap individually in waxed paper or cellophane, twisting the ends.

Marzipan Butter
From Molly Yeh

For anyone who loves the almondy flavor of marzipan, wunderblogger Molly Yeh discovered a version that puts it in spreadable, spoonable form to keep around and work into desserts at will. All you have to do is leave your food processor running for a very, very long time. Layer the marzipan butter in a trifle (involve fresh peaches if you can!), swirl it into brownies (page 22) or on top of pavlova (page 76), or serve it with cubes of toasted bread or fruit for dunking, Sweet Tahini Fondue style (page 185). And yes, of course, eat it on toast anytime plain almond butter feels too buttoned-up.

How to make it: In a food processor, blend **2 cups (220g) blanched slivered almonds** (untoasted for a classic marzipan flavor, or toasted for a deeper flavor and color—your call), scraping down the sides occasionally, until creamy and spreadable, 10 to 12 minutes. Add **¾ cup (90g) confectioners' sugar**, **¼ teaspoon kosher salt**, and **1 teaspoon almond extract** and blend, scraping down the sides occasionally, until very creamy, 12 to 15 minutes more. Caution: The mixture will be quite hot when it's finished blending. Let cool completely and store in an airtight container at room temperature. It will keep well for a very long time, but you might need to stir it before using to reincorporate the almond oil. Makes 1 cup.

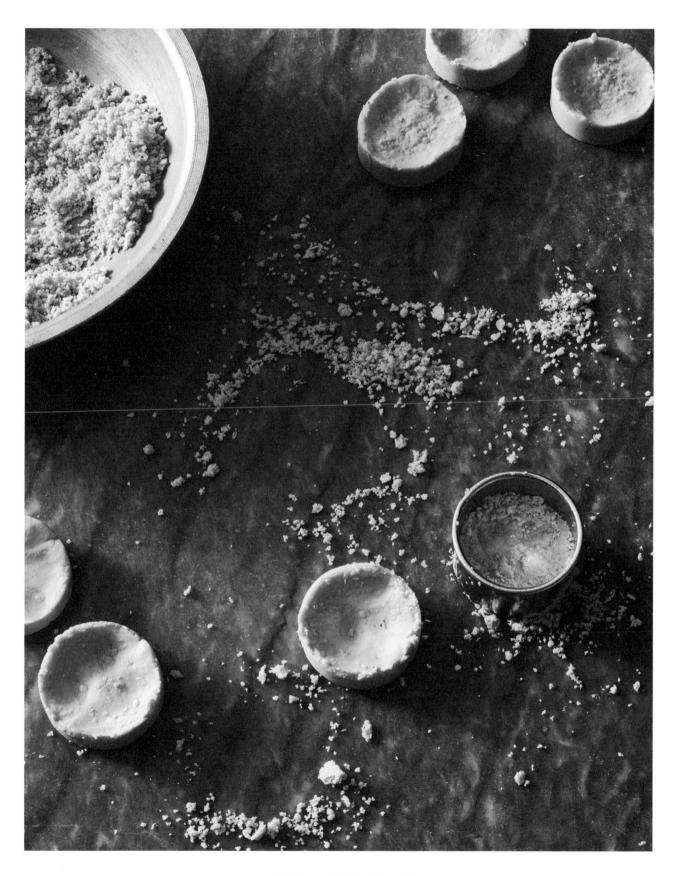

HOW TO TURN A LOAF OF BREAD INTO DESSERT

Yes, these are excellent ways to conjure up dessert without really baking and give new life to bread that's going stale. But more thrillingly, you get to eat toast in ways you wouldn't dream of at breakfast.

Apricot, Nectarine & Plum Bruschetta
From the River Café

Just like tomato bruschetta, this is half about the fruit, half about the toast, and all about the soft-juicy-crunchy melding in the middle.

How to make it: In a large bowl, stir together a **variety of halved (or quartered or sixthed, depending on size) pitted ripe stone fruits** (like nectarines, plums, and apricots) with **vanilla sugar (see page 152) to taste** and a **splash of brandy.** Set aside to macerate until a pool of juices has formed, about 20 minutes. Heat the oven to 400°F (200°C). Pile the fruit and juices with some of the fruit cut side down onto **well-buttered slices of sourdough** on a baking sheet and bake until the fruit is cooked through and soft and the toasts are crisp, about 25 minutes. Serve warm with **crème fraîche** spooned on top.

Toasted Bread Crumb Ice Cream
From Emily Luchetti

Bread crumbs leave a nubbly texture and a sweet-salty-yeasty flavor that plays off vanilla with more subtlety than, say, balls of cookie dough. This ice cream goes extremely well with Olive Oil Chocolate Sauce (page 182).

How to make it: For 1 quart (915g) of bread crumb ice cream, you'll need about **1 cup (100g) bread crumbs.** Heat the oven to 350°F (175°C). Cut ⅓ loaf of crusty sourdough bread (100g) into 1-inch (2.5cm) cubes. Place the bread cubes on a large, rimmed baking sheet, lightly sprinkle with olive oil and kosher salt, and toss. Bake until golden, about 30 minutes, tossing as needed. Let cool, then pulse in a food processor to medium-fine crumbs (not big pieces, but not dust either). Scoop **1 quart (815g) of very good vanilla ice cream** into a large bowl and let stand at room temperature until slightly softened. Stir in 1 cup (100g) bread crumbs or mix in a stand mixer with the paddle attachment. Scoop into a container, cover, and freeze until firm and scoopable, about 4 hours. Sprinkle with extra bread crumbs for serving.

Sugared Croutons
From Jeni Britton Bauer

Even meek sandwich breads can make bang-up sweet croutons for ice cream, but when butter and sugar cling to croissants' feathery layers, it's a little like eating caramelized clouds.

How to make them: Tear **6 croissants (or other stale bread)** into 1-inch (2.5cm) chunks. In a large saucepan, melt **a stick of butter (110g)** with **¾ cup (150g) sugar** and **½ teaspoon ground cardamom**, stirring to dissolve the sugar. Toss the croissant chunks with the sugary butter, then scatter across a baking sheet in one layer, leaving any extra butter behind in the saucepan. Bake in a 350°F (175°C) oven until the croutons are crispy, about 20 minutes, stirring and flipping with a spatula midway through. Serve warm or cool on top of ice cream. For a crunchy, vegan version: Try tossing tiny bread cubes in melted coconut oil and sugar before toasting like Jessica Koslow at Sqirl does (use unrefined coconut oil if you want it to taste like coconut).

Raspberry Ripple Sandwich
From Nigel Slater

This sandwich is a joyously messy experience and nostalgic even if you didn't grow up in England eating raspberry ripple ice cream (which is vanilla with a raspberry swirl, for the rest of us).

How to make it: Crush together a **mixture of fresh raspberries and any other berries you like** with a fork or potato masher. Softly whip **heavy cream**, sweetening it to taste with **superfine or confectioners' sugar** and **pure vanilla extract**. Fold the crushed berries into the whipped cream, leaving it streaked with berries, then heap the mixture onto **toasted brioche, challah, or white sandwich bread**. Eat immediately, while the toast is still warm and ripple cold.

No-Bake Chocolate Coconut Cookies
From Alexandra Stafford

Most no-bake cookies call for peanut butter as a binder, but using bread crumbs instead makes this a nut-free treat. With the addition of toasted coconut, this tastes like a Mounds bar in cold, crunchy cookie form.

How to make it: Combine **½ cup (110g) unsalted butter, ¾ cup (150g) sugar, ¼ cup (60g) milk, 1½ tablespoons unsweetened cocoa powder**, and **½ teaspoon kosher salt** in a medium saucepan and bring to a gentle boil over medium-high heat. Cook until the mixture is slightly thickened and sticky and coats the back of a spoon, about 2 minutes, stirring constantly. Stir in **1 teaspoon pure vanilla extract, ¾ cup (60g) lightly toasted unsweetened shredded dried coconut**, and **1¼ cups (80g) bread crumbs (panko or homemade)**. Remove from the heat and let cool slightly. Roll the mixture into tablespoon-size balls, then flatten them into 2-inch (5cm) cookies. Refrigerate until chilled, at least 30 minutes, before serving, then refrigerate in an airtight container. Makes 2 dozen cookies.

See also: French Toast Crunch on page 155, Sweet Tahini Fondue on page 185.

Cakes

East 62nd Street Lemon Cake

FROM MAIDA HEATTER & TONI EVINS

In the days when cookbooks were lucky to feature a handful of color photographs inset in the middle, if they had any at all, Maida Heatter's late daughter, Toni Evins, illustrated all of her mom's books. (This is also why Heatter's book jackets often pictured dozens of desserts crammed onto a buffet table, with her next to them, beaming.)

This stately lemon cake is the work of the two of them, named for a time when Evins lived on East 62nd Street in Manhattan. Though it's as simple as any cake to make, it has two smart, memorable little tricks. First, the pan is dusted with bread crumbs instead of flour, as Heatter did with almost all of her cakes. For more on this, see the Genius Tip below. The second trick is the no-cook lemon juice glaze, which is painted on liberally as the cake cools. As the glaze soaks in, it leaves behind faint sparkles of sugar and a bright-tasting edge that helps protect it from going stale.

SERVES 10

CAKE
Fine dry bread crumbs, for dusting the pan

3 cups (330g) sifted all-purpose flour

2 teaspoons baking powder

½ teaspoon fine sea salt

1 cup (225g) unsalted butter, softened

2 cups (400g) sugar

4 large eggs

1 cup (245g) whole or low-fat milk

2½ tablespoons finely grated lemon zest (from 2 large lemons)

GLAZE
⅔ cup (135g) sugar

⅓ cup (80g) freshly squeezed lemon juice

1 To make the cake, heat the oven to 350°F (175°C), with a rack in the lower third. Butter a 9-inch (23cm) tube pan (with 12-cup/2.8L capacity) and dust with bread crumbs, tapping out the excess.

2 Whisk together the flour, baking powder, and salt in a bowl.

3 In the bowl of a stand mixer fitted with the paddle attachment, beat the butter on medium-high speed until creamy, about 2 minutes. Add the sugar and beat until well incorporated, about 3 minutes. Beat in the eggs, one at a time, scraping down the bowl as needed with a rubber spatula. The mixture might look curdled—don't worry.

4 With the mixer on low, add the dry ingredients in three additions, alternating with the milk in two additions, and beat only until incorporated after each addition. Stir in the lemon zest by hand and scrape the batter into the tube pan. Level out the batter by rotating the pan briskly back and forth, a bit like a steering wheel.

5 Bake until a toothpick stuck in the middle comes out clean or with just crumbs clinging, 65 to 70 minutes.

6 Let the cake cool in the pan for 5 minutes, then cover with a rack and invert the cake onto the rack. Remove the pan, leaving the cake upside down on the rack. Place the cake and rack over a rimmed baking sheet.

7 To make the glaze, stir together the sugar and lemon juice in a small bowl. Immediately brush it all over the hot cake. The cake will drink it up.

8 Let the cake cool completely and then transfer it to a cake plate. Wait a few hours to cut the cake if you can, to give the glaze more time to absorb. Store leftovers airtight at room temperature.

GENIUS TIP: A MORE NONSTICK (AND MORE DELICIOUS) WAY TO PREP A CAKE PAN

It's no wonder Maida Heatter dusted (almost) all of her cake pans with fine dry bread crumbs, save for the occasional ground nut wildcard. Toasted bread crumbs are inherently more delicious and pleasantly textured than toasted flour, should any excess linger on the cake. But better yet, the crumbs are more effective at helping the cake's edges release from the pan.

Brazilian Carrot Cake *(Bolo de Cenoura)*

FROM DANIELLE NOCE

This is, in fact, a carrot cake, though at first glance it seems to have nothing in common with the chunky, cream cheese–frosted spice cake that's so beloved in many corners of the world.

The defining trait these cake sisters share is, of course, the carrots, which bring moisture and sweetness to both. But in this sort, raw chunks of carrot go straight into the blender with eggs, oil, and sugar to whirl into a simple batter. It bakes up into a downy, orange-tinted pound cake—without you having to grate (or even peel) a thing. Although cream cheese frosting would taste just fine here (there are few places it wouldn't), the cake is instead hugged by a shiny dark chocolate ganache, which offsets the gentle carrot sweetness with bitter and rich flavors instead of creamy tang.

This sleeker style of carrot cake is a classic made in homes across Brazil. Blogger Danielle Noce noticed that some of the more casual, handed-down recipes could be fickle, at times turning out dry or dense. She created this dependable version for her blog *I Could Kill for Dessert* by watching her mother-in-law, weighing the ingredients carefully so her readers wouldn't get tripped up by the vagary of "3 medium carrots" again.

SERVES 12

CAKE
2 cups (270g) ½-inch (1.3cm) carrot slices (from about 3 medium carrots, scrubbed but not peeled)

1¾ cups (360g) sugar

¾ cup + 1 tablespoon (175g) neutral oil (such as grapeseed)

3 large eggs

1¾ cups plus 2 tablespoons (240g) all-purpose flour (see page 5)

1½ teaspoons baking powder

1 teaspoon fine sea salt

GLAZE
6 ounces (170g) bittersweet chocolate, coarsely chopped

7 tablespoons (100g) unsalted butter, cut into ½-inch (1.3cm) slices

1 teaspoon honey

1 To make the carrot cake, heat the oven to 425°F (220°C), with a rack in the center. Butter a 10-cup (2.4L) Bundt pan and dust with bread crumbs or flour, tapping out the excess.

2 Pile the carrots, sugar, oil, and eggs in a blender and blend until completely smooth. Pour the carroty mixture into a large bowl and sift the flour and baking powder over the top. Add the salt and stir in the dry ingredients with a spatula until no streaks of flour remain.

3 Pour the batter into the pan and bake for 5 minutes. Turn the oven down to 400°F (200°C) and bake until a toothpick stuck midway between the center and outer edges of the pan comes out clean or with just crumbs clinging, about 30 minutes more.

4 Let the cake cool in the pan for 10 minutes, then turn it out onto a rack set over a rimmed baking sheet to finish cooling.

5 Once the cake is fully cooled, make the glaze. Melt the chocolate, butter, and honey in a heatproof bowl set over but not touching gently simmering water in a saucepan, or microwave in a microwave-safe bowl in 20-second bursts, stirring between bursts. The glaze should be completely melted and smooth.

6 Spoon the glaze over the cake. You can leave it to set for a half hour or more, or just leave it shiny and gooey, before slicing and serving.

7 Store leftovers airtight at room temperature. If you don't have a domed container and you don't want to disturb the glaze, poke a few toothpicks in the top of the cake and drape plastic wrap over the top, tucking the edges beneath the cake.

Olive Oil Cake

FROM MAIALINO & RACHEL BINDER

Olive oil cake at its best has a crackling crust and an aromatic oil-rich center, which, if it held any more moisture, would be pudding. Pulling this off should be easy: the batter is stirred together by hand, without any egg whites to whip and fold or butter to cream. But anyone who's been hunting for the perfect recipe knows that olive oil cake can be surprisingly temperamental—heavy or dry or sodden with egg—because it's all about balance. Now we can all stop searching: the one served at Maialino in New York City is it.

To develop their perfect version—a cake like the ones they'd had in Italy, but that still felt original—Maialino's then pastry chef, Rachel Binder, worked with Gerri Sarnataro, a pastry instructor at the Institute of Culinary Education. "We didn't want it to scream olive oil," Binder told me. The recipe they came up with is astonishingly simple—whisk wet and dry ingredients in separate bowls, then whisk together and bake. It turns into the crackly crust and rich middle of dreams, flirty with orange but otherwise agreeable to any way you want to serve it—say, with the Slow-Roasted Strawberries (page 258) pictured here. Maialino also offers it at breakfast in muffin form, and they've been known to turn it into a birthday cake, layered with mascarpone buttercream.

SERVES 10

2 cups (250g) all-purpose flour (see page 5)

1¾ cups (350g) sugar

1½ teaspoons kosher salt

½ teaspoon baking soda

½ teaspoon baking powder

1⅓ cups (285g) extra-virgin olive oil

1¼ cups (305g) whole milk

3 large eggs

1½ tablespoons finely grated orange zest

¼ cup (60g) freshly squeezed orange juice

¼ cup (55g) Grand Marnier or Cointreau

1 Heat the oven to 350°F (175°C), with a rack in the center. Oil or butter a 9-inch (23cm) round cake pan that is at least 2 inches (5cm) deep and line the bottom with parchment paper. (If your cake pan is less than 2 inches/5cm deep, divide the batter between 2 pans and start checking for doneness at 30 minutes.)

2 Whisk together the flour, sugar, salt, baking soda, and baking powder in a medium bowl. Whisk together the olive oil, milk, eggs, orange zest and juice, and Grand Marnier in a larger bowl. Add the dry ingredients to the wet ingredients and whisk until just combined. Scrape the batter into the pan.

3 Bake until the top is golden and firm to the touch and a toothpick stuck in the middle comes out clean or with just crumbs clinging, about 1 hour. Let the cake cool in the pan on a rack for 30 minutes.

4 Run a knife around the edge of the pan, invert the cake onto the rack, then invert back so the cake is right side up. Let cool completely, about 2 hours.

5 Store at room temperature. If you want to keep the crust crisp, cover only the cut side of the cake with parchment, not the top, and don't let it hang around too long.

GENIUS TIP: OIL, THE SECRET TO NEVER-DRY CAKES

For most of the cake recipes she developed for her eye-opening baking-science manual *BakeWise*, biochemist Shirley Corriher used a mix of half butter (for flavor) and half oil (for tenderness and moisture). Oil coats flour better than butter or other solid fats and keeps it from absorbing liquids and forming gluten, which means a more tender, moister cake. "Every time I bite into a horribly dry muffin, I think, 'They should have used oil,'" Corriher writes. Of course, here olive oil provides plenty of flavor, too—a win-win.

Dark Chocolate–Marzipan Scone Loaf

FROM MOLLY YEH

This charming loaf may look like a pound cake, act like a pound cake, travel well and make a sweet gift like a pound cake, but it has a slew of hidden perks. It takes all of 20 minutes to throw together, and in fact, the faster you slide it into the hot oven—and the colder it is when it goes in—the better). There is no glaze or icing to whip together, only a scruffy, sugar-dusted top and a side dollop of jam.

And perhaps most astonishingly, it's a cake where the sugar is measured in a few slim tablespoons, rather than cups. The secret to this genius loaf cake is that, in its bones, it's not really a cake. It's a scone dough devised by baking genius Molly Yeh that just happens to bake up handsomely in a loaf pan.

What's more: loafing offers some major advantages to the scone experience. By baking all the dough at once in a loaf pan, it's less likely than individual scones to accidentally get overbaked or overworked, and it keeps longer (chalk it up to less exposed surface area and a higher ratio of fluffy-soft innards).

SERVES 8

7 to 8 ounces (200 to 225g) marzipan, chopped into ½-inch (1.3cm) pieces

1 tablespoon confectioners' sugar

½ cup (85g) bittersweet chocolate chips

2 cups (250g) all-purpose flour (see page 5)

2 tablespoons plus 1 teaspoon sugar

1 tablespoon baking powder

½ teaspoon kosher salt

¾ cup (170g) unsalted butter, very cold and cut into ½-inch (1.3cm) cubes

2 large eggs

½ cup (120g) buttermilk or heavy cream

½ teaspoon pure vanilla extract

½ teaspoon almond extract

Raspberry jam, for serving

1 Heat the oven to 400°F (200°C), with a rack in the center. Line an 8 by 4-inch (20 by 10cm) loaf pan with parchment paper, leaving a 1-inch (2.5cm) overhang on the long sides. (A 9 by 5-inch/23 by 13cm loaf pan will also work—the loaf will just be a little squatter.)

2 In a large bowl, toss the marzipan with the confectioners' sugar to coat. Add the chocolate chips and toss to coat.

3 In a food processor, pulse the flour, 2 tablespoons of the sugar, the baking powder, and the salt to combine. Add the cold butter cubes and pulse until the biggest pieces of butter are pea-size. (If you don't have a food processor, quickly cut the butter into the flour mixture with your hands or a pastry blender.) Dump this mixture into the bowl with the marzipan.

4 Whisk together the eggs, buttermilk, and the vanilla and almond extracts in a small bowl. Add the wet ingredients to the dry ingredients and use a wooden spoon or spatula to stir until just combined.

5 Scrape the mixture into the loaf pan and pat it into an even layer with your hands, but leave the top a bit rough and craggy. Sprinkle the top with the remaining 1 teaspoon sugar. Bake until deep golden brown on top and firm when you poke it with your finger, with no squishy give (indicating an undercooked middle). Begin checking for doneness at 40 minutes. If you want to be extra sure it's done, an instant-read thermometer should read 205°F to 212°F (95°C to 100°C) in the middle.

6 Let the loaf cool in the pan for 10 minutes. Lift up the overhanging ends of the parchment paper and transfer the loaf to a rack to let cool completely. Once cool, slice with a serrated knife (not a dull butter knife like you see pictured here—do as we say, not as we do) and serve with jam. Store airtight and eat as quickly as you can.

Almond Cake

FROM AMANDA HESSER

In the early years at Food52, I saw a lot of these cakes go by as our cofounder Amanda baked them and packed them up—to thank people for helping the company grow, as an extra comfort to go with a condolence card, or just a simple thinking-of-you-so-you-get-a-cake. She kept the perfect box size on hand and started to call this our Thank-You Cake. Sometimes we carried them across the city on the subway, but often they went much farther. The cake gets better over days or even weeks, and it's sturdy enough to mail cross-country.

Watching her confidently ship them off, I realized that one of the smartest things you can do as a baker is to know a few trusted recipes to whip out fast when you want a dessert to say something, and how to send them out into the world without fear—and without carrying a warm cake to the post office without a plan. For your sake, never do that.

You can borrow our dependable Thank-You Cake to start. It first came from Elizabeth Friend, Amanda's late mother-in-law, who developed the recipe after a bakery in East Hampton wouldn't share theirs. It has a fine, sandy crust protecting a rich, buttery middle that's formed after it poufs in the oven and then gloriously collapses. This is part of why it's so shippable—there's nowhere left to fall.

As Elizabeth told Amanda, "This is the Shar-Pei of cakes. It doesn't look very pretty; it crumbles on the edges and invariably falls in the middle. No matter—it's still delicious." I only disagree on one point—in much the same way that an intriguing scar or a bold stripe of gray hair can make you want to get to know a person, this is, in fact, a deeply alluring and beautiful cake.

SERVES 10

1 cup (225g) sour cream, at room temperature

1 teaspoon baking soda

2 cups (220g) sifted all-purpose flour

½ teaspoon kosher salt

1 cup (225g) unsalted butter, softened

1½ cups (300g) sugar

One 7-ounce (200g) tube almond paste

4 large egg yolks, at room temperature

1 teaspoon almond extract

Confectioners' sugar, for dusting (optional)

1 Heat the oven to 350°F (175°C), with a rack in the center. Butter a 9-inch (23cm) springform pan. Line the bottom with parchment paper and butter the parchment. Stir together the sour cream and baking soda in a small bowl (but not *too* small—the baking soda reacts with the acid in the sour cream, so it will start to puff up). Whisk together the flour and salt in a medium bowl.

2 In a food processor, cream the butter and sugar together until pale and fluffy, 3 to 5 minutes. Crumble the almond paste into small pieces and add a few pieces at a time through the top, pulsing until the mixture is very smooth. Add the egg yolks, one at a time, pulsing until incorporated after each addition. Add the sour cream mixture and almond extract and pulse to combine.

3 With a rubber spatula, scrape the batter into a large bowl. Fold in the flour mixture just until the batter is smooth and no streaks of flour remain. Scrape the batter into the pan and smooth the top.

4 Set the pan on a rimmed baking sheet and bake until the cake shrinks from sides of the pan and the top is golden and springs back when lightly pressed, 50 to 60 minutes. Let the cake cool completely in the pan on a rack.

5 When ready to serve, remove the sides of the pan, and slide the cake onto a cake plate or stand, peeling away the parchment. Sift confectioners' sugar over the top and serve in wedges. Store airtight, in or out of the refrigerator. The cake improves with age and can be made up to 2 weeks ahead.

Weird & Wonderful Banana Cake

FROM LUCY CUFFLIN

This is not the kind of baking project that will transport you to a calmer place, like massaging cold butter into pie dough or smoothing frosting over the top of a cake.

Instead, you'll turn your head and hold your breath as you scrape a cup of wobbly mayonnaise onto a pile of mashed banana and brown sugar, and then stir it in as fast as you can. But that mayo—a secret ingredient that you might actually want to keep secret—is what makes this the fluffiest, softest, moistest banana cake you'll ever have. Just remember that mayonnaise is essentially emulsified egg yolks and oil (which this recipe otherwise lacks), plus a little vinegar and salt—all perfectly reasonable things to put in a cake.

In fact, mayonnaise cakes have been around since at least the 1920s, though usually made with chocolate or spices. With the gooeyness of bananas, this one from Lucy Cufflin is even more puddingy and rich. Cufflin, a caterer, former ski chalet cook, and author of books on baking shortcuts, serves it warm with toffee sauce or cold from the refrigerator. I keep it at room temperature and pull it off in big, soft palmfuls, because I know I won't be keeping it long.

SERVES 8

1 cup (250g) well-mashed, very ripe banana (from about 3 bananas)

1 cup (200g) lightly packed light brown sugar

1 cup (250g) mayonnaise (preferably Hellmann's or Best Foods)

3½ ounces (105g) freshly brewed strong coffee or water

2 cups (250g) all-purpose flour (see page 5)

1¾ teaspoons baking soda

Big pinch of kosher salt

1 to 2 tablespoons raw sugar

1 Heat the oven to 350°F (175°C), with a rack in the center. Line a 9 by 5 by 2½-inch (23 by 13 by 6.5cm) loaf pan with parchment paper, leaving a 1-inch (2.5cm) overhang on the long sides. (Note: This cake will fill the loaf pan to the brim, so if your pan is smaller, scrape some of the batter into the wells of a muffin tin and bake them alongside the loaf pan, checking them for doneness after 20 minutes.)

2 Stir together the bananas, brown sugar, and mayonnaise in a large bowl until well combined, then stir in the coffee. Add the flour, baking soda, and salt and stir until well combined. Scrape into the pan and sprinkle the top with raw sugar.

3 Bake until risen and firm to the touch or until a toothpick stuck in the middle comes out with just crumbs clinging, 50 to 60 minutes. Lift up the overhanging ends of the parchment paper, turn the cake onto a rack, and peel off the parchment. Let cool completely, sugar side up.

4 Store in an airtight container in a cool place. It will stay deliciously moist for up to 5 days, though the sugared top will lose some of its crunch over time.

GENIUS TIP: GIVE STALE CAKES A NEW LEASE ON LIFE

Any cake that's starting to dry out and lose its luster on day 3 or 4 will be gloriously restored with a quick blast of heat. You can either toast slices in a toaster oven or under the broiler, or sizzle them in a skillet with butter to warm and soften their middles and crisp up the edges. Top the toasted slices with jam, fruit, yogurt, or Pumpkin Butter (page 261), and they're fancy enough to serve to company.

Rhubarb Buckle with Ginger Crumb

FROM CORY SCHREIBER & JULIE RICHARDSON

The definition of *buckle*—like slumps and grunts and other charmingly named fruit desserts—seems to shift region by region and house by house. There's little point in trying to neatly categorize them, though we try. All you need to know is that they're sweet batter wrapped around seasonal fruit, in all manner of glorious, lumpy guises.

This buckle—from Portland, Oregon restaurateur Cory Schreiber and baker Julie Richardson's runaway hit cookbook *Rustic Fruit Desserts*—is essentially a cake, with an especially gorgeous crumble on top. To make it, you simply fold tart fresh rhubarb into a thick buttermilk batter, and then shower it with a sugary crumb, which is frozen first to make sure it doesn't melt into the cake.

It would be a pretty perfect recipe at that, but the Schreiber-Richardson team snuck in ginger—twice. There's fiery candied ginger minced up in the crumb topping and ground ginger in the cake—just enough to give it a warm, flirty *je ne sais quoi*. As it bakes, the rhubarb bleeds into downy cake, and a golden crust puffs and then dips under the weight of the craggy crumb top.

SERVES 8 TO 12

TOPPING
⅓ cup (65g) sugar

¼ cup (30g) all-purpose flour (see page 5)

¼ cup (25g) finely chopped candied ginger

2 tablespoons unsalted butter, melted

CAKE
1¾ cups (220g) all-purpose flour (see page 5)

1 teaspoon baking powder

1 teaspoon ground ginger

½ teaspoon baking soda

½ teaspoon fine sea salt

¾ cup (170g) unsalted butter, softened

1 cup (200g) sugar

2 large eggs

¾ cup (185g) buttermilk, at room temperature

1 pound (450g) rhubarb, trimmed and thinly sliced

1 Heat the oven to 325°F (165°C), with a rack in the center. Butter a 9 by 13-inch (23 by 33cm) baking pan. (A buttered 12-inch/30cm cast-iron skillet also works beautifully; rhubarb slices that touch the pan may turn darker in less-seasoned pans, but they will still taste just fine.)

2 To make the topping, stir together the sugar, flour, and candied ginger in a bowl and then stir in the melted butter. Freeze the topping while you mix the cake batter.

3 To make the cake, whisk together the flour, baking powder, ground ginger, baking soda, and salt in a bowl. In the bowl of a stand mixer fitted with the paddle attachment, or using a handheld mixer in a large bowl, cream the butter and sugar together on medium-high speed until light and fluffy, 3 to 5 minutes. Add the eggs, one at a time, scraping down the sides of the bowl after each addition. Add the flour mixture in three additions, alternating with the buttermilk in two additions, and beat on low speed only until incorporated after each addition. Scrape down the sides of the bowl occasionally. Gently fold in the rhubarb.

4 Spread the batter into the pan. Sprinkle the frozen crumb topping over the cake and immediately put the cake in the oven. (If the topping has a chance to thaw, it will melt into the cake instead of staying streusel-like on top.) Bake until the top is lightly golden and firm and a toothpick stuck in the middle comes out clean or with just crumbs clinging, about 1 hour. Let cool in the pan on a rack and then serve directly from the pan in squares or wedges.

5 Store airtight at room temperature for up to 3 days.

Blueberry Snack Cake with Toasted Pecans

FROM BROOKE DOJNY

Snack cakes like this one have no use for a frosting or glaze, because they make their own jammy filling. All you need is a modestly stocked pantry, a little lead time, and a stash of willing fruit.

Brooke Dojny, an expert on cooking New England style (no kidding, she's written cookbooks on lobster, beans, and clam shacks), built this blueberry number out of an old regional standard. "I gathered lots of community cookbooks and virtually all of them seemed to have a recipe of that ilk," Dojny told me. "But I found the standard formula to be somewhat boring."

So she added more butter, a sprinkling of crunchy pecans, and a little cornmeal. Her additions make the cake a study in textures. There's just enough cornmeal to give it structure and a yellow tint, without weighing down the batter. It bakes up airy and tender, with a crackly sheen and a top dotted with pecans.

If you can get wild blueberries, they're usually tiny enough to stay suspended in the cake, like a blueberry muffin. The larger cultivated blueberries available to most of us tend to sink to the bottom and meld into a blueberry pudding topped with cake and crunchy pecans. Neither could possibly be bad.

SERVES 8

1 cup (125g) all-purpose flour (see page 5)

3 tablespoons fine- or medium-ground cornmeal

1 teaspoon baking powder

½ teaspoon kosher salt

½ cup (110g) unsalted butter, softened

1 cup (200g) plus 1 tablespoon sugar

2 large eggs

⅓ cup (80g) whole or low-fat milk

1½ teaspoons pure vanilla extract

½ teaspoon finely grated lemon zest

2 cups (300g) fresh or frozen blueberries

1 cup (120g) coarsely chopped pecans or walnuts

1 Heat the oven to 350°F (175°C), with a rack in the center. Butter a 9-inch (23cm) square baking pan.

2 Whisk together the flour, cornmeal, baking powder, and salt in a large bowl.

3 In the bowl of a stand mixer fitted with the paddle attachment or in a food processor, or using a handheld mixer in a large bowl, cream together the butter and 1 cup (200g) of the sugar on medium-high speed until smooth. Add the eggs, milk, vanilla, and lemon zest and beat until well incorporated. It might look a little curdled here—that's okay! Add the flour mixture and mix just until the flour is incorporated. If you're using a food processor, transfer the batter to a large bowl.

4 Gently fold the blueberries into the batter, just until combined. Scrape the batter into the pan, smoothing the top. Sprinkle with the nuts followed by the remaining 1 tablespoon sugar.

5 Bake until the nuts are deep brown, the cake is golden, and a toothpick stuck in the middle comes out clean or with just crumbs clinging, 40 to 45 minutes. Set the pan on a rack and let the cake cool. Once completely cool, cut into squares in the pan and serve.

6 Store airtight at cool room temperature for up to 1 day or freeze for up to 1 month.

Chocolate Oblivion Truffle Torte

FROM ROSE LEVY BERANBAUM

This flourless chocolate torte is a better and purer vehicle for chocolate than chocolate itself, scientifically speaking. "When you just have a chocolate bar, you can't taste the chocolate until it starts melting in your mouth. But this is just the right texture, so that the minute you put it in your mouth, the flavors start exploding," Rose Levy Beranbaum explains.

The recipe calls for just three ingredients, takes less time to mix together than your average cookie, and bakes for only *15 minutes*. So why did baking it seem so scary, when in fact it takes no more skill than the next chocolate cake? Why was I emailing Beranbaum pictures of the cracked surface of my torte, only to slice into it later to find it was perfectly smooth and delicious inside?

I found that while Beranbaum's recipes are famously detailed and precise, it's not because there's only one way to get them right. It's because she tests them until she finds the most proven path to making them the best they can be. So I asked her which parts of the recipe were the most important to get right.

"The biggest deal breaker is scorching the chocolate, because that will ruin the flavor of it. And not beating the eggs enough, because then you won't have the moussey texture—but it's not going to be devastating, it just won't be as wonderful," Beranbaum said. "And of course one of the biggest things is, don't use cheap chocolate." Perish the thought!

SERVES 16

1 pound (450g) best-quality dark chocolate (preferably 55 to 62%), coarsely chopped

1 cup (225g) unsalted butter, cut into small pieces, at room temperature

6 large eggs (300g out of the shell), at room temperature if possible

Whipped cream, for serving (optional)

1 Heat the oven to 425°F (220°C), with a rack in the center. Butter an 8-inch (20cm) springform pan that's at least 2½ inches (6.5cm) deep. Line the bottom with parchment paper and butter the parchment. Wrap the outside of the pan with a double layer of heavy-duty aluminum foil so that no water can sneak in. You will also need a larger roasting pan or cake pan to serve as a water bath. (If using a larger cake pan, be sure it is a one-piece pan.)

2 Melt the chocolate and butter in a large heatproof metal bowl set over but not touching hot (not simmering) water in a saucepan, or microwave in a microwave-safe bowl in 20-second bursts, stirring between bursts. Set the bowl aside but keep the pan of water on the stove, turning the heat up so that the water simmers.

3 Set a stand mixer bowl over but not touching the simmering water and heat the eggs, stirring constantly with a whisk, until just warm to the touch. Immediately transfer the bowl to a stand mixer fitted with the whisk attachment. Whisk the eggs on high speed until the eggs triple in volume and are billowy and lighten in color, about 5 minutes. (If using a handheld mixer in a bowl, beat the eggs over the simmering water until they are hot, then transfer the bowl to the counter and beat until the eggs cool down to room temperature, about 5 minutes.) Use a large whisk or rubber spatula to fold half of the eggs into

CONTINUED

Chocolate Oblivion Truffle Torte

the chocolate mixture until almost evenly combined. Fold in the remaining eggs until almost no streaks remain. Use a rubber spatula to finish folding, scraping the bottom to make sure that the heavier chocolate mixture is all mixed in.

4 Scrape the mixture into the springform pan, smoothing the top, and set it inside the larger pan. Place the larger pan on the oven rack and carefully pour 1 inch (2.5cm) of hot water into the larger pan. Bake for 5 minutes. Cover the pan loosely with a sheet of buttered aluminum foil and bake for 10 minutes more. The cake will still wobble when moved but shouldn't look sloshy. Remove the cake pan from the water bath and let cool on a rack for about 45 minutes. Cover tightly with plastic wrap and refrigerate until very firm, at least 3 hours.

5 Once it's very firm, unmold the cake. Gather a serving plate that has at least an 8-inch (20cm) flat center portion, as well as an 8-inch (20cm) flat loose bottom of a tart pan or plate, covered with plastic wrap, to help with inverting.

6 Use a kitchen torch, hair dryer, or hot damp towel to warm the sides of the pan to loosen the torte. Run a thin metal spatula or knife around the edges of the torte and remove the sides of the pan. Gently set the plastic-wrapped plate on top and invert the torte onto it. Heat the bottom of the springform pan, remove it, and then peel off the parchment and invert the torte onto the serving plate.

7 The torte is the most moussey and delicious served at room temperature, though it's also delicious chilled and keeps very well in the refrigerator for a week or more. To serve, slice the torte using a thin-bladed knife dipped in hot water and wiped dry between each slice. Serve with whipped cream on the side.

GENIUS TIP: WHAT EXACTLY DID YOU MEAN BY "FOLDING"?

Lots of recipes in this book (and all over the baking universe) will tell you to fold ingredients together, which is not the most intuitive wording, given what folding means for sheets and sweaters. I saw a much better, though lengthier, way to explain it in Portuguese on the original recipe for the Brazilian Carrot Cake on page 90: *misture com uma espátula de baixo para cima*, which translates to "mix with a spatula from the bottom up." Instead of banging around in a bowl with a wooden spoon (which knocks out the air you've whipped into cream or egg yolks or whites), think of folding as gracefully sliding the edge of a rubber spatula through the middle and across the bottom and sides of the bowl, then pulling the mixture up over itself, protecting the precious air bubbles as you go. This is much easier if the mixtures you're folding together are similar in consistency, so if you need to lighten a stiffer mixture, start by whisking or stirring in about a third of the lighter mixture to loosen it up before folding the remainder in all at once.

GENIUS TIP: NEVER TRUST A TWO-PART PAN

Baking pans that disassemble for easy unmolding— like springforms and cake and tart pans with loose, removable bottoms—aren't the most trustworthy carriers of sloshy batters and bubbling fruit fillings. To prevent liquids from escaping and protect your oven floor, Rose Levy Beranbaum recommends always putting two-part pans on a rimmed baking sheet before baking. And wrap any springforms going into a water bath doubly—or even triply!—in heavy-duty aluminum foil to keep your cheesecakes and truffle tortes from flooding.

Chocolate Cloud Cake

FROM RICHARD SAX

Here is where we learn that flourless chocolate cake can mean many different things, depending on ratios and technique. Both this recipe and the preceding one from Rose Levy Beranbaum are known and loved as flourless chocolate cakes and use the same basic three ingredients (eggs, chocolate, and butter), with wildly different appearances and textures.

This one was a signature dessert of the late, beloved writer and cooking instructor Richard Sax. For the same amount of eggs as Beranbaum's, he calls for half the chocolate and butter, and—instead of heating and whipping six whole eggs until billowy—he has you whip four of the whites with sugar to make a fluffy meringue, then gently fold them into the rest. Far from a dense and creamy torte, these three changes produce a poufy soufflé of a cake that intentionally caves in the center, leaving a craggy, wafer-like rim behind and a moussey hollow that you fill up with cold whipped cream. The effect is dramatic and bold, giving you, as Sax famously said, "intensity, then relief, in each bite."

SERVES 8 TO 12

CAKE
8 ounces (225g) best-quality bittersweet chocolate, coarsely chopped

½ cup (110g) unsalted butter, at room temperature and cut into 1-tablespoon pieces

6 large eggs

1 cup (200g) sugar

2 tablespoons Cognac or Grand Marnier (optional)

Finely grated zest of 1 orange (about 1 tablespoon; optional)

WHIPPED CREAM
1½ cups (355g) heavy cream, very cold

3 tablespoons confectioners' sugar

1 teaspoon pure vanilla extract

Unsweetened cocoa powder and/or bittersweet chocolate shavings, for topping

1 To make the cake, heat the oven to 350°F (175°C), with a rack in the center. Line the bottom of an 8-inch (20cm) springform pan with parchment paper. (Do not butter the pan and parchment.)

2 Melt the chocolate in a heatproof bowl set over but not touching gently simmering water in a saucepan. You can whisk it occasionally to help it along. When it's melted, remove the bowl from the heat and whisk in the butter until smooth.

3 In two small bowls, separate 4 of the eggs. In a large bowl, whisk 2 whole eggs and the 4 egg yolks with ½ cup (100g) of the sugar just until combined. Slowly whisk in the warm chocolate mixture. Whisk in the Cognac and the orange zest. Using a handheld mixer in a separate bowl, beat the 4 egg whites until foamy, about 2 minutes. Gradually add the remaining ½ cup (100g) sugar and beat until beautifully glossy, soft peaks form that hold their shape but aren't quite stiff, about 5 minutes more. Very gently fold about a quarter of the beaten egg whites into the chocolate mixture to lighten it, then gently fold in the remaining whites. Scrape the batter into the pan and smooth the top.

4 Set the pan on a rimmed baking sheet and bake until the top is puffed and cracked and the center is no longer wobbly, 35 to 40 minutes. Be careful not to bake the cake beyond this point.

5 Let the cake cool in the pan on a rack. The center of the cake will sink as it cools, forming a sort of crater—this is good! Let the cake cool completely on a rack.

6 To make the whipped cream, whip the cream, confectioners' sugar, and vanilla in a large bowl with a handheld mixer until billowy, soft—not stiff—peaks form.

7 Using a spatula, fill the sunken center of the cake with the whipped cream, swirling the cream to the edges of the crater. Dust the top lightly with cocoa powder.

8 Run the tip of a knife around the edge of the cake, carefully remove the sides of the pan, and cut into wedges to serve.

9 Store any leftovers airtight in the refrigerator—they won't be very presentable but they'll make a delicious moussey snack.

Hazelnut–Brown Butter Cake with Sautéed Pears

FROM SUZANNE GOIN

Suzanne Goin—chef-owner of Lucques and A.O.C., pioneering restaurants in Los Angeles—loved this cake so much that she served it at her wedding (it required 25 pounds of hazelnuts, 25 pounds of brown butter, and 150 eggs).

Brown butter makes everything taste better, richer, and more captivating, and here it doubles down with ground toasted hazelnuts. This pairing plays off the French term for brown butter (*beurre noisette*), which translates literally to hazelnut butter for its color and roasted nutty flavor. Whether the wordplay was intentional or not, the effect is the same—a haunting nutty richness to an exponential degree.

The cake is stunning served with handsome butter-seared pears, but there's no reason to limit it to one season. Deb Perelman's riff with chocolate ganache on *Smitten Kitchen* has been understandably popular (use your favorite, or try the one on page 237), and it would be just as good with whatever fruit is ripe near you, or without any. The whipped cream is important, however—don't skip it.

SERVES 12

CAKE
1 cup (225g) unsalted butter, plus 1 tablespoon melted butter

5 ounces (140g) hazelnuts, skinned or not

½ vanilla bean

1⅓ cups (165g) confectioners' sugar

⅓ cup (40g) all-purpose flour (see page 5)

¾ cup (180g) egg whites (from 5 extra-large or 6 large eggs)

3 tablespoons sugar

PEARS
2 pounds (900g) Comice or Bartlett pears

½ vanilla bean

2 tablespoons unsalted butter, or more as needed

¼ teaspoon kosher salt

2 tablespoons sugar

WHIPPED CREAM
1 cup (235g) heavy cream, very cold

1 To make the cake, heat the oven to 350°F (175°C) with a rack in the center. Brush a 9-inch (23cm) or 10-inch (25cm) round cake pan with the melted butter and line the bottom with parchment paper.

2 Spread the hazelnuts on a large rimmed baking sheet and toast in the oven until they turn golden brown and smell nutty, 12 to 15 minutes. Crack one open to make sure it's golden throughout—if not, keep toasting. (If your hazelnuts have skins, wrap them in a kitchen towel and let steam for 10 minutes, then use the towel to rub off any loose skins, but don't worry about removing them all.) Let the nuts cool completely.

3 Put the remaining 1 cup (225g) butter in a medium saucepan. Split the half vanilla bean lengthwise with a paring knife and scrape the seeds onto the butter. Throw the vanilla pod into the pan and cook over medium heat, shaking the pan occasionally, until the butter melts, and then browns and smells nutty, 6 to 8 minutes. Set aside to cool.

4 In a food processor, pulse the cooled hazelnuts and the confectioners' sugar until the nuts are finely ground. Add the flour and pulse just to combine.

5 In the bowl of a stand mixer fitted with the whisk attachment, whip the egg whites and sugar on high speed until very stiff peaks form, 4 to 5 minutes. When you turn the whisk upside down, the peaks should hold. Scrape the whites gently into a large bowl.

6 Remove the vanilla pod from the brown butter and discard (or wash, dry, and save for another use—see page 152). Fold the nutty flour mixture into the egg whites in three additions, alternating with the brown butter in three additions. Be sure to scrape the bottom of the pan with a rubber spatula to get all the butter's little brown bits.

7 Pour the batter into the cake pan, smooth the top, and bake until the edges of the cake start to pull away from the

CONTINUED

Hazelnut-Brown Butter Cake with Sautéed Pears

pan and it springs back in the center when lightly pressed with a finger, 40 to 50 minutes. Let cool in the pan on a rack for 30 minutes. Run a knife around the inside edge of the pan and invert the cake onto a plate. Peel off the parchment and turn the cake right side up onto a serving platter, and let finish cooling to warm or room temperature, however you'd prefer to serve it.

8 To make the pears, cut the pears in half lengthwise, leaving the stems intact. Cut each half into 1-inch (2.5cm) wedges. (Don't remove the core—it's pretty.)

9 Split the half vanilla bean lengthwise with a paring knife and scrape the seeds onto the butter.

10 Heat a very large sauté pan over medium-high heat for 2 minutes. Add the butter, vanilla seeds, and the vanilla pod to the pan. When the butter foams, arrange the pear wedges in the pan, cut side down (if they don't all fit, cook them in batches). Season with the salt and cook until the pears are starting to soften and turn golden at the edges, about 2 minutes. Sprinkle the sugar over the pears and shake the pan to distribute the sugar and help it caramelize in the butter. Cook the pears, basting them often with the butter using a heatproof pastry brush, until they're caramelized on the first side, about 6 minutes. (If you don't have a pastry brush, you can add a bit more butter and baste the pears with foaming butter by tilting the pan and using a spoon.)

11 Carefully turn the pears over and cook, continuing to baste them, until the second cut side is golden and the pears are tender but not mushy, 3 to 4 minutes more. Transfer the pears to a platter and keep them in a warm place.

12 To make the whipped cream, whip the cream in a large bowl with a handheld mixer until soft peaks form. Cut the cake into wedges. Spoon the pears and their caramel juices over the cake and top with dollops of whipped cream. Store any cake leftovers airtight at room temperature, and pears airtight in the refrigerator.

GENIUS TIP: THE BALANCING POWER OF WHIPPED CREAM

Whipped cream is important—not a needless indulgence nor an afterthought. Suzanne Goin learned this maxim from Catherine Brandel, her mentor at Chez Panisse: "Sometimes you just need to lighten things up with a little heavy cream," which isn't as puzzling as it sounds. A swipe of clean, cold whipped cream gives your palate a needed, energizing break from more intense or sweet flavors. To add even more nuance, San Francisco pastry chef Emily Luchetti likes to minimize the distance between her whipped cream's sweetness and the dessert it serves. She won't try to make up for a less-sweet dessert with a sweetened whipped cream, which would clash on your tongue. As she told me, "It's like ping-pong in your mouth."

Rum-Scented Marble Cake

FROM NICK MALGIERI

Irked by marble cake batters that swirled unpredictably into muddled beige instead of zebra stripes of chocolate and vanilla, pastry instructor and cookbook author Nick Malgieri found the magic formula. Start with a single base vanilla batter, leaving two-thirds as is and spiking one-third with good, strong chocolate, and then swirl them together in the pan. Following his swirling method precisely instead of going willy-nilly helps, too—it won't feel like you've done enough, so just trust.

The dark rum is a swinging alternative to vanilla extract, playing well with the chocolate without tasting like a tiki drink. And along with the melted chocolate in the second batter, the rum helps preserve the cake in a soft and fluffy state for days longer than it ought to.

MAKES ABOUT 24 SLICES

Fine dry bread crumbs,
for dusting the pan

BASE BATTER
2²/₃ cups (335g) all-purpose
flour (see page 5)

1²/₃ cups (335g) sugar

2 teaspoons baking powder

¼ teaspoon fine sea salt

1½ cups (340g) unsalted
butter, softened

7 large eggs

3 tablespoons dark rum

CHOCOLATE BATTER
2 tablespoons dark rum

2 tablespoons milk

½ teaspoon baking soda

6 ounces (170g) bittersweet
chocolate, melted and cooled

Confectioners' sugar,
for dusting (optional)

1 Heat the oven to 325°F (165°C), with a rack in the lower third. Butter a 16-cup (3.8L) tube or Bundt pan and dust with bread crumbs, tapping out the excess. To be even more sure the cake won't stick, Malgieri sprays with a coat of vegetable oil spray, too.

2 To make the base batter, in the bowl of a stand mixer, stir together the flour, sugar, baking powder, and salt using a large rubber spatula. Fit the mixer with the paddle attachment, add the butter, and beat on low speed until it's a smooth, heavy paste, 1 to 2 minutes.

3 Whisk together the eggs and rum in a medium bowl. With the mixer on medium speed, add one-third of the egg mixture and beat for 1 minute. Stop and scrape down the sides of the bowl and the paddle. Add the remaining egg mixture in two additions, beating 2 minutes more after each addition.

4 Remove the bowl from the mixer and give the batter a final stir with the rubber spatula, scraping the bottom to incorporate any pockets of dry ingredients.

5 To make the chocolate batter, in a medium bowl, whisk together the rum, milk, and baking soda until the baking soda dissolves. Whisk in the cooled melted chocolate. Add 2 cups (475ml) of the base batter and whisk well to combine.

6 Scrape half of the remaining base batter into the pan with the rubber spatula and smooth the top. Cover this layer with all of the chocolate batter, making sure that the layer is as even as possible. Top the chocolate layer with the remaining base batter and smooth the top.

7 To marble the batter, use a wide-bladed table knife or a thin metal spatula (see image, page 116). Insert the knife into the batter at the center tube with the flat side of the blade facing you. Curving the blade in an arc like a backward C as you go, pull the blade through the batter toward

CONTINUED

Rum-Scented Marble Cake

the bottom of the pan and up and out the side of the pan closest to you, repeating the motion every inch (2.5cm) or so around the pan, creating a spiral in the batter, almost as though you were folding egg whites into it (reference the photo opposite). Don't bother wiping off the knife blade in between. Stop when you get back to the point where you started. Don't bother to smooth the top of the batter—it might disturb the marbling.

8   Bake the cake until it is well risen and firm to the touch and a toothpick stuck midway between the center and outer edges of the pan comes out with just crumbs clinging, about 1 hour.

9   Let the cake cool in the pan on a rack for 5 minutes. If the cake doesn't appear to be loose in the pan, loosen the center and outer edges by inserting a thin knife or spatula in any places that appear attached. Top with a cooling rack and invert the cake onto the rack. Remove the pan and let the cake cool completely. Dust with confectioners' sugar and cut into wedges to serve. Store any leftovers in an airtight container. The crust will be the best on the first day, but it keeps surprisingly well for several days.

GENIUS TIP: WE DON'T LIKE BURNT BUNDTS

Nick Malgieri isn't fond of the modern Bundt pans that have a thick, black nonstick coating. (If you've ever overbaked a Bundt, it's not you—it's the pan.) Lighter-colored modern pans are A-okay, and he also likes looking for old-fashioned, lightweight metal ones (usually pressed aluminum) at flea markets and secondhand stores. Even faux copper or pewter ones that were designed as Jell-O molds will work. If you have to use the darker pans, always decrease the oven temperature by 25°F (about 15°C) and watch it closely.

All-Occasion Downy Yellow Butter Cake with Neoclassic Buttercream

FROM ROSE LEVY BERANBAUM

In one proud layer cake, you get two of Rose Levy Beranbaum's claims to fame from her industry-changing 1988 book *The Cake Bible*: a renegade technique for tender, unruinable yellow cake and a classic French buttercream that doesn't require a candy thermometer.

Most standard butter cake batters start with creaming butter with sugar to beat in lots of air, plopping in eggs one by one, then adding in the flour, salt, and chemical leaveners like baking soda or powder at the end.

But for all her butter cake batters, Beranbaum reverses the order of ingredients to give the cake more structure and protect the batter from overbeating: she first mixes the dry ingredients with butter and a little milk, which coats the flour with fat and prevents the gluten from linking up too much. She then beats for a surprisingly long time to develop structure, and finally, she adds egg yolks and the rest of the liquid. The cakes have a smooth, never-tough crumb and are the perfect midpoint between dense, buttery pound cake and airy sponges. She calls this an all-occasion cake because it lines up beautifully in layers, but it also holds its own if you just want a simple tea cake to serve with fruit and cream.

For the buttercream, Beranbaum outsmarts the classic technique that requires cooking a simple syrup to exactly 238°F (114°C) to thicken the egg yolks just enough to emulsify with a generous amount of softened butter. By replacing some of the sugar and water with corn syrup (or honey or maple syrup), there's no need for a candy thermometer (in this proportion, it hits a rolling boil at precisely the right temperature), and the sugar is protected from crystallizing, too. This is the frosting to make if you are looking for a butter cloud to float over your cake.

MAKES 2 (9-INCH/23CM) CAKE LAYERS AND 4 CUPS (800G) BUTTERCREAM; SERVES 12

CAKE

6 large egg yolks (112g), at room temperature

1 cup (240g) whole or low-fat milk

2¼ teaspoons pure vanilla extract

3 cups (300g) sifted bleached cake flour

1½ cups (300g) sugar

1 tablespoon plus 1 teaspoon baking powder

¾ teaspoon fine sea salt

¾ cup (170g) unsalted butter, softened

BUTTERCREAM

6 large egg yolks (112g), at room temperature

¾ cup (150g) sugar

½ cup (165g) corn or maple syrup (or use ⅓ cup [110g] honey and omit the sugar)

2 cups (450g) unsalted butter, softened and cut into tablespoons

2 to 4 tablespoons liqueur or eau-de-vie of your choice (optional)

1   To make the cake, heat the oven to 350°F (175°C), with a rack in the center. Butter two 9-inch (23cm) round cake pans that are at least 1½-inches (4cm) deep. Line the bottoms with parchment paper and butter the parchment and dust with bread crumbs or flour, tapping out the excess.

2   Lightly whisk the egg yolks, ¼ cup (60g) of the milk, and the vanilla in a medium bowl.

3   In the bowl of a stand mixer fitted with the paddle attachment, or using a handheld mixer in a large bowl, combine the flour, sugar, baking powder, and salt. Mix on low speed for 30 seconds to blend. Add the butter and the remaining ¾ cup (180g) of milk. Mix on low speed just until the dry ingredients are moistened, then increase to medium speed (or high speed if using a handheld mixer) and beat for 1½ minutes to aerate the batter to help develop the cake's structure. Scrape down the sides of the bowl. Add the egg yolk mixture in three additions, beating for 20 seconds on medium speed after each addition to strengthen the structure. Scrape down the sides of the bowl again. Scrape the batter evenly into the pans and smooth the tops.

CONTINUED

All-Occasion Downy Yellow Butter Cake
with Neoclassic Buttercream

4 Bake until the cakes spring back when pressed lightly in the center and a toothpick stuck in the middle comes out clean, 25 to 35 minutes. The cakes should start to shrink from the sides of the pans only after removing them from the oven.

5 Let the cakes cool in the pans on racks for 10 minutes. Loosen the sides with a small metal spatula or knife and invert onto buttered racks or baking sheets. To prevent the layers from splitting, invert them once more so that they're right side up. Let cool completely. The texture is most perfectly moist the same day as baking; serve at room temperature. Alternatively, store in an airtight container for up to 2 days at room temperature, 5 days in the refrigerator, or 2 months in the freezer.

6 To make the buttercream, butter a 1-cup (240ml) heatproof glass measuring cup or other heatproof bowl and set it near the stove.

7 In the bowl of a stand mixer fitted with the whisk attachment, or using a handheld mixer in a medium bowl, beat the egg yolks on high speed until light in color, about 2 minutes.

8 Meanwhile, combine the sugar and corn syrup in a small saucepan (preferably nonstick) and cook over high heat, stirring constantly, until the sugar dissolves and the syrup comes to a rolling boil with large bubbles covering the entire surface. Immediately pour the syrup into the glass measuring cup to stop the cooking.

9 If using a stand mixer, pour a small amount of syrup over the yolks with the mixer turned off. Immediately beat on high speed for 5 seconds, then stop the mixer. Add a larger amount of syrup and beat on high speed for 5 seconds more. Continue adding the remaining syrup and beating on high speed for 5 seconds after each addition. Use a rubber spatula to scrape out the syrup clinging to the glass measuring cup and continue beating until completely cool.

10 If using a handheld mixer, pour the syrup into the yolks in a steady stream. Don't let the syrup fall on the beaters or they will spin it onto the sides of the bowl. Use a rubber spatula to scrape out the syrup clinging to the glass measuring cup and continue beating until completely cool.

11 Gradually beat in the butter, a tablespoon at a time, adding each tablespoon once the preceding tablespoon has blended in thoroughly. Add the liqueur and beat just until combined. Use the buttercream right away or refrigerate airtight. Let come to room temperature before using, beating briefly to restore texture.

12 Once the cakes are cooled and the frosting texture is smooth, frost and decorate the cake as you like (see extra-credit tips on page 128). To store any leftovers, cover the cut sides with plastic wrap and store the cake in an airtight container in the refrigerator. Bring it back down to room temperature before serving.

GENIUS TIP: FOR SILKIER BUTTERCREAMS

To get the silkiest buttercream, *The Fearless Baker* author Erin Jeanne McDowell likes to switch to the paddle attachment for the last minute or two of beating to knock out some of the air bubbles whipped up by the whisk attachment. Try it if you want a smoother frosting on your cake, with fewer teeny air bubble holes.

Coffee Cardamom Walnut Cakes

FROM CLAIRE PTAK

It's silly how much of a difference a simple reorientation can make. What could have been only a muffin (not dessert) or a frosting-swirled cupcake (maybe too much dessert) is now an entirely changed experience.

By baking these little cakes in standard muffin tins and then inverting them, not only do they give off the fancy vibe of a canelé without having to buy special molds, but the muffin bottom is no longer an afterthought.

Were you to keep these right side up and muffinish, they could hold a stiff frosting or streusel just fine, but a glaze would pour off the top like a fountain, leaving the bottom untouched. And if you'd tucked them into crinkly liners, they'd be quite soggy and sad. This way, the coffee glaze can trickle attractively over more surfaces, and both top and bottom retain their integrity. This cake recipe in particular is a fittingly playful one—floral, floaty cardamom, anchored by earthy coffee and walnut—for turning on its head.

MAKES 12 MINI CAKES

CAKES
¾ cup (75g) walnut halves

1½ cups (190g) all-purpose flour (see page 5)

¾ teaspoon baking powder

¾ teaspoon baking soda

½ teaspoon kosher salt

1 teaspoon ground cardamom

1 teaspoon ground pink peppercorns (or substitute freshly ground black pepper)

¾ teaspoon ground cinnamon

⅛ teaspoon ground cloves

¾ cup plus 1 tablespoon (180g) unsalted butter, softened

¾ cup (150g) sugar

2 large eggs

1½ teaspoons pure vanilla extract

¾ cup plus 2 tablespoons (210g) crème fraîche

ICING
1½ cups (185g) confectioners' sugar

2 to 3 tablespoons freshly brewed strong coffee or espresso

1 To make the cakes, heat the oven to 350°F (175°C), with a rack in the center. Generously butter a 12-cup muffin tin and dust with bread crumbs or flour, tapping out the excess.

2 Spread the walnuts on a large rimmed baking sheet and warm them through in the oven for no more than 5 minutes—you're not toasting them, just bringing out the fragrant oils. Let the nuts cool to the touch, then transfer them to a cutting board and finely chop them.

3 Sift together the flour, baking powder, baking soda, salt, cardamom, pink peppercorns, cinnamon, and cloves in a large bowl. Whisk in the chopped nuts.

4 In the bowl of a stand mixer fitted with the whisk attachment, cream the butter and sugar on medium-high speed until light and fluffy, 3 to 5 minutes. Add the eggs, one at a time, beating until incorporated after each addition. Add the vanilla and beat just to combine. With the mixer on low speed, add the flour mixture and mix just until no streaks of flour remain. Add the crème fraîche and mix just until combined.

5 Divide the batter among the 12 muffin wells. Bake until the cakes spring back to the touch, about 20 minutes, rotating the pan halfway through baking. Let the cakes cool in their wells for about 10 minutes, then gently slide them out (you may need to run a small paring knife around the inside of the wells to ease the cakes out). Turn the cakes upside down on a rack and let cool completely.

6 To make the icing, whisk together the sugar and 2 tablespoons of the coffee in a bowl. Add up to 1 more tablespoon coffee, whisking until the consistency of the icing is thick but pourable. Spoon the icing over the cakes, using the back of a spoon to nudge it toward the edges so that it drips over the sides. Let the icing set, about 30 minutes, before serving. Store any leftovers airtight at room temperature.

Superstable Fruity Whipped Cream Frosting
From Stella Parks

This whipped cream frosting is astonishingly bright and fruity, thanks to a base of pulverized freeze-dried fruit (the kind sold as a space-age snack in health food stores, and in bulk online), which also absorbs any excess moisture that would normally seep out. By making it all in a food processor, this is a quick one-bowl move, and the whipped cream stays dense, creamy, and highly spreadable for up to a week, rather than fluffing up too much (and then, inevitably, deflating).

How to make it: In a food processor, pulse **2 ounces (55g) freeze-dried fruit** (like berries, cherries, apples, or even corn!) and **½ cup (100g) sugar** until powdery and fine, about 1½ minutes. Add **3 cups (705g) cold heavy cream** and stir with a rubber spatula or fork to ensure no dry ingredients are stuck in the corners. Pulse again until well combined, thick, and creamy (it should be close to the consistency of Greek yogurt), about 2 minutes. Don't overdo it, or it will turn into butter. Store airtight in the refrigerator until you need it to frost a cake. It's fluffiest on day 1, but holds up remarkably well for up to a week. Just give it a stir before using. Makes about 4 cups (1L) of frosting, or enough to cover an 8-inch (20cm) double-layer cake.

White, Milk, or Dark Chocolate Mousse for Layer Cakes
From Joanne Chang

At her Flour Bakery locations in Boston, Joanne Chang layers white, milk, and dark chocolate mousses between skinny stripes of flourless chocolate cake, then floods the whole surface with a thin ganache. At home, you can take it easier, but the mousse will whip up smoothest if you refrigerate it overnight.

How to make it: The day before you want to frost your cake, scald **1½ cups (355g) heavy cream** in a saucepan (just until small bubbles form along the sides of the pan) over medium-high heat. Optionally, while the cream is scalding, scrape the seeds from **½ vanilla bean**, split lengthwise, into the cream and toss in the pod, or add a **teaspoon of ground dark-roast coffee or espresso**. Finely chop **3 ounces (85g) white, milk, or dark chocolate** and place in a small heatproof bowl (don't use chips—they don't melt as nicely). Pour the scalded cream over the chocolate, let stand for a minute or so, and whisk until the chocolate is completely melted and smooth. Pour the mixture through a fine-mesh sieve into a small container, stir in **⅛ teaspoon kosher salt**, cover, and refrigerate overnight. The next day, whip the mousse until it holds stiff peaks, in a mixer or by hand. Use it to frost your cake, or skip the cake and serve it in a bowl topped with berries or a scoop of passion fruit, seeds and all. This makes 2½ cups (590ml) of frosting, or enough mousse for an 8 by 12-inch (20 by 30cm) sheet cake.

superstable fruity whipped cream frosting

milk chocolate mousse

sweet potato frosting

Two-Ingredient Sweet Potato Frosting
From Genevieve Ko

This is one ultra-easy, barely sweetened, vegan magic trick of a frosting. It tastes very grown-up and faintly tangy, like a soft dark chocolate ganache that happens to be made from a vegetable.

How to make it: Empty a **15-ounce (425g) can of pure sweet potato purée** into a large saucepan and bring to a simmer over medium heat, stirring often with a rubber spatula. Remove from the heat and stir in **10 ounces (285g) finely chopped bittersweet chocolate** until smooth. Let cool, stirring once in a while, until the mixture is frosting-like in thickness and holds soft peaks when you lift the spatula. Serve at room temperature for the most luscious texture. Store it in the refrigerator for up to 3 days, but bring it to room temperature before frosting the cake. Makes 2½ cups (590ml) frosting, or enough to cover a 9 by 13-inch (23 by 33cm) cake.

Vegan Chocolate Birthday Cake with Superfluffy Frosting

FROM ANITA SHEPHERD

Two unexpected ingredients and some brilliant tinkering helped make this birthday cake vegan—but better yet, they led to a fudgier cake and a frosting that's as fluffy as Swiss buttercream with less fuss. The tinkerer in question is Anita Shepherd, the vegan pastry chef and coconut yogurt pioneer behind Anita's Yogurt.

Instead of relying on whipped eggs or airy creamed butter for leavening, her cake batter harnesses the fizz from vinegar reacting with baking soda (remember the "volcano" from the fourth-grade science fair?). This is also when she adds secret ingredient number one: a couple of mashed avocados, which give the cake a sly richness and a soft, bouncy crumb.

But the frosting is where our tinkerer really got going. After studying the back of a Cool Whip container and seeing that the third ingredient was high-fructose corn syrup, she started playing with the wholesome equivalent: brown rice syrup (secret ingredient number two). Added on its own, the syrup made frostings sleek and glossy, but still heavier and stickier than she wanted. But she discovered that the syrup helped stabilize the base enough that pouring in almond milk made it turn into pillowy ripples in the mixer instead of thinning back into a glaze.

The frosting that comes out is lustrous and smooth. The flavor is moored by salt, vanilla, chocolate, and something less familiar: the earthy, molasses-like hint of the brown rice syrup, which doesn't overpower the chocolate but makes it more rounded and intriguing— yet still recognizable enough to remind you of the best birthday cakes of yore.

SERVES 12

CAKE
3 cups (375g) all-purpose flour (see page 5)

¼ cup plus 2 tablespoons (30g) unsweetened cocoa powder (see page 5)

2 teaspoons baking powder

2 teaspoons baking soda

½ teaspoon fine sea salt

2 cups (475g) water

1 cup (230g) smooth mashed avocado (puréed or passed through a fine mesh strainer, from 2 avocados)

¼ cup (55g) neutral oil (such as grapeseed) or nut oil (such as almond)

2 tablespoons white vinegar

2 teaspoons pure vanilla extract

2 cups (400g) sugar

FROSTING
7 ounces (200g) best-quality unsweetened chocolate (such as 100% Dagoba)

1 cup plus 2 tablespoons (230g) non-hydrogenated shortening

3 cups (375g) confectioners' sugar

¾ cup (180g) almond milk

2 teaspoons pure vanilla extract

¼ teaspoon fine sea salt

¾ cup (250g) brown rice syrup

1 To make the cake, heat the oven to 350°F (175°C), with racks in the upper and lower thirds. Oil two 8- or 9-inch (20 or 23cm) round cake pans and dust with bread crumbs or flour, tapping out the excess.

2 Sift together the flour, cocoa powder, baking powder, baking soda, and salt in a large bowl. Whisk together the water, mashed avocado, oil, vinegar, and vanilla in a separate bowl. Add the sugar to the wet ingredients and whisk until combined. Pour the wet ingredients into the dry all at once and whisk together until smooth.

3 Pour the batter evenly into the cake pans. Bake until a toothpick stuck in the middle comes out with just crumbs clinging, 30 to 40 minutes.

4 Let the cakes cool in the pans for 15 minutes, then turn out onto racks to cool completely before frosting.

CONTINUED

Vegan Chocolate Birthday Cake with Superfluffy Frosting

CONTINUED

5 To make the frosting, melt the chocolate in a heatproof bowl set over but not touching gently simmering water in a saucepan. You can stir it occasionally to help it along. Set aside to cool completely. If you're in a rush, you can set the bowl of melted chocolate in a bath of cold water and whisk to cool it down faster, but don't let the chocolate get solid again!

6 In the bowl of a stand mixer fitted with the paddle attachment, beat the shortening on medium speed until smooth. Add the sugar and beat on low speed until smooth. Add ¼ cup (60g) of the almond milk, the vanilla, and the salt and beat until combined. If at any point the frosting starts to look ugly and separated, don't worry—just keep beating on high until it smooths out. If your kitchen is hot and the frosting looks separated or flat, stick the bowl in the refrigerator to cool it down, then continue.

7 With the mixer on medium-high speed, slowly pour in the brown rice syrup, followed by the remaining ½ cup (120g) almond milk, and beat until the frosting gets superfluffy. Add the cooled chocolate and beat until incorporated. Taste and adjust the salt or sweetness if you like. Let cool completely to firm up, chilling if needed, then whisk again and use to frost the cooled chocolate cakes. Store any leftovers airtight at room temperature.

GENIUS TIP: AN EVEN MORE PANTRY-FRIENDLY CAKE

If you don't have ripe avocados on hand, omit them. You'll have what was known during the Depression as a wacky cake or crazy cake, since it (wackily) lacked eggs, butter, and milk and still worked beautifully (and cheaply). The cake will be less fudgy, but still do the trick.

GENIUS TIP: PRETTIER CAKE TRICKS—NO FANCY TOOLS NEEDED

You don't need a well-equipped pastry kitchen or loads of experience to feel confident baking cakes for a celebration. Here are a few tricks using tools and doodads that are probably lying around in your kitchen drawers.

- If you don't want uneven layers in your birthday cake, don't eyeball it when slicing the cake in two or shearing off a rounded top—even Ina Garten pokes skewers laterally through the middle of each cake as a guide to make sure she's slicing straight and even.

- For exciting swirly streaks in your buttercream, dribble runny jams down the inside of your piping bag (or zip-top bag) before decorating, à la Sarah Kieffer of the *Vanilla Bean Baking* blog, and smear some onto the sides of your cake for good measure (check out the beauty on page 119). It's helpful to experiment a bit on a plate first and thin the jam as needed, before you get going.

- What goofy-looking cake? Confectioners' sugar cures all gnarly surfaces and battle scars—and anything can be a stencil (doilies, noodles, ribbons, cheese graters, pressed leaves from the backyard—see page 139). Sprinkle right before serving so the sugar doesn't disappear on you. A PSA: A fine-mesh strainer is a perfectly good sifter (and garnish delivery system)—no need to own both.

Whole Orange Cake

FROM *SUNSET* & STEPHANIE SPENCER

You might be thinking this is one of the genius breed of cakes made with whole citrus boiled for hours to make a custard-like base. (I included Claudia Roden's famous Orange and Almond Cake in the *Genius Recipes* cookbook, and Nigella Lawson is known for a few with clementines.) It's not! This one doesn't bother with boiling at all, instead chucking fresh chunks of orange—skin, pith, and juicy flesh—right in the food processor and blitzing until only tiny flecks of skin remain.

After mixing this pulpy orange slush into the batter, the cake that comes out is incredibly moist (and gets more so by the day), with a flavor that's marmalade-like but brighter, for people who prefer a bit of bitterness and complexity to straight sweet. And for those who don't, the glaze is a good distraction.

SERVES 12

CAKE
1 cup (225g) unsalted butter, softened

1¼ cups (250g) sugar

3 large eggs

2 oranges (about 1 pound/ 450g), unpeeled but ends trimmed, then cut into chunks and seeded

2½ cups (315g) all-purpose flour (see page 5)

2 teaspoons baking powder

¼ teaspoon baking soda

¼ teaspoon fine sea salt

GLAZE
1½ cups (185g) confectioners' sugar, plus more as needed

2 tablespoons plus 1 teaspoon freshly squeezed orange juice

1 To make the cake, heat the oven to 325°F (165°C), with a rack in the center. Butter a 10-cup (2.4L) Bundt pan.

2 Using a handheld mixer in a large bowl, cream the butter and sugar until fluffy, 3 to 5 minutes. Add the eggs, one at a time, beating until incorporated after each addition.

3 In a food processor, pulse the orange chunks until the pulp is mostly smooth but not completely puréed. Spoon out 1½ cups (355ml) of the orange mixture and add this to the batter, then beat again until blended. (Compost any remaining orange mixture.) Add the flour, baking powder, baking soda, and salt and beat just until smooth. Scrape the batter into the pan and smooth the top.

4 Bake until the cake is risen, evenly golden, and firm to the touch and a toothpick stuck in the middle comes out with just crumbs clinging, about 55 minutes. Let the cake cool in the pan on a rack set over a rimmed baking sheet for 10 minutes, then invert the cake onto the rack and let cool completely.

5 To make the glaze, once the cake is cool, whisk together the confectioners' sugar and orange juice in a small bowl. If you'd like the glaze to be thicker, whisk in more confectioners' sugar. Test the glaze's consistency on a small area of the cake, if you like. Once the consistency is as you like it, spoon the glaze over the top. Let the glaze set, about 30 minutes, before serving. Cut the cake into slices and serve. Store any leftovers airtight at room temperature. If you don't want to disturb the glaze, see the tip in step 7 on page 90.

Parsnip Cake with Blood Orange Buttercream

FROM PETER MEEHAN & MARY-FRANCES HECK

With its gentle spice and swirly, tangy frosting, this parsnip cake is closer to what much of the world thinks of as carrot cake than the actual carrot cake recipe on page 90. But because it was developed by the *Lucky Peach* crew for their book *Power Vegetables,* it's a little kooky and very, very good.

There are no carrots here, only shredded parsnips—the first, more elusive of this cake's surprises. Parsnips make the cake moist and sweet, just like carrots would, and give the cake a bonus spicy kick. The second surprise gives itself away: blood orange juice, reduced to an intense syrup and spun into a tart, bright pink buttercream. When I can't find blood oranges, I serve this cake with *Fine Cooking* magazine's excellent Brown Butter Cream Cheese Frosting (page 135) as a throwback to its carrot cousin. Apply either frosting liberally.

SERVES 12 TO 16

CAKE

3 large eggs

1 cup (200g) sugar

½ cup (110g) neutral oil (such as grapeseed)

½ cup (125g) milk

1 teaspoon kosher salt

½ teaspoon pure vanilla extract

1½ cups (190g) all-purpose flour (see page 5)

2 teaspoons baking powder

1 teaspoon ground cinnamon

¼ teaspoon freshly grated nutmeg

¼ teaspoon ground allspice

¼ teaspoon ground cloves

1 pound (450g) parsnips, peeled and grated (about 2 cups)

1 teaspoon grated peeled fresh ginger or ½ teaspoon ground ginger

BUTTERCREAM

½ cup (120g) freshly squeezed blood orange juice (from 5 small blood oranges)

1 cup (225g) unsalted butter, softened

3 to 4 cups (375 to 500g) confectioners' sugar

1 To make the cake, heat the oven to 350°F (175°C). Lightly butter or oil a 9 by 13-inch (23 by 33cm) cake pan and line the bottom with parchment paper.

2 Whisk together the eggs, sugar, oil, milk, salt, and vanilla until smooth. Add the flour, baking powder, cinnamon, nutmeg, allspice, and cloves and whisk together until smooth and homogenous, about 2 minutes. Fold the parsnips and ginger into the batter.

3 Pour the batter into the pan—the batter won't rise much, so you can fill the pan to within ½ inch (1.3cm) of the top. Bake until a toothpick stuck in the middle comes out with just crumbs clinging, about 24 minutes, rotating the pan halfway through baking. Let cool in the pan for 10 minutes, then turn out onto a rack and cool completely.

4 To make the buttercream, pour the blood orange juice into a small saucepan and bring to a simmer over high heat. Reduce the heat and continue to simmer until the juice is reduced to a syrup, about 10 minutes. Remove from the heat and let cool completely.

5 In the bowl of a stand mixer fitted with the paddle attachment, cream the butter on medium-high speed until fluffy, about 2 minutes. Add the blood orange syrup and beat until incorporated (the buttercream won't come together at first, so start on low speed, and then turn the speed way up by the end). Drape a kitchen towel over the top of the mixer to contain any flying sugar, then add the confectioners' sugar to the mixture 1 cup (125g) at a time, blending well on low speed, until it's a spreadable consistency (and sweetness level) you like. Slather the frosting on the cake and serve. Store any leftovers airtight at room temperature.

CONTINUED

Brown Butter Cream Cheese Frosting

From Fine Cooking *& Jeanne Kelley*

By taking your average cream cheese frosting and replacing the butter with brown butter (and some of the confectioners' sugar with brown sugar), you still get a swiftly made frosting that's blessedly tangy and smooth—but with richer, warmer notes that get along nicely with spice cakes. The original recipe called for leaving the bits of toasty milk solids behind in the bottom of the bowl after chilling the brown butter, which you can do if you're looking for a perfectly smooth, coffee-colored buttercream. But I like to leave them in to intensify the brown butter flavor (and I don't mind the freckly appearance one bit).

How to make it: Melt ½ cup (110g) unsalted butter in a small, heavy saucepan over medium heat, swirling occasionally until the butter turns golden brown and smells nutty, about 4 minutes. Pour the butter into a small bowl and chill in the freezer until just firm and no liquid butter remains, about 20 minutes. In a stand mixer fitted with the paddle attachment, beat the brown butter, **8 ounces (225g) room-temperature cream cheese**, and ¼ cup (55g) packed **light brown sugar** on medium-high speed until the brown sugar has dissolved and the mix is light and fluffy, about 2 minutes. Gradually beat in **1¼ cups (155g) confectioners' sugar** and continue beating until fluffy, about 2 minutes. Makes about 2½ cups (590ml) frosting, or enough to frost one 9 by 13-inch (23 by 33cm) sheet cake.

GENIUS TIP: HOW TO REVIVE BADLY BEHAVING BUTTERCREAM

If your buttercream starts to look broken and separated, counterintuitively, it probably just needs a bit of heat. Keep beating it on high speed while warming the bowl with a hair dryer, or scoop out about a third of the frosting, warm it in the microwave or on the stovetop, then slowly blend it back in to restore the glossy emulsion. (On the flip side, if the frosting is looking smooth but runny, it probably needs to cool off—whisk the frosting in a bowl set over an ice bath to firm it up.)

Parsley Cake

FROM ROBERTA'S & KATY PEETZ

If we can put mint in ice cream, what's stopping parsley from stumbling into sweets? It's an herb with as much leeway as all the rest—it just hasn't made the leap in our imaginations yet. For that, we can thank the punk rock crew at Roberta's restaurant in Brooklyn, namely former pastry chef Katy Peetz.

In its DNA, Peetz's recipe is a relatively normal sheet cake, with a little cornstarch slipped in to help guarantee a tender crumb. But the real stars are the five bunches of parsley (and two of mint), blitzed up into a vivid green oil that makes the batter bright and refreshing, two words not often associated with cake. If you can, let the batter sit for a few hours or overnight, and it will be even greener.

At the restaurant, the cake is served with fennel caramel gelato, lemon zest granita, and more parsley cake crumbles. We did the lazy equivalent: store-bought vanilla ice cream, candied lemon, and a few finishing swoops of olive oil. Alternatively, eat it warm with butter for breakfast.

> "Whenever there's an abundance of green things at the farmers market or in our garden, green inevitably spills over into our desserts." —Roberta's team

SERVES 12 TO 14

4 cups (150g) firmly packed fresh flat-leaf parsley leaves (from 5 small bunches)

1 cup (30g) firmly packed fresh mint leaves (from 2 small bunches)

¾ cup (165g) good olive oil

2⅓ cups (290g) all-purpose flour (see page 5)

1 tablespoon plus 2 teaspoons cornstarch

2¼ teaspoons kosher salt

1½ teaspoons baking powder

4 large eggs, at room temperature

1⅔ cups (335g) sugar

Vanilla ice cream, candied lemon peel or fresh lemon zest, and/or a drizzle of olive oil, to serve (optional)

1   Combine about one-quarter of the parsley and one-quarter of the mint in a high-speed blender or food processor and process on low speed, scraping down the sides as needed. Continue adding the remaining herbs in two or three additions until you have a blender full of fine green mulch.

2   With the blender on medium-low speed (or pulsing, if using a food processor), pour in half of the olive oil in a steady stream. Add the remaining olive oil all at once and process for no longer than 10 seconds. The mixture will look loose and stringy—that's okay. Scrape it into a bowl and refrigerate until ready to use.

3   Whisk together the flour, cornstarch, salt, and baking powder in a medium bowl. In the bowl of a stand mixer fitted with the paddle attachment, whip the eggs on medium-high speed for about 30 seconds. Add the sugar and mix on high speed until very thick and pale yellow, about 3 minutes. With the mixer on low speed, pour in the herb-oil mixture, followed by the flour mixture and mix until just combined. Pour the batter into a container and refrigerate for 6 to 24 hours, if possible (the cake will be greener if you can).

4   When you're ready to bake, heat the oven to 350°F (175°C) and lightly oil a 10 by 15-inch (25 by 38cm) rimmed baking sheet. Line with parchment paper and lightly oil the parchment. Pour the batter into the baking sheet and smooth the top with a spatula.

5   Bake until a toothpick stuck in the middle comes out with just crumbs clinging, 12 to 18 minutes, rotating the cake halfway through baking. If the top begins to brown before the inside of the cake is done, turn the heat down to 325°F (165°C) and cook a couple of minutes longer. Let the cake cool in the pan on a rack.

6   To serve, tear serving-size squares of cake into a few large pieces and divide them among individual plates, along with vanilla ice cream, candied lemon peel, and a drizzle of olive oil. Store any leftover airtight at room temperature.

Guinness Stout Ginger Cake

FROM CLAUDIA FLEMING

This is one of those recipes that comes up again and again when you ask home cooks and pastry chefs alike for their favorite dessert. What is it that makes it so memorable? I have a theory or two.

For one thing, thanks to the molasses and oil, the cake stays good and moist for days, which is extra handy for a spice cake, as the nutmeg, cinnamon, and clove really come into their own on days two and three. (For more on how oil works its wonders in cakes, see page 93.)

As for theory number two, ginger cake recipes calling for stout—instead of the typical hot water or coffee—were extremely uncommon before Claudia Fleming published her version in her book *The Last Course* in 2001. Since then, the combination has taken hold, as bakers have recognized the dark, malty, slightly bitter depth that dry stouts can bring to cakes that are flavored with molasses and warm spices. Fleming's version was inspired by Dona Abramson and Stuart Tarabour at Bright Food Shop, a pioneering fusion restaurant for 22 years in the Chelsea neighborhood of Manhattan (in their case, it was Mexican-Asian—neither of which has much to do with ginger cake, but such was the loosey-gooseyness of fusion). Fleming added her own tweaks and a more complete roster of spices and sent it to the moon.

SERVES 8 TO 12

1 cup (210g) Guinness stout

1 cup (340g) molasses (preferably mild, not blackstrap)

1½ teaspoons baking soda

3 large eggs

½ cup (100g) sugar

½ cup (110g) packed dark brown sugar

¾ cup (160g) neutral oil (such as grapeseed)

2 cups (250g) all-purpose flour (see page 5)

2 tablespoons ground ginger

1½ teaspoons baking powder

¾ teaspoon ground cinnamon

¼ teaspoon ground cloves

¼ teaspoon freshly grated nutmeg

⅛ teaspoon ground cardamom

1 tablespoon grated peeled fresh ginger

Confectioners' sugar, for dusting (optional)

Whipped cream, ice cream, or crème fraîche, for serving (optional)

1   Heat the oven to 350°F (175°C), with a rack in the center. Butter a 9 by 13-inch (23 by 33cm) pan, line the bottom and sides with parchment, and grease the parchment. Alternatively, butter and dust a 10-cup (2.4L) Bundt pan with fine, dry bread crumbs or flour, tapping out the excess.

2   Combine the stout and molasses in a large (preferably 4-quart [3.8L] or larger) saucepan and bring to a boil over high heat. Immediately turn off the heat and stir in the baking soda. Let sit until the foam settles down.

3   Meanwhile, whisk together the eggs and sugars in a medium bowl, followed by the oil. In a large bowl, whisk together the flour, ground ginger, baking powder, cinnamon, cloves, nutmeg, and cardamom.

4   Pour the stout mixture into the egg mixture and whisk together. Pour the stout-egg mixture into the flour mixture in two additions, whisking to combine after each addition. Stir in the grated ginger.

5   Pour the batter into the pan and bake until the top springs back when gently pressed and a toothpick stuck in the middle comes out with just crumbs clinging, about 35 minutes for the 9 by 13-inch (23 by 33cm) pan and 1 hour for the Bundt. Don't open the oven until the cake is almost done, or the center may fall slightly. Let the cake cool completely in the pan on a rack, then loosen the edges with an offset spatula before unmolding from the pan onto a serving plate. For the 9 by 13-inch (23 by 33cm) pan, you may want to invert the cake one more time to be right side up. (Alternatively, serve from the pan.)

6   Dust with confectioners' sugar (see the Genius Tip on page 128), cut into slices, and serve at room temperature with whipped cream, ice cream, or crème fraîche. Store any leftovers airtight at room temperature—they'll keep well.

New-Fashioned Apple Cider Doughnuts

FROM IDEAS IN FOOD

This recipe harnesses the power of time to make better, fluffier doughnuts and, as an extra make-ahead perk, means that you get to roll out of bed with your dough ready to cut, fry, and eat (and, sure, share). You can stir together a cider paste one day, the dough the next, and the day after that you become a local hero when you set them—the doughnuts, holes, and cult-favorite crunchy scraps called "debris"—out at a brunch or barbecue or bar mitzvah, or just a casual Friday at your office.

They're the work of Aki Kamozawa and H. Alexander Talbot, the founders of Ideas in Food, a pioneering food science blog, consulting company, and series of cookbooks. In 2015, the duo opened Curiosity Doughnuts, to the delight of central New Jerseyans and road-tripping food geeks everywhere. The reason they use this stop-start routine is a good one and borrows from the technique used to make soft, ultrafluffy Japanese milk bread with *tangzhong* (a simple cooked starch paste). "As a kid, I grew up eating Japanese milk bread, and for years I chased after that firm yet tender and fluffy texture in my baking," Kamozawa told me.

By cooking a portion of the flour in liquid (here, cider and butter) to form a starch paste, you're gelatinizing the flour, so you're able to both add more moisture to the dough and gently develop the gluten's structure without kneading, which allows the doughnuts to capture (and rise with) extra steam. The moisture in the dough also sticks around, so they keep longer, too. The results are much like the cider doughnuts you might pick up at an apple orchard, but extra-fluffy and plush inside, with a spicy quirk in the cinnamon-sugar coating that's hard to pin down (it's cardamom!).

MAKES 1 BAKER'S DOZEN CIDER DOUGHNUTS
WITH HOLES AND DEBRIS

CIDER PASTE (TANGZHONG)
¼ cup plus 2 tablespoons (90g) apple cider

3 tablespoons unsalted butter

⅓ cup plus 1 tablespoon (50g) all-purpose flour (see page 5)

DOUGHNUTS
1 cup (250g) apple cider

1 cup plus 2 tablespoons (250g) heavy cream

1 cup (200g) sugar

2 large eggs

4 teaspoons pure vanilla paste or extract

5 cups plus 3 tablespoons (650g) all-purpose flour (see page 5)

4 teaspoons baking powder

1 teaspoon baking soda

4 teaspoons Diamond Crystal kosher salt

Neutral oil (such as rice bran or grapeseed), for frying

CINNAMON-CARDAMOM SUGAR
2½ cups (500g) sugar

2 tablespoons ground cinnamon

1 teaspoon ground cardamom

1 To make the cider paste, combine the apple cider and butter in a small saucepan and cook over medium heat until the butter melts and the mixture comes to a boil. Add the flour and cook, stirring constantly with a heatproof spatula, until the flour is absorbed and the mixture turns into a paste that pulls away from the sides of the pan, 1 to 2 minutes. Scrape the cider paste into a small stainless-steel bowl or other heatproof container to cool. Refrigerate airtight for at least 4 hours and up to 3 days. The paste should be completely chilled before using.

2 To make the doughnuts, put the chilled cider paste, cider, heavy cream, sugar, eggs, and vanilla in a blender (preferably a high-speed blender) or food processor and process until the mixture is a smooth, lump-free liquid. (If using a high-speed blender, start the blender at low speed, and then increase to medium-high.) Whisk together the flour, baking powder, baking soda, and salt in a large bowl. Pour the wet ingredients into the dry ingredients and use a rubber spatula to stir everything together just until the dry ingredients are absorbed—no longer. The mixture should look like a thick, sticky biscuit dough. Line

CONTINUED

New-Fashioned Apple Cider Doughnuts

a rimmed baking sheet with plastic wrap and scrape the dough onto it. Cover the dough with more plastic wrap and gently press the dough with your hands into an even layer—it doesn't need to be perfect since you'll be rolling it out later. Refrigerate the dough for at least 4 hours and up to 2 days.

3 To make the cinnamon-cardamom sugar, whisk together the sugar, cinnamon, and cardamom in a wide shallow bowl.

4 To fry the doughnuts, line two large rimmed baking sheets with parchment paper and set them near the stove. Gather a rolling pin, a 3-inch (7.5cm) ring cutter, and a 1-inch (2.5cm) ring cutter (if you have them, otherwise find comparable cutting tools among your juice glasses and melon ballers—get creative!). Generously dust a large countertop or other work surface with flour.

5 Remove the top piece of plastic wrap and invert the dough onto the floured workspace. Peel off the remaining layer of plastic wrap. Generously dust the top of the dough with more flour. Use a rolling pin to roll the dough into a rough rectangle that's about ½ inch (1.3cm) thick. Use the 3-inch (7.5cm) ring cutter to cut out doughnuts. Use the 1-inch (2.5cm) cutter to cut out the center hole of each doughnut. Place the doughnuts and holes on one of the baking sheets. If there is space to cut out more holes from your scraps, do so and then add them to the baking sheet with the doughnuts. Put the remaining dough scraps— no matter their shape—on the second baking sheet. You will fry these separately to create delicious doughnut debris.

6 Set a large pot on the stovetop and fill halfway with oil. Bring the oil to 375°F (190°C) over medium heat. (If you don't have a thermometer, you can gauge the temperature by tossing in a doughnut hole; the oil is ready when the hole browns in 1½ minutes). Either way, you will need to adjust the heat as you go, depending on how quickly your doughnuts are browning. Meanwhile, set racks over two additional baking sheets and place them next to the pot of oil. (Out of baking sheets? Transfer the uncooked

doughnuts to a cutting board, or another workspace near the stove, and use the racks set over the baking sheets for draining the fried doughnuts.) Have a heatproof slotted spoon or spider skimmer nearby to turn the doughnuts in the hot oil.

7 When the oil is hot, use the slotted spoon to put one-third of the scraps into the pot. Set a timer for 1 minute (yes, Curiosity Doughnuts uses a timer every single time). When the timer goes off, flip the scraps and set the timer for 1 minute more. When the timer goes off again and the scraps are deep golden brown, transfer them to a rack to cool. Continue frying the remaining scraps in two more batches, monitoring the heat to make sure the oil temperature stays around 375°F (190°C). Do not overcrowd the pot or the temperature will drop, resulting in greasy doughnuts.

8 After the scraps are fried, use the slotted spoon to gently lower the doughnut holes into the hot oil. Set a timer for 1½ minutes. As the holes fry, use the slotted spoon to gently stir the holes in the hot oil to flip and turn them so they cook evenly. When the timer goes off and the holes are deep golden brown, use the slotted spoon to transfer them to the rack alongside the scraps.

9 Position the empty rack next to the cooking oil. Put 3 doughnuts into the pot. Set a timer for 1½ minutes. When the timer goes off, flip the doughnuts with the slotted spoon and set the timer for 1½ minutes more. When the timer goes off again and the doughnuts are a deep golden brown on both sides, transfer them to the rack to cool. Continue frying the remaining doughnuts, 3 at a time.

10 Let the doughnuts, holes, and scraps cool for 10 minutes, then roll them all in the cinnamon-cardamom sugar to coat evenly. Serve immediately or return the doughnuts to a rack to continue cooling. Holding them on the rack will help preserve the crispy crust underneath the sugar. Store any leftovers on a rack at room temperature, covered in plastic wrap or aluminum foil. Poke the plastic or foil with air holes to help preserve the crust.

Wonder Dough
Sponge Cake (& Cookie) Base Recipe

FROM ALEX RAIJ

After an obsessive few weeks trying to perfect a Victoria sponge cake recipe, chef and restaurateur Alex Raij found her freezer brimming with cake trimmings. Each time the freezer filled up, she repurposed the scraps into a crumbly topping for warm roasted or poached fruit. She named the dessert *migas dulces*, after the family of (usually savory) dishes in Spain called *migas* for using up stale bread (*migas* means "crumbs," so *migas dulces* literally translates to "sweet crumbs"). These dolled-up leftovers became so popular at Txikito, her restaurant in the Chelsea neighborhood of Manhattan, that she had to start making the cake just to get the crumbs.

She's since developed a batter that's drier than the Victoria sponge, which has made the recipe even more versatile. She uses it not only to make dense cakes for soaking with liquor and fruit (*bizcochos borrachos*, or drunken cakes), or turn into the now famous *migas dulces* (page 147)—but the very same batter works just as well for making crunchy *langue de chat*–style butter cookies, which in turn make delicious layered trifles with booze and cream (page 147). In her hands, and now in yours, a single batter can become endless desserts.

MAKES 2 (8 BY 12-INCH/20 BY 30CM) CAKES
OR 12 DOZEN COOKIES

BASE BATTER
¾ cup plus 2 tablespoons (170g) sugar

¾ cup (170g) unsalted butter, very cold and cut into ½-inch (1.3cm) cubes

3 large eggs

½ teaspoon pure vanilla extract

1⅓ cups (170g) cake flour (see page 5)

1½ teaspoons baking powder

1 Heat the oven to 350°F (175°C), with racks in the upper and lower thirds. To make the base batter, in a food processor, pulse together the sugar and butter until combined, scraping down the sides if needed. Let the motor run until the batter is smooth and lighter, 1 to 2 minutes. With the processor running, add the eggs, one at a time, processing until combined after each addition. Add the vanilla and process until combined. Turn off the processor, add half of the cake flour and the baking powder, and pulse just until smooth. Scrape down the sides of the processor, add the remaining cake flour, and pulse just until smooth. Line two large rimmed baking sheets with parchment paper or silicone baking mats. Proceed either to Sponge Cake or Cat's Tongue Cookies from here (or both!).

Sponge Cake

1 Using a spatula, spread half of the batter onto the center of each baking sheet, smoothing it into a rough oval or rectangle that's about ⅓-inch (8mm) thick; try to smooth the batter into a relatively even layer. Bake until evenly golden brown and the top springs back when gently pressed, about 15 minutes. Let the cakes cool on the baking sheets. Once cool, store airtight at room temperature. Serve the sponge cake as is (perhaps with a splash of booze, juicy summer fruit, or jam) or proceed straight to the *Migas Dulces* recipe on page 147. (One cake should give you just the right amount of crumbs.)

Cat's Tongue Cookies

1 Load the batter into a piping bag or zipper bag. Snip the tip of the bag to make a ¼-inch (6mm) opening and pipe the batter into small cat tongue–shaped or round cookies, spacing them at least 2 inches (5cm) apart. Alternatively, drop teaspoonfuls onto the baking sheet. Bake until golden, about 12 minutes. Let cool completely on the baking sheets on racks. Store airtight at room temperature or proceed straight to the Cookie Trifle on page 147.

migas dulces

cookie trifle

CAKE & COOKIE SPIN-OFFS

Migas Dulces **from Sponge Cake (page 145) or Any Cake Trim:** If the cake isn't already quite dry, heat the oven to 350°F (175°C), with a rack in the center. Line a baking sheet with parchment paper or a silicone baking mat. Break the cake into pieces roughly the size of a shelled walnut and arrange on a baking sheet. You should have about 4 cups (275g) cake crumbs. Bake until dried, about 15 minutes.

In a food processor, pulse the **cake crumbs, 2 cups (200g) walnut pieces, 1 cup (100g) powdered milk (optional), ½ cup (110g) butter, 5 tablespoons (60g) light brown sugar, ½ teaspoon kosher salt**, and any optional flavorings like **fennel seeds, lemon or orange zest, rosemary, or cinnamon** until it's the texture of coarse meal. Add a **large egg** and pulse just to combine. Using your hands, clump the crumble into pieces, aiming for roughly the size of a shelled walnut, and arrange them on the baking sheet. Bake until lightly brown, about 20 minutes, stirring gently every 6 minutes or so. They'll break apart into a variety of sizes—this is okay, just watch to make sure the small bits don't burn.

To serve, poach or roast fruit to taste (for example, poach pears, apples, or peaches using the instructions on page 253, or roast figs or plums until softened and juicy, but not mushy). Place the fruit in small bowls, splash with Armagnac or other brandy, top with crumble, and finish with a scoop of ice cream or cinnamon whipped cream.

Cookie Trifle from Cat's Tongue Cookies (page 145): Pick 6 pretty glasses or 1 pretty glass bowl and calculate 5 cookies per person. Whip **2 cups (470g) heavy cream** to soft peaks, sweetening and **flavoring to taste with sugar and vanilla**; or stir together **half whipped cream and half Greek yogurt, crème fraîche, or mascarpone**. Pour a little **sherry or Marsala** or even great **añejo tequila** in a shallow dish. Dip the cookies into the booze and layer the drunken cookies and the flavored cream in the glasses or bowl, refrigerate until chilled and serve. You can hack this dessert with other butter cookies but it's almost as easy to make these homemade cookies and store them, so you always have them on hand.

Custards, Puddings & Frozen Things

Greek Yogurt Chocolate Mousse

FROM MARIA SPECK

Not only is this mousse quicker and more casual to make than the frillier traditional French version, but serious lovers of dark chocolate may also find themselves liking it more. You don't need to whip cream or egg whites; just simply stir together hot milk and chocolate to make a ganache, then fold in Greek yogurt. The tart yogurt and total absence of cream and eggs let the fruity side of good dark chocolate really break free, for a bright, tangy mousse that won't make you want to crawl into bed after a few spoonfuls.

The recipe comes from Maria Speck, cookbook author and ancient grain guru, who riffed on a version she spotted in a Greek magazine. In an especially delightful move, Speck tops each cup with a dollop of orange marmalade, which won't at all remind you of one of those foil-wrapped chocolate oranges. Instead, the bittersweet jelly plays off the more intensely chocolaty notes and the Grand Marnier (and it looks pretty and gem-like on top, too). Of course, if you're not in the mood for orange, strip this down to the basic mousse and stir in another booze, or garnish with fresh berries or crumbled brittle or halvah, as you like.

SERVES 4

6 ounces (170g) best-quality bittersweet chocolate (70% cacao), finely chopped

½ cup (125g) whole milk

1 cup (225g) whole or 2% Greek yogurt (don't use nonfat)

1 to 2 tablespoons Grand Marnier or other good-quality orange liqueur

4 teaspoons orange marmalade

1 Place the chocolate in a medium heatproof bowl. In a small heavy saucepan, bring the milk just to a boil over medium heat. Pour the hot milk over the chocolate and let sit for 2 minutes. Stir with a spatula or wooden spoon until smooth.

2 In a small bowl, beat the Greek yogurt with a small whisk or a fork until smooth. Using a spatula, fold the yogurt into the chocolate mixture until thoroughly combined and then stir in 1 tablespoon of the Grand Marnier. Taste, and if you'd like a boozier dessert, add the second tablespoon.

3 Spoon the mousse into four small serving cups and refrigerate until firm, at least 1 hour. You can store, covered with plastic wrap, for up to 1 day.

4 Just before serving, spoon a teaspoon of marmalade onto the top of each mousse cup. Serve cold.

Vanilla Bean Rice Pudding

FROM MOLLY WIZENBERG

The goal—and the surprising challenge—of making rice pudding is to coax the grains of rice to sweeten and plump fully in milk, yet stay wholly themselves and not blur into mush.

I tried a good dozen rice pudding techniques as I stumbled down this path, looking for comfort. The most extreme (and most consoling) recipes called for baking or simmering the rice for three hours at the lowest possible heat, to get the rice to soak up as much milk as it could without falling to bits. But in times when we want comfort, we want it a lot sooner than three hours from now.

Molly Wizenberg's recipe is my favorite of them all, as it's the fastest route to perfect pudgy grains. She uses a simple two-step process, by steaming the rice for 10 minutes and then adding in milk and cream to finish the job—all in one pot. As it simmers, the pudding fills the kitchen with the aromas of bubbling sweet milk and vanilla, taking just long enough to make you yearn, and then fixes everything.

SERVES 6 TO 8

1½ cups (355g) water	1 cup (235g) heavy cream
¾ cup (135g) basmati rice	½ cup (100g) sugar
¼ teaspoon fine sea salt	½ vanilla bean, split lengthwise
3 cups (735g) whole milk	

1 Bring the water, rice, and salt to a simmer in a large heavy saucepan over medium-high heat. Turn the heat to low, cover, and simmer gently until the water is absorbed, about 10 minutes.

2 Pour in the milk, cream, and sugar. Scrape the seeds from the vanilla bean with the tip of a paring knife and then add the seeds and vanilla pod to the pot and stir to combine. Turn the heat to medium-low and simmer gently, uncovered, stirring occasionally and scraping the bottom of the pot with a rubber spatula, until the rice is tender and the mixture thickens to a soft, loose pudding texture, about 30 minutes.

3 Remove from the heat and set aside the vanilla bean (see the Genius Tip). Spoon the pudding into 6 to 8 small bowls. Serve warm or press plastic wrap onto the surface of each pudding to keep a skin from forming and refrigerate thoroughly to serve cold.

GENIUS TIP: HOW TO STRETCH A VANILLA BEAN FOR MANY, MANY DESSERTS

Never throw away a used vanilla pod—they have much more life to give you. Stick it into your sugar container (clean and dry it first, if needed—there, you just made vanilla sugar!). In a couple of days, that same sugar will bring deeper, more nuanced vanilla notes to your baked goods, without having to buy a pricey specialty ingredient. Alternatively, simmer the pods in simple syrup to add to your iced coffee or to brush onto a cake layer. Or dry the pods out in a low oven, then grind them into vanilla powder to use in Chocolate Magic Dust (page 43).

French Toast Crunch

FROM ANTHONY MYINT

One night at the original Mission Street Food pop-up restaurant in San Francisco, faced with the demands of coming up with a new dessert each night with scant time and space, Anthony Myint served milk toast. But he gave it a little flash, by caramelizing a buttery, sugary crust onto slices of brioche and serving them in warm, chamomile-scented cream.

You can't eat this and not be happy. A loud, unflinching bite of the broiled, sugared toast is a joy matched only by the crack of a spoon breaking through the glassy top of a crème brûlée. The airy toast will have drunk up the warm, milky puddle like a tres leches cake while the candied top floats above it, keeping its crunch pristine.

When would you serve it, besides a quiet moment alone? A weeknight dinner party. A brunch. Valentine's Day. An afternoon snack for your children, if you don't want your children to ever eat plain toast again.

In his *Mission Street Food* cookbook, Myint includes a chart of thirteen twists on French Toast Crunch, from matcha to baklava. You can vary the flavors endlessly, but this is comfort food, so you can also just revel in keeping it simple.

SERVES 4

1 cup (240g) half-and-half

¼ cup (7g) whole chamomile buds or 2 or 3 chamomile tea bags

1 tablespoon sweetened condensed milk, or to taste

6 to 8 tablespoons (85 to 110g) unsalted butter, at room temperature

Four 1-inch-thick (2.5cm) slices sturdy white bakery bread (such as brioche or pain de mie)

About ½ cup (100g) sugar

1   In a small saucepan, warm the half-and-half over medium heat until small bubbles appear at the edges and it's almost at a simmer. Remove from the heat and stir in the chamomile. Cover and steep for 10 minutes, then strain through a fine-mesh sieve set over a bowl. Stir in the tablespoon of condensed milk, taste, then add more if you like. (Save the rest of the can for sweetening ice coffee.) Keep warm.

2   Generously butter one side of each slice of bread, all the way to the edges, using as much as 2 tablespoons per slice. Broil the buttered bread on both sides, starting buttered side up, until the edges are lightly browned—watch it closely.

3   Spread the sugar in a shallow dish and dip the buttered side of each piece of toast in the sugar, then sprinkle on a little more sugar to make sure it's evenly coated. Broil the toast again, sugared side up, just till the toast is well browned and crackly, again watching closely so that it doesn't burn. (Alternatively, use a kitchen torch to brûlée the sugared toast on a flameproof rack set over a baking sheet. Holding the torch nozzle 2 to 3 inches [5 to 7.5cm] above the toast, move it slowly across the surface of the bread slices. Carefully tip the pan as needed to coax melted sugar toward unmelted sugar. Avoid torching the edges— uncovered bread could ignite.)

4   To serve, spoon the warm milk into 4 shallow bowls, then place a piece of brûléed toast in each bowl. Serve immediately with spoons.

Mango Cream with Berries *(Crema de Mango con Moras)*

FROM ROBERTO SANTIBAÑEZ

Here we have more ingredient magic thanks to the chef, cookbook author, and genius who changed the way so many cooks think about guacamole, Roberto Santibañez: a custard without making a custard; a cream with no cream; a bright, rich dessert that comes from your pantry (and fruit bowl).

Instead of doing the more formal work of making a custard, you put fresh mango and lime juice into a blender with two kinds of canned milk and whir until it turns into a pudding. The acid of the fruit thickens the milks, with help from the abundant natural pectin in mango. (You might remember pectin as the gelling agent you can add to jams and jellies, but it also naturally occurs in a lot of fruit.) You can spoon this up with just berries, or layer it into a more elaborate trifle with Yogurt Whipped Cream (page 258) and whatever cookies and bits you have on hand, say Nibby Buckwheat Butter Cookies (page 49) or any of the several forms of Alex Raij's Sponge Cake (& Cookie) recipe (page 145).

SERVES 10 TO 12

1½ pounds (680g) ripe mangoes (about 2 large), peeled and pitted

1 (14-ounce/396g) can sweetened condensed milk

1 (12-ounce/354ml) can evaporated milk, shaken

3 tablespoons freshly squeezed lime juice, or more to taste

3 cups assorted fresh berries or berry compote

1 Combine the mangoes, milks, and lime juice in a blender and blend on high for 30 seconds. Taste and add more lime juice, if you like, and then continue blending to thicken the cream, about 2½ minutes more. It should resemble the texture of yogurt.

2 Transfer the mango cream to a large airtight container and refrigerate for at least 4 and up to 24 hours. It will continue to thicken as it chills.

3 Halve or quarter any large berries. Spoon the mango cream into serving bowls or glasses, layered with the berries or compote. Serve cold. Refrigerate any leftovers in an airtight container.

> "This recipe is for lazy cooks, as sometimes we all can be." —Roberto Santibañez

Ten-Minute Lime Cracker Pie

FROM J. KENJI LÓPEZ-ALT

This icebox cake has the spirit of a Key lime pie and can be layered up in 10 minutes (if you're not too precious about lining things neatly), then sent to the refrigerator to meld into a glorious tart-sweet-creamy-cakey pudding. But it has a salty secret: its structure comes from Ritz crackers.

A recipe this slapdash is a bit unusual coming from J. Kenji López-Alt, Serious Eats' Food Lab columnist-wizard who famously published a 21-ingredient meatloaf recipe, including gelatin, Marmite, anchovies, and soy sauce. But smart kitchen hacks are smart kitchen hacks. This one comes by way of his wife, Adriana, who learned it from her aunt Gloria in Colombia, though there they use Ducales, a local buttery cracker, instead.

This is not the first time we've seen Ritz tiptoe into a dessert—the original Mock Apple Pie, a Depression-era invention, was crackers masquerading as apple slices when the fruit was unavailable or too expensive. But it does serve as a good excuse for a PSA: (almost) anything can be an icebox cake. You can use any dry, crunchy cookie-like thing, store-bought or homemade. Excellent contenders include crispy chocolate chip cookies like Tate's, graham crackers, brown-sugary Biscoff cookies, the Pains d'Amande (page 53) and Thin & Crispy Black Sesame Oatmeal Cookies (page 50) in this book, and now (insert your favorite salty cracker here).

SERVES 8 TO 10

2 (14-ounce/396ml) cans sweetened condensed milk

2 cups (470g) heavy cream

1 tablespoon finely grated lime zest, plus more for serving

½ cup (120g) freshly squeezed lime juice (from about 8 limes)

10 ounces (285g) Ritz crackers (85 crackers, from about 3 sleeves)

1 Whisk together the condensed milk and heavy cream in a large bowl until combined. Add the lime zest and juice and whisk until thickened, about 1 minute.

2 Spread 1 cup (240ml) of the condensed milk mixture on the bottom of a deep-dish pie plate, an 11-inch (28cm) oval casserole, or a similar large shallow dish. Top with a single layer of Ritz crackers. Repeat, alternating layers of filling and crackers, until the dish is full, finishing with a layer of filling. Cover and refrigerate for at least 2 hours or overnight—the longer you wait, the more the crackers will soften and meld with the filling. Serve cold, zesting more fresh lime over the top, if you like.

Butterscotch Budino

FROM NANCY SILVERTON & DAHLIA NARVAEZ

Although this *budino* is technically just butterscotch pudding, it reaches deeper, scratching some itch that, until 2006, diners didn't even realize they had. After Los Angeles baking icon Nancy Silverton and her longtime pastry chef Dahlia Narvaez built it together for their opening menu at Pizzeria Mozza, it quickly became their signature dessert.

Their butterscotch takes what's typically a fairly one-note sweetness and drives it into dark, bitter caramel territory, with licks of butter and rum, making the pudding one of the most dynamic-tasting bites in one of the smoothest, most singular textures. It's topped with more caramel—this one sweeter—plus whipped cream with a bold top-heavy proportion of tart crème fraîche and crunches of sea salt. Though it's all served innocently enough in a clear glass, no one will see what's coming.

> "If the smoke alarm in your house doesn't go off while you're cooking the sugar, chances are you haven't cooked the caramel long enough." —Nancy Silverton

SERVES 10

BUDINO
3 cups (705g) heavy cream

1½ cups (370g) whole milk

1 cup plus 2 tablespoons (225g) lightly packed dark brown sugar

½ cup (120g) water

1½ teaspoons kosher salt

1 large egg plus 3 large egg yolks

5 tablespoons (40g) cornstarch

5 tablespoons (70g) unsalted butter, cut into a few pieces

1½ tablespoons dark rum

CARAMEL SAUCE
½ cup (120g) heavy cream

Seeds scraped from ⅛ vanilla bean

2 tablespoons unsalted butter

2 tablespoons corn syrup

½ cup (100g) sugar

WHIPPED CREAM
¼ cup (60g) heavy cream

¾ cup (170g) crème fraîche

Fleur de sel, for topping

1 To make the budino, in a large bowl or measuring cup, combine the cream and milk and set it near the stove. In a large heavy pot with a light-colored interior, combine the brown sugar, water, and salt and cook over medium-high heat, without stirring, until it's a smoking, dark caramel, 10 to 12 minutes. The sugar will get thicker, bubble more slowly, and then smell caramelized and nutty and turn a deep brown.

2 Immediately whisk the cream mixture into the caramel to stop the cooking (be careful—the mixture will steam, and the sugar will seize). Bring the caramel up to a boil and then turn the heat down to medium.

3 In a medium heatproof bowl set in a damp kitchen towel nest to keep it steady (see the Genius Tip on page 163), whisk together the egg, egg yolks, and cornstarch. While whisking constantly, pour about half of the caramel into the bowl, a cupful at a time, until incorporated. Pour the egg mixture back into the remaining caramel in the pot and cook, whisking constantly, until the custard is very thick and the cornstarch is fully cooked, about 2 minutes.

4 Remove from the heat and whisk in the butter and rum. Pour the custard through a fine-mesh strainer set over a large bowl to remove any lumps. Divide among 10 (6-ounce/175ml) clear glasses or ramekins, filling them no more than ½ inch (1.3cm) from the top. Cover with plastic wrap and refrigerate for several hours or up to 3 days.

5 To make the caramel sauce, pour the cream into a medium saucepan. Scrape the seeds from the vanilla bean over the cream and cook over medium heat until simmering, about 3 minutes. Add the butter and remove from the heat.

6 In a large heavy pot with a light-colored interior, stir together the corn syrup and sugar. Add just enough water to make a wet sandy texture, about ¼ cup (60g). Cook over medium-high heat, swirling the pan just slightly to watch

CONTINUED

Butterscotch Budino

the caramelization, but not stirring, until the sugar turns a medium amber color, about 10 minutes.

7 Remove from the heat and carefully whisk in the cream mixture (it will steam and bubble up, so stand back) until smooth. Set the pan in a large bowl of ice water to cool.

8 To make the whipped cream, whisk the cream in a chilled bowl until it starts to thicken. Add the crème fraîche and whip just until thick and fluffy.

9 Just before serving, warm the caramel sauce over medium heat. Spoon about 1 tablespoon on top of each budino (less than what we used in the photo on page 161—we went a little overboard), sprinkle with a big pinch of fleur de sel, and add a spoonful of whipped cream. Refrigerate any leftovers airtight.

GENIUS TIP: A TRICK FOR STEADYING YOUR MIXING BOWL

The best way to keep your mixing bowl grounded in delicate operations where you're whisking with one hand and pouring things in with the other—from tempering custards to emulsifying vinaigrettes—is to make your bowl a little nest, a trick I learned in culinary school at the Institute of Culinary Education.

Roll a damp kitchen towel into a long tube shape, then set it on the counter and curl the tube into a tight circle to form a nest that the bowl can set into snugly (see the photo at left). At school, we learned to form the tube quickly by grabbing opposite corners of the towel and twirling it wildly as if we were getting ready to whip someone with it, but I couldn't tell you if this was necessary or just fun.

GENIUS TIP: THE EASIEST WAY TO CLEAN A STICKY, SUGARY MESS

Next time you have a pot or tart pan that looks hopelessly globbed with caramel residue (in this recipe, there are potentially two), douse it in boiling water. For cooking vessels, it's especially easy: simply fill them with water, bring them to a boil, and then carefully pour the water down the drain. The stickiness will be freed, too. Repeat if needed. I bet more people would make caramel if they knew about this time- and agita-saver.

Apple Granita with Crème Fraîche Tapioca

FROM NICOLE KRASINSKI

This recipe starts with the funny act of putting whole apples in the freezer and ends with one of the most electric desserts you've ever had. In the middle, when you rip the thawed apples in half with your bare hands, you get to feel like a bodybuilder on Muscle Beach or a very strong raccoon.

In developing this technique, Nicole Krasinski, pastry chef and co-owner of State Bird Provisions in San Francisco, was inspired by her former co-pastry chef Mikiko Yui, who taught her about the Japanese trick for storing the fall apple harvest in the snow, which not only preserved them through winter but also made for extra-juicy apples.

Freezing swells the water inside the apple as it turns into ice and makes its structural cell walls burst, which means that once the ice melts, the apple is much softer and you can easily squeeze out the fresh juice without the aid of an expensive juicer. One of those handheld lemon squeezers (or simply your hands) will do the trick.

What you end up with is pure juice with a bit of body and a bright, spangly apple flavor that frames up nicely with a little maple, lemon, sparkling water, and salt stirred in before you freeze and scrape it into granita. Alone, this is as refreshing as desserts come, but served in a bowl with tart, creamy tapioca pudding and blackberries, it's downright euphoric— bouncy spheres and melting shards, icy pink juice and biting cream, cold and colder.

SERVES 4

GRANITA

2 pounds (900g) Gravenstein, Red Gala, or Honeycrisp apples

2 teaspoons freshly squeezed lemon juice

½ cup (120g) sparkling water

¼ cup (80g) maple syrup

¼ teaspoon kosher salt

TAPIOCA

1½ teaspoons sugar

1¾ cups (430g) whole milk

¼ cup (40g) small tapioca pearls

5 tablespoons (70g) crème fraîche

2 cups (300g) fresh blackberries

1 At least a day before you plan to serve the granita, clear a shelf in your freezer, arrange the apples on a large baking sheet in a single layer, and freeze uncovered until frozen solid, at least 8 hours.

2 The next day, defrost the apples on a rimmed baking sheet at room temperature until they're defrosted and very soft but still quite cold, about 3 hours. Do not rush the process by heating them or leave them out long after defrosting, or else the apples will start to turn brown. If you need to leave them to defrost longer, defrost in the refrigerator instead.

3 Pour the lemon juice into a nonreactive bowl. Set a fine-mesh sieve over the bowl. Using some combination of a handheld lemon squeezer and your hands, break the apples into halves or quarters, squeeze them (be prepared for squirting juice!) through the strainer, and then stir and press on the solids to help extract as much juice as possible— you should be able to get at least 2 cups (475ml) of juice if you keep squeezing and pressing. Whisk in the sparkling water, maple syrup, and salt until well combined. Taste and adjust the flavors—the juice should seem a bit too sweet and salty, since the flavors will mute once frozen.

4 Pour the mixture into a 9 by 13-inch (23 by 33cm) baking pan and freeze, uncovered, until the liquid has an icy border, about 1 hour. Take the pan out of the freezer

CONTINUED

and scrape with a fork to loosen the frozen edges and stir them evenly throughout the mixture.

5 Return the pan to the freezer, scraping and stirring every 30 minutes or so, until you have a semi-flaky, completely frozen granita, 1½ to 2 hours more. Remove the pan from the freezer and use a sturdy fork to thoroughly scrape the granita into flakes, starting with the surface and working your way to the bottom. Cover tightly with plastic wrap and freeze for up to 4 days.

6 To make the tapioca, whisk together the sugar and milk in a small pot. Bring to a simmer over medium heat, whisking occasionally to prevent burning and watching to make sure it doesn't boil over, which can happen quickly.

While whisking, slowly pour in the tapioca pearls (this will prevent them from sticking to the bottom of the pan and clumping together). Turn the heat to low and simmer until the tapioca is tender and clear, with a small white center, 12 to 16 minutes. Let the tapioca rest in the pot for 1 minute and then set the pot in an ice bath, stirring occasionally to prevent clumping—it will thicken as it cools. Once the tapioca is cool, stir in the crème fraîche with a rubber spatula. Store airtight in the refrigerator for up to 3 days.

7 To serve, place a large spoonful of cold tapioca in chilled bowls, add a heaping cup of granita, and top with a few blackberries. Serve immediately.

Tiramisu

FROM BROOKS HEADLEY

At Del Posto restaurant in Manhattan, pastry chef and former punk rock drummer Brooks Headley took pride in serving his legendary tiramisu "impossibly small"—as it was printed on the menu—in an eggcup, then refusing to give out second servings. Think espresso clouds suspended in soft, rum-twisted cream that can only be served from a spoon, never by the slice.

The one step that adds fuss is that the coffee-drenched layers are made not with the crunchy store-bought Italian ladyfinger cookies called *savoiardi*, but with an actual airy sponge cake you make yourself. But the cake comes together quickly and makes for far lighter tufts—and *savoiardi* were never that easy to find anyway.

Headley considers the raw egg yolks in this recipe an essential part of its flavor and silky texture—he uses this trick in all his gelatos, too. If you're concerned, seek out pasteurized eggs. It will still be good.

> "Although we pride ourselves on hospitality, giving our guests whatever they want, we refuse second servings. 'Can I have another?' *Nope. That's all you need.*"
> ——Brooks Headley

SERVES 8

SPONGE CAKE
9 large eggs, separated

2 cups (400g) sugar

¼ cup (60g) water

1 cup (125g) all-purpose flour (see page 5)

½ cup (65g) cornstarch

A pinch of salt

TIRAMISU CREAM
2 cups (450g) mascarpone

½ cup (100g) sugar

4 large egg yolks

2 tablespoons heavy cream

2 tablespoons dark rum

A pinch of salt

¾ cup (180g) freshly brewed espresso or very strong coffee, cooled

A few tablespoons best-quality natural unsweetened cocoa powder

1   To make the sponge cake, heat the oven to 375°F (190°C), with racks in the upper and lower thirds. Line two large rimmed baking sheets with parchment paper or silicone baking mats.

2   Put the egg whites in the bowl of a stand mixer fitted with the whisk attachment. With the mixer on low speed, slowly add 1 cup (200g) of the sugar, gradually increasing the speed to medium to create a stable, fluffy meringue that holds stiff peaks. Scrape the meringue into a separate bowl to refrigerate briefly, but don't wash the mixer bowl.

3   In the still-messy mixer bowl, combine the egg yolks, water, and the remaining 1 cup (200g) sugar and whip on high speed until you have a ribbony mixture, about 6 minutes.

4   In a wide shallow bowl, combine the egg yolk mixture and the egg white mixture and use a rubber spatula to fold together very gently, leaving some streaks of egg white visible.

5   Sift together the flour, cornstarch, and salt into a bowl and gently fold them into the eggs until no streaks of flour remain. Using the spatula, very gently place half of the batter on each baking sheet and smooth it into a relatively

CONTINUED

Tiramisu

CONTINUED

even layer that's about 1 inch (2.5cm) thick (it might not go to the edges). You can roughly form it into the shape of your serving dish, which should be about 12 by 9 inches (30 by 23cm), but don't worry about making it perfect.

6 Bake until the tops of the cakes are golden brown and still soft to the touch, 7 to 14 minutes, rotating the baking sheets from front to back and top to bottom halfway through baking. Let the cakes cool on the baking sheets.

7 To make the tiramisu cream, in the bowl of a stand mixer fitted with the whisk attachment, beat the mascarpone, sugar, egg yolks, cream, rum, and salt on low speed, gradually increasing to medium-high speed as it starts to thicken, until you have a very fluffy cream that just barely holds soft peaks, as in the photo at left. Don't go beyond

this point or it may curdle and separate.

8 To assemble the tiramisu, find a shallow rimmed serving dish about 12 by 9 inches (30 by 23cm) and trim cake layers to fit. Remove the parchment from the cakes. Spread about one-third of the tiramisu cream evenly in the bottom of the serving dish and cover with one cake layer. Pour half of the cooled espresso all over the cake to soak it completely. Spread one-half of the remaining tiramisu cream on top of the soaked cake layer, followed by the second layer of cake and the remaining espresso. Top it all with the remaining cream, spreading it to the edges. Sift the cocoa onto the finished tiramisu—it should be fully blanketed. Serve immediately with a large spoon, or refrigerate for up to 8 hours.

One-Step, No-Churn Coffee Ice Cream

FROM NIGELLA LAWSON

Not having an ice cream maker has never *really* stopped anyone from making ice cream. Common hacks include vigorously shaking (or kicking) coffee cans full of cream or returning obsessively to the freezer to stir. But instead of doing any of this, you can glide over to your cupboard like you're Nigella Lawson, find four ingredients, whip them into a featherbed, then freeze—they will become ice cream while you go on with your day.

It's really as simple as that—there's no egg to deal with, nothing to heat or temper or strain, because the ingredients do the work. Booze keeps the mixture from getting hard and icy; whipped cream provides air (and, yes, cream); condensed milk helps do the thickening work of a custard.

The ice cream has a creamy, almost buttery smoothness, and its ease and versatility come in handy especially when layering into more complicated desserts like ice cream cakes, mud pies, and Baked Alaskas. Use this technique and basic proportion with any flavors you like, but it's important to include a little bitterness or sharpness to keep it from skewing too sweet. (This is why Lawson also has versions spiked with bourbon, salty caramel, margarita fixings, and pomegranate and lime juice—follow her lead!)

MAKES ABOUT 3 CUPS (710ML)

1¼ cups (295g) heavy cream, very cold

⅔ cup (175g) sweetened condensed milk

2 tablespoons instant espresso powder

2 tablespoons espresso liqueur

1 In the bowl of a stand mixer fitted with the whisk attachment, whip all the ingredients together on medium speed just until the mixture is airy and the whisk leaves trails of soft peaks on the surface. Scrape into two airtight 1-pint (475ml) containers and freeze for at least 6 hours or overnight before serving.

> "My absolute favorite way of eating this is by squidging it into little brioches, like sweet burger buns, as they do in the south of Italy."
> —Nigella Lawson

Chocolate Sorbet

FROM DAVID LEBOVITZ

In this sorbet from ice cream whisperer David Lebovitz, the chocolate flavor is deep and true—like a square of good dark chocolate, lifted to ice cream form. But despite having no dairy or eggs (that's right, vegans), it's impossibly creamy, thanks to the wonders of emulsification and a high proportion of bittersweet chocolate, rich with cocoa butter. It also remains perfectly scoopable without turning hard or icy after several days in the freezer.

Even with standard-issue Dutch-processed cocoa and supermarket brand bittersweet chocolate, this sorbet is miraculous—and you can only go up from there.

MAKES ABOUT 1 QUART (1L)

2¼ cups (530g) water

1 cup (200g) sugar

¾ cup (75g) Dutch-processed cocoa powder (see page 5)

Big pinch of salt

6 ounces (170g) bittersweet chocolate, finely chopped

½ teaspoon pure vanilla extract

1 Whisk together 1½ cups (355g) of the water, the sugar, cocoa powder, and salt in a large saucepan. Bring to a boil over high heat, whisking frequently, then let it continue to boil, whisking continuously for 45 seconds.

2 Remove the pan from the heat and stir in the chocolate until it's melted; then stir in the vanilla extract and the remaining ¾ cup (175g) water. Pour the mixture into a blender, cover, and open the hole in the top of the blender and cover with a kitchen towel to let steam escape without splashing. Blend on high for 15 seconds.

3 Refrigerate the mixture for at least an hour before churning. If the mixture has become too thick to pour into your ice cream maker, whisk it well to thin it out. Churn in your ice cream maker until the sorbet thickens to a soft serve–like consistency. Transfer to an airtight container and freeze several hours until firm before serving.

Sweet Pistachios in Olive Oil
From Suzanne Goin

This sauce perks up desserts as much with its aroma—fruity olive oil, dizzy whiffs of orange—as its texture and splashy color. In *The A.O.C Cookbook,* Suzanne Goin spoons the sweet pistachios over slices of chocolate mascarpone tart and plum cake. I like spooning it over ice cream—just be sure to eat it quickly, before the olive oil starts to firm up like Magic Shell.

How to make it: Heat the oven to 350°F (175°C), with a rack in the center. Spread **¾ cup (90g) shelled pistachios** on a rimmed baking sheet and warm in the oven for 3 to 5 minutes—don't let them brown, to keep the sauce vibrant green. Cool, then coarsely chop the pistachios. Whisk together **½ cup (110g) best–quality extra-virgin olive oil, 1½ teaspoons sugar, ½ teaspoon freshly squeezed lemon juice, ½ teaspoon finely grated orange zest**, and **¼ teaspoon kosher salt** in a bowl until the sugar and salt dissolve. Stir in the pistachios, leaving behind any loose papery skins. Store leftovers in the refrigerator for up to 1 week, bringing the sauce to room temperature before serving. Makes 1 cup (240ml).

Best (& Easiest) Frozen Yogurt

FROM MAX FALKOWITZ & ETHAN FRISCH

It took Pinkberry's world takeover in 2005 to help us realize how much we love—really, really love—frozen yogurt that actually tastes like yogurt.

That bright, undeniably yogurty flavor should have been our first clue to how easy frozen yogurt would be to make at home. As it turns out, making tart, sweet, creamy, soul-rebirthing-on-a-hot-day frozen yogurt is literally as simple as sticking yogurt in an ice cream maker along with a little salt and sugar.

This formula was developed and stress-tested by Max Falkowitz, then food editor at Serious Eats, and Ethan Frisch, founder of Guerrilla Ice Cream. "Frozen yogurt, despite the dairy, behaves basically like sorbet," Falkowitz wrote to me. "You want about four parts liquid to one part sugar by volume for something scoopable." This means that even if you pack it up in the freezer, it will stay creamy and yielding, or you can eat it like soft serve (like Pinkberry) straightaway.

A few tips: don't substitute nonfat yogurt (or it will be unpleasantly icy). Yes, you can use Greek yogurt, but you might want to cut it with a little liquid to keep it from being too creamy, like a bizarre and delicious version Falkowitz makes with dry white wine. Yes, you can play around with different sweeteners and mix-ins and infusions (see the Genius Tip on page 180). If you don't have an ice cream maker, pack it into a shallow, covered dish, pop it into the freezer, and stir occasionally as it freezes.

MAKES 1 QUART (1L)

1 (32-ounce/907g) container full-fat plain yogurt (see note above about substituting Greek yogurt)

1 cup (200g) sugar

¼ teaspoon kosher salt

1 Whisk together the yogurt, sugar, and salt in a medium bowl until the sugar has completely dissolved. Chill in an ice bath or refrigerate until the yogurt registers 45°F (7°C) on an instant-read thermometer (it should be thoroughly chilled—this is roughly refrigerator temperature).

2 Churn in your ice cream maker until the yogurt thickens to a soft serve–like consistency. Scoop and eat like soft serve or, for a more scoopable texture, transfer the frozen yogurt to an airtight container and freeze for at least 4 hours before serving.

XL Granola Crumbles
From Alanna Taylor-Tobin

Former pastry chef and blogger Alanna Taylor-Tobin taught me this trick for making the best granola crumbles, quickly, without adding egg whites, flours, or starches. By baking granola pressed between two baking sheets and never stirring, you allow the sticky, slow-toasting oats to fuse into one big sheet you can break up into whatever size clumps you like. The extra insulation and diffused heat from the top baking sheet protects the granola from burning. Try this trick with any of your favorite granola recipes; this one tastes especially good on tart frozen yogurt (see right) or lemon ice cream (page 179).

How to make it: Heat the oven to 325°F (165°C), with a rack in the center. In a bowl, stir together **2½ cups (225g) old-fashioned rolled oats, ½ cup (70g) raw almonds, ½ cup (65g) raw cashews, ⅓ cup (65g) lightly packed light brown (or unrefined granulated) sugar, the finely grated zest of a small orange, ½ teaspoon ground cinnamon, ½ teaspoon freshly grated nutmeg, 6 tablespoons (85g) melted unsalted butter, ¼ cup (80g) maple syrup,** and **1 teaspoon kosher salt.** Spread mixture into a thin layer, with the edges slightly thicker than the center, on a parchment paper–lined baking sheet. Cover the granola with another sheet of parchment paper and then top with a second baking sheet, right side up, making a granola sandwich. Bake until the granola is a rich golden brown, 30 to 40 minutes, rotating the baking sheet front to back and peeking under the parchment once or twice to make sure the edges aren't burning. When it's done, the granola will still be soft, but it will crisp up as it cools. Let the granola cool on the baking sheet, then break up and store airtight. Makes 3 to 4 cups (about 500g).

No-Churn Fresh Lemon Ice Cream

FROM DORI SANDERS

When it's too hot to make a custard or do much at all, it's nice to know that you can still have sweet-tart, bracing lemon ice cream all the same. This recipe—from Dori Sanders, a peach farmer, novelist, and cookbook author—only asks you to juice, zest, and stir. If you want to chat with her about it, most summer days she's selling peaches at her family's farmstand in Filbert, South Carolina.

While Nigella Lawson's no-churn ice cream on page 172 relies on cream whipped with sweetened condensed milk for its lush, scoopable texture, here it's the acid in lemon juice that magically thickens the cream without whipping or churning. Sugar both balances out the pucker of the lemon and keeps the ice cream from freezing too hard. In Sanders's cookbook and memoir *Dori Sanders' Country Cooking*, she serves the ice cream at a family reunion next to her cousin's celery cake and a warm apple bread pudding. The message is it plays well with others, if you need a strategic dessert for a potluck. And it plays *really* well with Estela's Candied Sesame Seeds on page 195, as pictured here. But it's pretty remarkable on its own, too.

MAKES 3 CUPS (710ML)

1 tablespoon finely grated lemon zest

¼ cup (60g) freshly squeezed lemon juice (from 2 lemons)

1 cup (200g) sugar

⅛ teaspoon fine sea salt

1 cup (235g) heavy cream

1 cup (245g) milk

1 Whisk together the lemon zest and juice, the sugar, and salt in a large bowl.

2 Whisk together the cream and milk in a measuring cup and gradually pour into the lemon and sugar mixture, whisking constantly. Continue to whisk until the sugar dissolves—you won't hear or feel it scraping against the bottom of the bowl anymore, about 2 minutes.

3 Pour the mixture into an 8-inch (20cm) square metal baking pan. Cover tightly with aluminum foil and freeze until the mixture is solid around the edges and mushy in the middle, 2 to 3 hours. Stir well, cover again with foil, and continue to freeze until completely firm, about an hour more. Once firm, scoop into chilled bowls to serve.

Coconut "Ice Cream" with Lime & Mango

FROM JULIA TURSHEN

This sunny dessert happens to be one of the friendliest in this book for a mixed-diet crowd. There's no gluten, eggs, or dairy, and if someone's allergic to coconut, well, at least they can eat the mango. And it gives you yet another clever way to churn ice cream at home without an ice cream maker: by freezing it into ice cubes, then pummeling them into soft serve in a food processor.

Like those smart people who freeze pesto or tomato paste in ice cube trays, then pop them into neatly labeled freezer bags so they're ready for *anything*, you can make these ice cream starter pods up to a week ahead.

MAKES 1 PINT (475ML)

1 (13½-ounce/400ml) can full-fat coconut milk, shaken

¼ cup (80g) maple syrup

1½ tablespoons finely grated lime zest

3 tablespoons freshly squeezed lime juice (from 2 limes), or to taste

Pinch of kosher salt

½ cup (40g) large unsweetened coconut flakes (optional)

1 ripe mango, peeled, pitted, and diced

1 Whisk together the coconut milk, maple syrup, lime zest and juice, and salt in a medium bowl. If the mixture doesn't smooth out by whisking, use a blender or immersion blender to force it into submission. Pour the mixture into a pitcher or measuring cup with a pouring spout and divide it evenly among the wells of two standard ice cube trays. Don't worry about filling the wells of the trays completely—the ice cream will be easier to blend if the cubes are smaller.

2 Freeze the cubes until solid, at least 4 hours. Once frozen, pop them into a resealable bag and store in the freezer. Don't leave them exposed in the open trays, which dulls the flavor over time and may infuse the ice cream with other, unpleasant odors from your freezer. The frozen cubes will keep in the freezer for up to 1 week.

3 When you're ready to serve the ice cream, toast the coconut flakes in a skillet over medium heat until they're golden brown at the edges, shaking frequently to keep them from burning, 5 to 8 minutes. Cool the coconut flakes in the skillet on a rack; they will continue to crisp up.

4 In a food processor, pulse the frozen cubes until coarsely chopped, then process until the mixture is smooth and looks like soft serve, stopping to scrape down the sides of the bowl a few times. If the mixture isn't getting smooth within a couple of minutes, let it stand for a few minutes to defrost slightly, then process again.

5 Scoop the ice cream into bowls and top with the toasted coconut flakes and mango. Serve immediately. (Store leftover ice cream airtight in the freezer for up to 1 week. Let sit at room temperature for about 10 minutes and then process again in the food processor, following the instructions in step 4, before serving.)

GENIUS TIP: ADDING FRUIT (THAT TASTES LIKE FRUIT) TO FROZEN TREATS

According to Fany Gerson, author of *Paletas* and *Mexican Ice Cream*, the key to mixing fresh fruit into ice creams and paletas and having it actually taste like fruit (and not chunks of flavorless ice), is to make sure the fruit is cooked or macerated in sugar first. She macerates strawberries, raspberries, and mango, letting the raw fruit sit in sugar for 30 minutes or so. But she lightly cooks stone fruit, pineapple, and blueberries until the fruits are swimming in syrup.

DUELING CHOCOLATE SAUCES

Both of these chocolate sauces can be pulled together at the last second and also happen to be dairy-free—but they give you completely different results. Choose one based on mood and what's on hand, or make them both for a mini tasting panel if you want to become very popular.

Hot Fudge
From Jeni Britton Bauer

Most hot fudge recipes call for cream or butter, but dairy fat tends to mute complex flavors. For a more pronounced chocolaty zing, skip the dairy entirely and use straight water instead (yes, that's right), just like Jeni's Splendid Ice Creams shops across the country do. Don't worry; it will still taste like the hot fudge sundaes you grew up with—just a little bit better.

How to make it: Mix ¼ cup (60g) water, ¼ cup (20g) **Dutch-processed cocoa powder** (see page 5), and **¼ cup (50g) sugar** in a small saucepan and bring to a boil, stirring. (You can also do this in the microwave.) Remove from the heat and add **¼ cup (35g) finely chopped dark chocolate (70% cacao)**. Let sit for 2 minutes, then stir. Spoon over ice cream. Makes ¾ cup (175ml).

Olive Oil Chocolate Sauce
From Brooks Headley

Brooks Headley developed this chocolate sauce to complete a plated dessert of grilled eggplant and ricotta stracciatella gelato. Strangely, in this complicated layered dessert, Headley specifically recommended avoiding pouring the sauce directly on the gelato, lest the sauce solidify. Any fan of Magic Shell will ignore his advice.

How to make it: In a microwave-safe bowl, microwave **1 cup (160g) chopped best-quality bittersweet chocolate** in 15-second bursts, stirring between bursts, until completely smooth. Be careful not to scorch it. (If you don't have a microwave, use a double boiler.) Stir in **¼ cup (55g) extra-virgin olive oil and sea salt to taste** (a healthy amount—more than you think you need). It should taste like all three ingredients. Makes 1¼ cups (300ml).

hot fudge

olive oil chocolate sauce

Tahini Semifreddo

FROM MICHAEL SOLOMONOV

One more smart path to churn-free frozen desserts is to make semifreddo, the Italian mousse–like concoction that freezes up soft and spoonable. Better yet, this tahini version, from Michael Solomonov, chef-owner of Zahav in Philadelphia, has extra insurance against icy stiffness.

Because tahini is made from ground toasted sesame seeds, it's rich in sesame oil, which turns out to be a good buffer against ice crystals, as well as a happy carrier for the smoky, nutty flavors that we love in tahini dishes both savory and sweet—it's like peanut butter, but with a huskier voice.

Solomonov serves this with bright fruits like strawberries and rhubarb in spring or passion fruit and lime in winter; with banana and streaks of chocolate; or with crumbled cookies on top (the Thin & Crispy Black Sesame Oatmeal Cookies on page 50, for example). If you don't want to wait for it to freeze, this also makes a stupefyingly good tahini mousse.

> "This requires a bit of a delicate touch, so sip a little chamomile tea and practice some deep breathing before you start."
> —Michael Solomonov

SERVES 8

2 cups (470g) heavy cream, very cold	1 cup (200g) sugar
7 large egg yolks	½ cup (125g) well-stirred tahini

1 In the bowl of a stand mixer fitted with the whisk attachment, or using a handheld mixer in a large bowl, whip the cream until it holds soft peaks. Refrigerate the whipped cream briefly as you proceed with the next step.

2 Whisk together the egg yolks and sugar in a small heatproof bowl set over but not touching gently simmering water in a saucepan. Whisk the eggs and sugar constantly until the sugar is dissolved and the yolks have lightened in color, about 2 minutes. Remove the bowl from the heat.

3 Scrape about one-third of the whipped cream into a large bowl with a rubber spatula and pour in the yolk mixture. Stir together until well combined. Scrape in half of the remaining whipped cream and fold it in gently with the spatula until just incorporated. (To brush up on your folding technique, see the Genius Tip on page 106.) Repeat with the last of the whipped cream.

4 In a separate large bowl, stir together ½ cup (120ml) of the whipped cream–egg yolk mixture with the tahini until well combined. You want the texture of each ingredient to be as similar as possible before folding them together, so be sure the tahini is well stirred.

5 Carefully fold in the rest of the whipped cream–egg yolk mixture with a rubber spatula until no streaks remain. Divide the mousse among eight 4- to 6-ounce (120 to 175ml) bowls or ramekins, cover with plastic wrap, and freeze until firm, about 4 hours or up to 3 days.

Sweet Tahini Fondue
From Engin Akin

This five-ingredient pantry dessert is yet another reason to keep a jar of tahini around always. "This dessert is an all-timer all around Turkey," *Essential Turkish Cuisine* author Engin Akin told me. "Families keep tahini in their pantry, and since sugar is always available, they make this sweet preparation after meals when they do not have another dessert." (This is served room temperature—only the style is like fondue!)

How to make it: Whisk together **1 cup (250g) well-stirred tahini, 8 to 10 tablespoons (100 to 125g) lightly packed light or dark brown sugar,** and **1 teaspoon ground cinnamon** until well combined. Serve a bowl of sweet tahini fondue with fondue (or regular) forks, alongside **cubes of bread, toasted or fresh,** and **½ cup (60g) coarsely chopped shelled pistachios.** Using the forks, guests dunk the bread first in the sweet tahini fondue, then dip into the pistachio pieces. Serves 8.

Cardamom & Rose Water Kulfi

FROM MEERA SODHA

Traditional kulfi is a dense, almost chewy, frozen treat that dates back to the 16th century in India. It takes hours of vigilant simmering and stirring to reduce milk down to a quarter of its volume. As you probably suspect, this recipe is not traditional kulfi.

This breezier version from Meera Sodha, author of *Made in India* and other cookbooks, combines the modern convenience of tinned evaporated milk with the fresh richness of cream. It requires nothing more than heating them to a boil, then cooling all the way down—either in traditional conical kulfi molds, or in ice pop molds or small paper cups. As the mix cools, the cardamom and rose water latch on and waft through with a spicy floral lightness, calming and sweet. Make it just like this for well-honed balance, or use the same basic recipe to infuse saffron, pistachios, vanilla beans, or other delicate flavors that shine best on a pure palate.

SERVES 6 TO 8

12 cardamom pods	2 tablespoons rose water
1 (12-ounce/354ml) can evaporated milk	Fresh fruit, for serving (optional)
1¼ cups (295g) heavy cream	Dried rose petals or chopped pistachios, for topping (optional, see Genius Tip, right)
½ cup (100g) sugar	

1 Crush the cardamom pods lightly to free the seeds inside; then discard the outer green pods. Using a spice grinder or a mortar and pestle, grind the seeds as finely as you can.

2 Combine the evaporated milk, cream, sugar, rose water, and ground cardamom in a saucepan. Bring the mixture to a gentle boil over medium-low heat, stirring often to keep it from sticking to the bottom of the pan.

3 When it starts to boil, remove from the heat and set the pot in a larger bowl of ice water to cool it down, stirring the mixture occasionally. When the mixture is cold, pour it through a fine-mesh strainer set over a large measuring cup or other container with a spout. Pour the strained mixture into kulfi molds, ice pop molds, or another freezable container. Cover tightly and freeze until firm, at least 3 hours.

4 To remove the kulfis from their molds, dip them into hot water for a second, turn them upside down over a plate and give them a sharp tap on the top.

5 Serve with fresh fruit or by themselves. Store any leftovers airtight in the freezer.

GENIUS TIP: PRETTIER POPS

For extra-fetching pops (and to give a sneak preview on the flavor), *The Fearless Baker* author Erin Jeanne McDowell sprinkles ingredients like dried rose petals or chopped pistachios on the exposed surface of her ice pops (or kulfi, as the case may be) once the base is firm enough that the topping won't sink in, usually after about 1 hour of freezing.

Grasshopper Shake

FROM JEFFREY MORGENTHALER

Not many of us have ordered a Grasshopper in the past 40 years, and it's easy to see why: traditionally, the drink is equal parts cheap crème de menthe, crème de cacao, and heavy cream—shaken and served in a martini glass—and is precisely the color of milky Astroturf.

But when classic cocktail savant Jeffrey Morgenthaler puts a Grasshopper on his menu, you pay attention. His version of the drink is based on the Midwestern style, which blends the unholy trinity with vanilla ice cream. But Morgenthaler takes what would in most other contexts be a painfully sweet and unsightly drink and makes it good. Really, first-sip-makes-you-laugh-it's-so-good, good.

To tame the inherent richness and sweetness of a cocktail made with sugary liqueurs and ice cream, he brings in a teaspoon of Fernet Branca, a bitter herbal digestif so powerful that bartenders and other industry folk have long seen it as a rite of passage. Then he mutes the Fernet with a little sea salt. The balance of crushed ice is important too, to keep the shake thick and frothy, but not heavy. The original Grasshopper was a struggle to get three sips deep; this one will be gone before you know it.

MAKES 1 TALL GLASS (OR 3 TINY ONES)

1½ ounces (45g) green crème de menthe

1½ ounces (45g) white crème de cacao

1 ounce (30g) half-and-half (or half milk and half heavy cream)

1 teaspoon Fernet-Branca

Big pinch of sea salt

½ cup (105g) vanilla ice cream

1 cup (140g) crushed ice, prepared by bashing in a tea towel with a rolling pin, or in a food processor

Mint sprig, for garnish

1 Stick a tall glass in the freezer. Add all ingredients except for the mint sprig to a blender. Blend on high speed until smooth and frothy. Serve immediately in the frozen glass, garnished with the mint sprig.

"Wanting to step away from the brown, bitter, and stirred drinks so prevalent on today's cocktail menus, my team and I started looking into drinks that you might consider—wait for it—fun."
—Jeffrey Morgenthaler

Meringue Gelato Cake with Chocolate Sauce

FROM NIGELLA LAWSON

Much of the wonder of this dessert may lie in its semihomemade ease—you're doing little more than bashing up store-bought meringues and folding them into whipped cream. But this gelato cake comes from quite literary roots, reminding us that we should be open to finding cooking inspiration in all sorts of places: dusty books at estate sales, our elders' recipe boxes, or the yellowed clippings that flutter out of an old birthday card. In this case, it did help that Nigella Lawson could read Italian.

Lawson is a self-proclaimed lover of languages (you can sense this as you read her lyrical recipe writing and occasional invented words). She found the basic notion of this recipe in an Italian book from 1986 by chef and culinary philosopher Gioacchino Scognamiglio. It called for an obscure liqueur, which she tracked down and studied; her version is modified for boozes we can more easily find. The frozen cake is downy, like a more weightless icebox cake, with gentle crackles of meringue and chocolate that melt away quickly on your tongue.

> "This is a no-churn affair. You mix everything together, wodge it into a loaf tin, freeze, and you're done." —Nigella Lawson

SERVES 6 TO 8

GELATO CAKE
1¼ cups (295g) heavy cream

1 ounce (30g) bittersweet chocolate (62% cacao or higher)

1 tablespoon coffee liqueur or rum, or better yet, a mix of the two

4 ounces (110g) crumbled store-bought or homemade meringue cookies (about 2 cups)

CHOCOLATE SAUCE
1 cup (235g) heavy cream

5 ounces (125g) dark chocolate (62% cacao or higher), finely chopped (about ⅔ cup)

2 tablespoons coffee liqueur or rum, or better yet, a mix of the two

1 To make the gelato cake, line a 9 by 5-inch (23 by 13cm) loaf pan with plastic wrap, leaving a 3-inch (7.5cm) overhang on the long sides so the plastic can cover the cake when freezing.

2 In the bowl of a stand mixer fitted with the whisk attachment, or using a handheld mixer in a large bowl, whip the cream until thick but still soft. Very finely chop the chocolate into splinters and fold them into the cream, followed by the liqueur and crumbled meringues.

3 Scrape the mixture into the loaf pan, packing it down as you go, and smooth the top. Pull the plastic wrap up and over to seal the top, then wrap more plastic wrap around the whole pan. Freeze until solid, at least 8 hours or overnight.

4 To make the chocolate sauce, pour the cream into a saucepan and add the chocolate. Gently heat over medium-low heat, whisking frequently, until the chocolate is almost all melted. Remove from the heat. (If the mixture gets too hot, the chocolate will seize, but it will continue melting nicely in the warm cream even off the heat.)

5 Add the liqueur, still off the heat, and whisk again until smooth. Pour the sauce into a pitcher, whisking occasionally, until it cools to just warm.

6 To serve, unwrap the outer layer of plastic wrap, then uncover the top, lift up the overhanging ends of the plastic, and flip the frozen cake onto a cutting board or platter, peeling away and discarding the rest of the plastic. Pour some of the chocolate sauce over the top and cut into thick slabs. Serve immediately with the rest of the chocolate sauce on the side. Rewrap up any leftovers to freeze airtight.

Frozen Lemon Cream Sandwiches

FROM GRACE PARISI

This ice cream sandwich recipe is more about clever grocery shopping than it is about baking, yet you'll still get a better and fresher dessert than you could buy—and prettier, too. The technique comes from Grace Parisi, a recipe developer and food editor who's written more than 1,400 recipes for *Food & Wine* alone and who knows a legitimate shortcut when she sees one.

Here, the recommended store-bought components all have lists of ingredients your grandmother would recognize, with no funny stuff: jarred lemon curd, crème fraîche, and thin, crunchy Belgian butter cookies that stay crisp even after a week in the freezer. If you can't find any one of the ingredients, riff on the idea that an ice cream sandwich doesn't really need ice cream in other ways—swap in other thin, crunchy cookies like the Thin & Crispy Black Sesame Oatmeal ones on page 50, or use the lemon cream on page 241 for a fully homemade version of the filling.

SERVES 6

¾ cup plus 2 tablespoons (200g) crème fraîche, very cold

¼ cup (80g) lemon curd (preferably Wilkin & Sons Tiptree brand)

Finely grated zest of 1 lemon (about 1 tablespoon)

12 crisp butter waffle cookies (preferably Jules Destrooper Butter Crisps)

¼ cup (30g) finely chopped unsalted pistachios

1 Line a small baking sheet with waxed paper. Using a handheld mixer in a chilled bowl, beat the crème fraîche, lemon curd, and lemon zest until it looks billowy and a spoonful is firm enough to mound onto a cookie without running off, about 2 minutes.

2 Lay half of the cookies on the baking sheet flat side up and spoon the lemon cream onto the centers, smoothing it almost to the edges. Top with the remaining cookies, pressing down very gently. Cover the baking sheet with plastic wrap, taking care not to squish the sandwiches, and freeze until firm, at least 4 hours.

3 Before serving, spread the pistachios on a plate and roll the edges of the sandwiches in them. Serve at once. The lemon cream sandwiches can be frozen in an airtight container for up to 1 week.

> "What I love about the development process is the elegance of efficiency—there is no wasted movement, no wasted ingredient, no wasted effort." —Grace Parisi

instant aged balsamic

double-chocolate cookie crumbles

MORE SAUCY & CRUNCHY TOPPERS

Instant Aged Balsamic
From America's Test Kitchen

Traditional aged balsamic vinegar is one of the most electrifying substances you can put on your food—the good stuff also takes decades to barrel-age and can cost hundreds of dollars for a tiny, precious bottle. But the MacGyvers at America's Test Kitchen came up with a smart way to hack the system. They don't just (gently) reduce supermarket balsamic; they also add a wingman ingredient or two—a bit of sugar and fruity port are all it takes to temper and round out the flavors.

How to make it: Stir together **⅓ cup (85g) balsamic vinegar, 1 tablespoon sugar,** and **1 tablespoon port** in a shallow, nonreactive pan and gently cook over very, very low heat—it should be barely simmering—until reduced to half of its original volume, about 5 minutes. Let cool to room temperature and drizzle over vanilla ice cream or panna cotta, ripe pears or strawberries, cheeses (especially, but not only, Parmesan), or anywhere else your food could use a hit of bright, sweet tang. Makes about ¼ cup (60ml).

Candied Sesame Seeds

From Estela

This is one of the more rewarding ways to spend 10 minutes. As you stir sesame seeds in a sticky syrup, suddenly the water disappears and a dry crystalline layer of sugar pops to the surface. At Estela, chef Ignacio Mattos's curve-shattering restaurant in New York City, they roll scoops of caramelized white chocolate in the candied seeds, but the seeds are also just as good sprinkled over ice cream or paletas, or topping a brownie or a slice of cheesecake—anywhere you want a little crunchy sesame-flavored twinkle.

How to make it: Line a baking sheet with parchment paper and set it by the stove. Heat **½ cup (100g) sugar** and **½ cup (120g) water** in a wide saucepan over high heat until the syrup just begins to bubble. Add **1 cup (150g) white sesame seeds** and stir constantly until the water evaporates and the surface of the seeds turns dry and powdery and just barely golden, 5 to 10 minutes—don't let them brown more. Pour the candied seeds onto the baking sheet, spreading them evenly, and let cool completely. Break up any big clumps and store airtight. Makes about 1 pint (250g).

Double-Chocolate Cookie Crumbles

From Nicole Krasinski

In this cookie that never becomes a cookie, Nicole Krasinski of State Bird Provisions in San Francisco adds frozen chocolate bits to a dough and barely bakes it, so the chocolate melts just enough to help hold the crumbles together. She says to serve them over ice cream, but they would also make a jazzy streusel-like layer to top fancier frozen desserts and layer cakes.

How to make it: In a food processor, pulse **8 ounces (225g) coarsely chopped dark chocolate (72% cacao)** until pea-sized. Freeze on a plate for 30 minutes. Heat the oven to 325°F (165°C). Sift together **1¾ cups (220g) all-purpose flour** (see page 5), **⅓ cup (40g) oat flour** (see page 5), **¼ cup plus 2 tablespoons (30g) unsweetened cocoa powder** (see page 5), **2 teaspoons baking soda**, and **1¼ teaspoons kosher salt** onto a sheet of waxed paper. Press any lumps through the sifter, then add any salt that's caught in the sifter. With a handheld mixer in a large bowl, beat **1 cup (225g) room-temperature unsalted butter**, **1 cup (200g) turbinado sugar**, and **⅓ cup plus 1 tablespoon (80g) sugar** on medium speed until very light and fluffy, about 5 minutes. Stir in the flour mixture until just combined, followed by the frozen chocolate. Drop crumbly clumps of the dough, no bigger than an almond, in a single layer onto two parchment paper–lined rimmed baking sheets (loose bits are okay). Bake until the top is dry but the crumble is still soft, about 10 minutes. Let cool completely. Store airtight at cool room temperature. (Also delicious straight from the freezer.) Makes 9 cups (1kg).

candied sesame seeds

Pies & Tarts

Atlantic Beach Pie

FROM BILL SMITH

If lemon meringue is the poodle of pies, this is the scraggly mutt you didn't plan on falling for. It might look rough around the edges, but that's half the charm.

Bill Smith, the longtime chef at Crook's Corner in Chapel Hill, North Carolina, developed the recipe based on the cracker-crusted lemon pies he grew up eating at seafood restaurants along the North Carolina coast, switching out the traditional meringue top for whipped cream and salt.

The crust is saltine crackers you can mash with your hands; its tart custard belly is only three ingredients. Just before serving it in cold slices, you blob on some unsweetened whipped cream and scatter it with sea salt.

This isn't just a lazy path to pie; it's a good one. The pale comfort of saltines turns into a toasted shell that holds together better than you'd think, once you crunch it all up with butter and sugar and parbake it. Unlike graham crackers, which seem designed to crumble into a fine-grained crust, saltines stay true to themselves, flaky and crisp.

Each bite of pie has the sweet rush of a lemon bar, cooled with thick cream and flanked by salt and crunch. Every flavor and texture is dialed up to eleven, which somehow keeps them all in check. It tastes of summer and the beach, like salt-rimmed margaritas and ice cream cones, sea and sun.

SERVES 12

CRUST
6 ounces (170g) saltine crackers (60 crackers, from about 1½ sleeves)

3 tablespoons sugar

½ cup (110g) unsalted butter, softened

FILLING
4 large egg yolks

1 (14-ounce/396g) can sweetened condensed milk

½ cup (120g) freshly squeezed lemon or lime juice (from about 3 lemons or 5 limes) or a mix of the two

TOPPING
1 cup (235g) heavy cream, very cold

Coarse or flaky sea salt

1 To make the crust, heat the oven to 350°F (175°C), with a rack in the center. Crush the crackers finely but not to dust, using a food processor, a rolling pin, or just your hands. Put the crumbs in a bowl.

2 Add the sugar, then knead in the butter until the crumbs hold together like dough. Press into an 8-inch (20cm) pie pan. Refrigerate for 15 minutes, then bake until the crust is deep golden brown, about 20 minutes. Cool slightly on a rack.

3 To make the filling, whisk together the egg yolks and condensed milk in a bowl, followed by the citrus juice. Be sure the filling is completely combined and smooth.

4 Pour the filling into the crust. Bake until the filling has set, about 16 minutes. Refrigerate the pie, uncovered, until chilled, at least 2 hours; it needs to be completely cold to be sliced.

5 To top the pie just before serving, in the bowl of a stand mixer fitted with the whisk attachment, or using a handheld mixer in a large bowl, whip the cream until it holds soft peaks. Spread the whipped cream over the top and sprinkle with sea salt. This pie is best served the day it's made. If you anticipate leftovers, they will keep better airtight in the refrigerator without the whipped cream topping; in that case, serve the whipped cream and salt on the side.

Italian Jam Shortbread Tart *(Fregolotta)*

FROM CINDY MUSHET

You can make this entire layered, jammy, crumbly tart in about an hour, including cleanup, and yet it comes out looking like a Byzantine mosaic. In the Veneto region of Italy, the tart would be called *fregolotta*, but as Chez Panisse alum and cookbook author Cindy Mushet says, it's "really more like a big cookie."

She's not kidding. The dough is one simple shortbread that you use for both the crust and the topping (you wonder why you'd ever make them separately). In between is a shiny layer of apricot jam, and on top, a flutter of sliced almonds.

As long as you have butter, sugar, and flour, you can use whatever jams and nuts are in your pantry. Try pine nuts, pistachios, pecans; the cherry preserves from summer, marmalade from winter, or rhubarb from spring, or mix them up at will. It's just jam and sundries, unbound by season or time.

SERVES 8 TO 10

¾ cup (170g) unsalted butter, softened

½ cup (100g) sugar

¼ teaspoon almond extract

1½ cups (190g) all-purpose flour (see page 5)

⅛ teaspoon fine sea salt

¼ cup (80g) not-too-sweet apricot jam or other jam

⅓ cup (30g) sliced almonds (preferably unblanched)

Yogurt Whipped Cream (page 258) or crème fraîche, for serving

1 Heat the oven to 350°F (175°C), with a rack in the center.

2 In the bowl of a stand mixer fitted with the paddle attachment, cream the butter and sugar on medium speed until the mixture is pale and fluffy, 3 to 4 minutes. Scrape down the sides of the bowl. Add the almond extract and mix until incorporated, 30 seconds more. (If you use a handheld mixer, just allow a little more time to reach each stage in the recipe.)

3 Whisk together the flour and salt in a medium bowl. Add the flour mixture to the butter-sugar mixture and mix on low speed just until the dough is well combined, about 30 seconds. Measure out ½ cup (130g) of the dough and pat it flat on a small plate; stick the plate in the freezer to chill (to make the dough easier to crumble).

4 Using your fingers, press the remaining dough into a 9- or 9½-inch (23 or 24cm) tart pan in an even layer (the edges can be a little higher than the rest, just make sure the center is not the thickest part). If the dough is sticking to your hands, refrigerate it briefly before continuing.

5 Use a small offset spatula or the back of a spoon to spread the jam in a thin, even layer over the surface of the dough, leaving a 1-inch (2.5cm) border uncovered around the edges.

6 Remove the reserved dough from the freezer and crumble it with your fingers into small pieces over the layer of jam, leaving some of the jam peeking through. Sprinkle the almonds evenly over the crumble.

7 Bake on a rimmed baking sheet until the topping is evenly golden brown, 30 to 40 minutes. Remove from the oven and cool completely on a rack. If your tart pan has a removable bottom, to unmold, center the tart pan on top of a large can or sturdy glass so that it balances midair as the rim of the tart pan falls to the counter. Leave the bottom of the pan under the tart for support, or be bold and remove it like so: run a large, thin spatula between the crust and the pan, using the spatula to ease the tart onto a serving plate. Serve with Yogurt Whipped Cream.

8 Store the tart covered in plastic wrap at room temperature. To freeze the unbaked tart for up to 1 month, assemble the tart, then cover it tightly in two layers of plastic wrap and freeze on a flat surface. Bake the tart from frozen; it may require a few extra minutes of baking time.

No-Bake Persimmon & Goat Cheese Cheesecake

FROM LOUISA SHAFIA

No-bake cheesecakes are a cheery genre of dessert—there's no water bath to fuss with and no worry about cracks or unset middles: they're firm and sliceable because a block of cream cheese is, too. But that doesn't mean all no-bake cheesecakes have to be quite so dense. This one, from Louisa Shafia, author of *The New Persian Kitchen*, holds up just as well, but is far lighter in texture and freer in spirit.

It starts with a base of fresh, tangy goat cheese, whose salty funk is mellowed just enough with coconut oil and whipped cream, then lifted into balance with lime juice, spicy whiffs of cardamom and cinnamon, and puréed fruit. Here, Shafia uses Hachiya persimmons (the oblong kind, shaped like a Roma tomato) in both the filling and spilled over the top. Hachiya need to be supersoft and ripe to make sure they don't taste chalky, but luckily if you can't find any, ripe peaches or mangoes (or Fuyu persimmons, the squatter kind, shaped like a beefsteak tomato) make excellent substitutes. If the market is really slim on good fruit, you could even plump up dried apricots in hot water for 30 minutes or so and blend that in. You're just looking for something bright and jolly to hold up its end.

MAKES ONE 9- OR 10-INCH (23 OR 25CM) CHEESECAKE

1½ cups (180g) shelled pistachios

½ cup (120g) heavy cream, very cold

1 cup (80g) finely crushed graham crackers (from just over 5 whole crackers)

¾ cup plus 3 tablespoons (185g) melted unrefined coconut oil, slightly cooled

½ teaspoon ground cinnamon

1½ teaspoons ground cardamom

1 cup plus 2 tablespoons (225g) sugar

Fine sea salt

5 very ripe Hachiya persimmons or other fruit (see above)

1 pound (450g) fresh goat cheese, at room temperature, crumbled

1 tablespoon freshly squeezed lime juice

1 Toast the pistachios in a large skillet over low heat, tossing occasionally, until they turn golden and smell nutty, about 5 minutes. Let cool. Lightly oil a 9- or 10-inch (23 or 25cm) springform pan with coconut oil.

2 In a medium bowl, using a handheld mixer or by hand, whip the cream to stiff peaks. Scrape the whipped cream into a small bowl to refrigerate briefly, but don't wash the mixer and bowl.

3 In a food processor, pulse together the pistachios, graham cracker crumbs, 3 tablespoons of the coconut oil, the cinnamon, cardamom, 2 tablespoons of the sugar, and a pinch of salt until the mixture clumps easily when pinched with your fingers. Scrape the crumb mixture into the springform pan and spread evenly over the bottom, pressing it down with your hands. Use the bottom of a juice glass to pack it down well.

4 Halve the persimmons, scoop the pulp into a blender, and puree at high speed until smooth. If you want an even smoother purée, you can pass it through a fine-mesh stainer. Set aside ½ cup (120ml) of the purée and store the rest airtight in the refrigerator.

5 With the still-messy mixer and bowl, whip the goat cheese, the remaining ¾ cup (150g) coconut oil, and the remaining 1 cup (200g) sugar until smooth, 2 to 3 minutes. Fold in the ½ cup (120ml) persimmon purée, the lime juice, and a pinch of salt, then fold in the whipped cream. Scrape the creamy mixture into the crust and smooth the top. Cover the pan tightly with plastic wrap or a lid and refrigerate until firm, at least 4 hours.

6 To serve, run a thin knife around the inside edge of the pan, remove the sides of the pan, and cut the cheesecake into wedges. Garnish each slice with a generous spoonful of the remaining persimmon purée and pass the rest of the purée at the table. Store leftovers in the refrigerator airtight.

Wonder Dough
No-Stress Pie Dough

FROM STELLA PARKS

There is so much genius embedded in this one recipe from Stella Parks, aka the baker, science whiz, and sugar historian behind the blog and book *BraveTart*, that I've opted to make her pie dough my default flaky crust in this book. Though there are lots of good ways to turn cold butter and flour into puffed, golden layers in the oven, this is the method that has surprised me the most and stands to make the biggest difference for a budding pie baker.

While most dough recipes take a bit of practice—you need to get comfortable discerning what the heck "coarse crumbs" look like, or how to *fraisage* butter across a counter—Parks provides an unexpected path that anyone can understand, without prior baking knowledge or intuition. She has you simply pinch cubes of butter in flour until they're flat, without working them in more. Then you stir in exactly ½ cup (120g) of cold water (again, no guessing!), and then roll and fold the dough once like a book to distribute the butter into big flakes—an act similar in spirit but not in intensity to making puff pastry. The crust is among the flakiest I've ever had, and yet a child could make it without having to look up "coarse crumbs."

The second game changer is that Parks doesn't blind-bake the crust with store-bought pie weights, or even dried beans. Instead, she fills the crust with sugar, which doesn't melt, but rather toasts and deepens in flavor, giving you a stash of golden, roasted sugar that you can use in *any other baking recipe*. I'm including her blind-baking instructions for single-crust pies, because she bakes at a lower temperature for longer than most, which results in less shrinking and disfigurement in the crust. But I also had the Food52 staff help me test this dough in all sorts of ways, at high heat and low, in slab galettes and latticed double-crust numbers, even as a quasi puff pastry, and it worked beautifully every time.

MAKES TWO 9-INCH (23CM) SINGLE PIECRUSTS OR ONE DOUBLE PIECRUST

8 ounces (225g) all-purpose flour (1¾ cups + 1 tablespoon), plus more for dusting (see page 5; Parks prefers the tenderness of Gold Medal bleached flour)

1 tablespoon sugar

1¼ teaspoons kosher salt (preferably Diamond Crystal)

8 ounces (225g) unsalted butter, very cold and cut into ½-inch (1.3cm) cubes

½ cup (120g) water, very cold

1 To make the dough, gather all your ingredients before your hands get messy, plus a medium bowl, a fine-mesh strainer or sifter, a whisk, a rubber spatula, a rolling pin, a 9-inch (23cm) pie pan (preferably glass), and a bench scraper or offset spatula (or other thin spatula-like thing). A ruler and a pair of kitchen shears will help, too.

2 Sift the flour into a medium bowl (if not measuring by weight, be sure to spoon the flour into the measuring cups and level with the back of a knife before sifting). Whisk in the sugar and salt, then add the butter. Toss the butter cubes in the flour, separating any stuck-together cubes with your fingers, then pinch each cube until it's flat and about ¼ inch (6mm) thick—don't work the butter in more! (See the top bowl in the photo to the right.) Stir in the cold water with a rubber spatula and press and knead together until the dough comes together in a shaggy ball. Dump the ball onto a heavily floured work surface, sprinkle the top with more flour, and use a rolling pin to roll out a rectangle that's about 10 by 15 inches (25 by 38cm), with a longer side closest to you, adding as much flour as you need along the way to keep it from sticking. (If at any point the butter gets melty and sticky, gather the dough onto a baking sheet and pop it into the refrigerator until it firms up a little, 15 minutes or so.)

3 To fold the dough, reference the handy photos on page 206. Slide the bench scraper under the dough to loosen it from the counter, then fold each 10-inch (25cm) side toward the middle so the edges meet, then close the packet like a book.

CONTINUED

fold in

fold in

fold over

fold down

cut

ta-da!

Fold the book in half, top to bottom, then slice the dough in half horizontally, so you have two roughly equal-size rectangles of dough. (If it's warmer than 72°F/22°C in your kitchen, you might want to refrigerate the dough for 15 to 20 minutes before proceeding.) Cover one portion of dough tightly in plastic wrap and refrigerate it while you get to work on the other one, or freeze for later it if you don't plan on using it right away.

4 Using as much flour as needed, roll out the remaining portion into a 14-inch (36cm) round that's ⅛ to ¼ inch (3 to 6mm) thick. (It can help to roughly shape it into a disk first, but starting from a rectangle is also fine.) Feel for sticky patches on top and underneath as you go, smoothing flour over them if needed. Brush off any excess flour, then drape the dough over your 9-inch (23cm) pie pan and lift the edges of the dough to drape the sides down into the corners without stretching the dough. Trim the excess to a 1¼-inch (3cm) overhang all around, then fold it under and press to seal it well, creating a ¾-inch (2cm) border. **If making a single-crust pie**, crimp with your fingers or a fork into whatever decorative edge you like. **If making a double-crust pie**, don't crimp, and roll out the second half of the dough as you did the first, then transfer it to a baking sheet or parchment-lined cutting board. **For both single- and double-crust pies**, cover all dough well in plastic and refrigerate for at least 2 hours or overnight. (Alternatively, the dough can be frozen for up to 3 months and thawed overnight in the refrigerator before baking.)

5 To blind-bake the crust for a single-crust pie, heat the oven to 350°F (175°C), with a rack in the lower middle. Line the chilled crust with a 16-inch (40cm) square of foil (not parchment or waxed paper), pressing it against the dough and letting the excess hang over the sides. Fill the crust to the brim with sugar, a no-waste blind-baking alternative to traditional options like rice or dried beans (for more on using the roasted sugar, see page 42).

6 Set the pie pan on a rimmed baking sheet and bake until the crust is cooked through and lightly browned, about 1 hour (using a glass pan makes it easy to check the underside to make sure it's nicely browned). Remove the crust from the oven and carefully lift out the foil with both hands and set aside on a plate until the sugar has fully cooled.

7 Let the crust cool to room temperature and use within 12 hours. Once cool, store the roasted sugar airtight at room temperature and use in any recipe in place of sugar. To use the other half of the dough if frozen, thaw in the refrigerator overnight before rolling out.

GENIUS TIP: THE MOST IMPORTANT RULE IN PIE DOUGH (PLUS TWO EXTRA TRICKS)

There is only one thing that separates the people who think they can't make pie dough from the people who are confident and fearless about it: the knowledge that anytime the dough starts to get sticky on you (whether you're in the midst of rolling or latticing or crimping), you can chill it for a few minutes and make your life easier. Leave it in the refrigerator just until the butter in the dough firms up, but not long enough for it to become rock solid and brittle.

If you want to make it extra easy on yourself, clear a section of your refrigerator (or freezer) and keep a baking sheet handy for speedy transfer.

- **TRICK 1** For even more insurance, cool down your countertop before rolling by filling gallon zip-top bags with ice cubes and a little cold water and laying them flat on the counter, like Stella Parks does.

- **TRICK 2** One more solution for stickiness (and using less flour): Lots of smart bakers, Rose Levy Beranbaum and Dorie Greenspan among them, like to roll out their pie dough between two layers of flour-dusted plastic wrap to minimize stress. The dough will be a more even thickness and less likely to stick to the counters or the rolling pin.

PIE DOUGH SPIN-OFFS

When using Stella Parks' No-Stress Pie Dough (page 204) in your flaky pie and galette adventures in the following pages, it would be a shame to waste even one scrap. Perhaps it should come as no surprise that three of the savviest uses for leftover pie dough trimmings come from three beloved Southern chefs, all masters of smart, thrifty baking.

Pie Dumplings: The late cooking legend Edna Lewis snipped her dough scraps into bite-size pieces and tucked them right into the filling of her deep-dish pies and cobblers. They cook up like chewy little bonus dumplings steeped in the bubbling fruity filling, leaving no need to find another use for them later.

Worms: The first thing the late Bill Neal, the founding chef of Crook's Corner in Chapel Hill, North Carolina, learned to cook was what his grandmother Inez called worms: sheets of leftover biscuit or pie dough rolled out thin; sprinkled with grated apple, cinnamon, and brown sugar; curled up jelly roll style; cut into ½-inch (1.3cm) slices; and baked, cut side up, in a 400°F (200°C) oven till golden, about 15 minutes. You can either bake the cut worms freestanding on a parchment paper–lined baking sheet or snuggled together into a buttered pan, but once baked, be sure to present them by saying, as Neal suggested in his book *Biscuits, Spoonbread, and Sweet Potato Pie*, "Would you care for some hot worms?"

Cobbler Toppers & Pandowdies: Food writer and *Sweet & Southern* author Ben Mims collects his pie dough scraps in the freezer until he's ready to top a fruit cobbler or pandowdy with wild, artsy-looking bits of dough (check out the photo to the left). If you want an extra-glossy, browned crust, instead of trying to brush egg wash (a mix of beaten egg and a splash of cream, milk, or water) onto each scrap, risking eggy pools on top, Erin Jeanne McDowell, Food52's baking consultant at large, recommends tossing the chilled scraps with the egg wash in a bowl before scattering them over the fruit and baking at 375°F (190°C) till bubbling and browned.

The Fruitiest Peach (or Nectarine or Apple) Pie

FROM ROSE LEVY BERANBAUM

The challenge of any pie stuffed with perfectly ripe fruit: where do all the juices go? If you let them run free, they flood the bottom crust; if you dam them up with starches or flours, you end up with a gummy paste in the filling. Neither does justice to the fruit.

In one of her more legendary moves, Rose Levy Beranbaum macerates fruits like peaches, nectarines, and apples in sugar and lemon juice for 30 minutes or more to draw out lots of liquid, then collects and cooks it down to a sticky syrup. This way, she's able to use half the thickener she would otherwise, and the sauce swimming around the fruit is less cornstarch and more concentrated jammy juices. Beranbaum has pulled out this trick time and again, from *The Pie & Pastry Bible* in 1998 to *The Baking Bible* in 2014. Here, I've combined her recipes into one all-purpose method for the best fruits you can find.

SERVES 6 TO 8

2¾ pounds (1.2kg) peaches or nectarines, pitted and cut into ½-inch (1.3cm) chunks, or 2½ pounds (1.1kg) tart-sweet baking apples like Honeycrisp or a mix of apples, cored and cut into ¼-inch (6mm) slices (in both cases, peeling is optional)

½ cup (100g) sugar, or ¼ cup (50g) lightly packed light brown sugar and ¼ cup (50g) sugar

1 tablespoon freshly squeezed lemon juice

¼ teaspoon fine sea salt

¼ teaspoon freshly grated nutmeg (for apple)

½ teaspoon ground cinnamon (for apple)

2 tablespoons unsalted butter

1 tablespoon plus 1 teaspoon cornstarch

½ teaspoon almond extract (for peach or nectarine)

1 recipe No-Stress Pie Dough (page 204, prepped through step 4 for a double crust)

2 tablespoons milk

1 tablespoon turbinado sugar

1 In a large nonreactive bowl, gently stir together the fruit, sugar, lemon juice, salt, and spices. Set aside to macerate, covered, at least 30 minutes and up to 3 hours.

2 Scrape the fruit and its juices into a colander set over a bowl and let drain. The mixture should release ½ to 1 cup (120 to 240ml) of liquid.

3 Combine the liquid and butter in a small saucepan and bring to a boil over medium-high heat. Cook until syrupy and lightly caramelized and reduced to about ⅓ cup (80ml), or slightly more if you started with more than ½ cup (120ml) of liquid. Swirl the liquid but do not stir it. Meanwhile, scrape the fruit back into the original bowl and toss it with the cornstarch and extract until no streaks of cornstarch remain. Pour the syrup over the fruit, tossing gently to coat. (Don't worry if the liquid hardens when it hits the fruit—it will dissolve during baking.)

4 Scrape the fruit mixture into the chilled bottom piecrust. Moisten the border of the crust by brushing it lightly with water, then place the top crust over the fruit. Alternatively, form a lattice crust (or something more casual, as in the Cranberry Sage Pie on page 223). Trim the overhang, leaving about a 1½-inch (4cm) border. Tuck the overhang under the bottom crust border and press down all around the top to seal it. Crimp the border with your fingers or a fork and, if using a solid top crust and not a lattice, slice about five evenly spaced 2-inch (5cm) vents in the center of the pie to let steam escape, starting about 1 inch (2.5cm) from the center and radiating toward the edge. Cover the pie loosely with plastic wrap and refrigerate for 1 hour before baking to chill and relax the pastry. This will help keep the crust flaky and avoid shrinking.

5 At least 20 minutes before baking, position an oven rack in the lowest position. Place a baking stone or large rimmed baking sheet on the rack. Lay a large piece of aluminum

CONTINUED

The Fruitiest Peach (or Nectarine or Apple) Pie
CONTINUED

foil on top of the stone to catch any juices. Heat the oven to 425°F (220°C). Brush the top crust with the milk and sprinkle with the turbinado.

6 Cover the outer edge of the pie with a ring of foil to protect it from burning. Set the pie directly on the foil-topped baking stone and bake until the juices bubble through the slashes and the fruit feels tender but not mushy when a cake tester or small, sharp knife is inserted through a slash, 45 to 55 minutes.

7 Let the pie cool on a rack for at least 3 hours before slicing and serving. Serve just warm or at room temperature. Store any leftovers in the refrigerator, airtight, for a breakfast treat.

GENIUS TIP: IF YOU ONLY SORT OF WANT TO PEEL YOUR FRUIT

If you don't want slips of peach skin in your pie, but don't feel like peeling (or wasting) them, Julie Richardson shared a clever fix in *Rustic Fruit Desserts*: poke the fruit all over with a fork before slicing it. The extra holes will encourage the peels to break down in the filling as they cook, instead of staying intact. Plus, less fruit for the compost and more for you!

GENIUS TIP: HOW TO SPEED-DRY STRAINERS AND WHISKS

Fine-mesh strainers and whisks can take their sweet time to air-dry, which can be a pain if you need to sift or mix dry ingredients again soon and don't want them to get clumpy. Alice Medrich's ingenious work-around is to wave metal tools over an open gas or electric burner until they're bone-dry—or blast them with a hair dryer. (If there are any plastic parts, the hair dryer is the better way to go.)

FLAKY VESSELS FOR FRUIT

Apple Galette

FROM CANAL HOUSE

Free-form loosey-goosey galettes are the most laid-back way to make pie—and the best entry point for anyone timid about handling dough, since they're deliberately open-faced and unkempt.

This recipe from Melissa Hamilton and Christopher Hirsheimer of Canal House has two bits of insurance against the unpleasant surprise of a soggy bottom crust. By cooking the apples down on the stovetop first, there won't be any major moisture releases to surprise you, plus you get to sweeten and season the filling to taste. The second trick is to bake the galette on an unheated pizza stone, if you have one. It's easier to transfer the cool stone into the oven with a galette on it than try to slide the galette onto a preheated stone, and even starting from cool, the bottom crust magically crisps up anyway.

SERVES 8

½ portion No-Stress Pie Dough (page 204, prepped through step 3)

2½ pounds (1.1kg) apples (such as Honeycrisp or Jonagold)

⅓ cup (65g) sugar

½ teaspoon ground cinnamon

3 tablespoons salted butter

½ vanilla bean, split lengthwise

2 tablespoons heavy cream

1 Refrigerate the pie dough for 1 hour. Meanwhile, peel and core the apples (save the peels! see the recipe at right), then cut them into 1-inch (2.5cm) wedges. In a large bowl, toss together the apples with the sugar and cinnamon.

2 Melt the butter in a very large skillet over medium heat, add the vanilla bean, followed by the apples, nudging the wedges into a single layer. (If the apples don't fit in a single layer, use two pans.) Cook the apples, turning occasionally with a fork or thin spatula, until the apples are tender, 30 to 45 minutes. Remove from the heat, scrape the seeds from the vanilla pod into the skillet, and spoon the pan juices over the apples. Transfer the pan to a rack to cool.

3 Heat the oven to 375°F (190°C), with a rack in the lower third. Line a room-temperature pizza stone or large rimmed baking sheet with parchment paper. When the apples are cool and you're ready to assemble the galette, roll out the pie dough on a lightly floured surface into a 13-inch (33cm) round that's ⅛ to ¼ inch (3 to 6mm) thick. Roll the dough around the rolling pin and unfurl on the pizza stone.

4 Starting in the middle of the dough, quickly arrange the apples in a tight circular pattern until about 3 inches (7.5cm) from the edge—it doesn't need to be perfect. Spoon the pan juices over the apples. Fold the edge of the dough over the apples, pleating the dough roughly as you go. Brush the exposed dough with the heavy cream.

5 Transfer the pizza stone to the oven and bake until the crust is golden, about 45 minutes. Remove from the oven and let cool for 10 minutes before cutting into wedges. Store any leftovers airtight at room temperature, or to extend their life, in the refrigerator.

Fried Apple Peels
From Paula Wolfert

Don't toss those apple peels! Panfry them until crisp and their flavor intensifies, like raspy curls of apple fruit leather. Paula Wolfert brought this recipe back from Provence in her cult favorite cookbook *Paula Wolfert's World of Food*. Use peelings from any apples and sprinkle them over roasted fruit, yogurt, or the very thing you're baking.

How to make it: Peel the **apples** so the peelings are thick. Wolfert then slices them thinly, but you can also leave them in their natural state, as you see in the photo at left. Heat **⅓ cup (70g) clarified butter** or ghee with **3 tablespoons neutral oil** (such as grapeseed) in a small skillet over medium heat until sizzling. Working in batches, fry the peelings, stirring occasionally, until nicely browned around the edges, 2 to 3 minutes. Using a slotted spoon, transfer them to a paper towel–lined baking sheet to drain—they will crisp up as they cool. They can be made several hours in advance—if they lose their crunch, crisp them up on a rack in a 250°F (120°C) oven, about 30 minutes. Store airtight at room temperature.

Slab Pie

FROM MARTHA STEWART

A slab pie is simply a shallow pie that's stretched to fit in a rimmed baking sheet. It feeds more revelers than a standard round pie does, with less mess. It's a pie in a sensible bar cookie outfit; a hand pie, without having to shape a bunch of hand pies; a boon to crust-lovers everywhere. It is, essentially, a Pop-Tart.

This is a pure distillation of all of Martha Stewart's various slab pie recipes: a template from *Martha Stewart's Baking Handbook* for any fruit growing near you. I'll be honest, trying to roll out pie dough into a perfect 18 by 13-inch (45 by 33cm) rectangle could rattle even experienced bakers, so don't worry about being perfect. If fissures emerge in the dough, or your rectangle is more of a trapezoid or triangle or trippy free-form starfish, patch it together by repurposing any long, scraggly edges. If the dough starts to get sticky, put it in the refrigerator (or freezer) for a few minutes, then flour and smooth out any sticky patches when it's cooler and more trustworthy.

Most important of all, remember this thing is called slab pie—it sounds like something even Barney Rubble could make. Call it shabby caveman and even Martha would approve.

SERVES 12

Double recipe No-Stress Pie Dough (page 204, prepped through step 3 and cut so that one half is slightly larger)

6 cups (750g) fresh or frozen assorted berries, 6 cups (750g) stemmed and pitted sour cherries, or 7 peaches, cut into ½-inch (1.3cm) wedges (about 8 cups, see note)

1¼ cups (250g) sugar

¼ cup (30g) cornstarch

1 tablespoon freshly squeezed lemon juice

¼ teaspoon fine sea salt

2 tablespoons heavy cream

¼ cup (50g) turbinado sugar

1 Refrigerate the pie dough for 1 hour. Heat the oven to 375°F (190°C), with a rack in the center. On a lightly floured surface or, preferably, between two large floured pieces of plastic wrap, roll out the larger half of the dough until it's ¼ inch (6mm) thick. Trim it down to an 18 by 13-inch (45 by 33cm) rectangle, saving any excess dough to patch holes. Carefully peel off the top sheet of plastic wrap and fold the dough into quarters to more easily transfer it to a 15 by 10-inch (38 by 25cm) rimmed baking sheet (also known as a jelly roll pan), then unfold. Lightly lift up the edges to drape the dough into the corners of the pan, leaving pastry to hang over the sides as evenly as you can. Refrigerate while mixing together the filling.

2 In a large bowl, stir together the fruit, sugar, cornstarch, lemon juice, and salt. Scrape the mixture into the chilled pie shell and spread evenly to the edges. Refrigerate again while you roll out the top crust.

3 Roll out the remaining smaller half of the dough ¼ inch (6mm) thick, trimming it down to a 16 by 11-inch (40 by 28cm) rectangle. Remove the bottom crust with the filling from the refrigerator and drape the top crust over the filling. Fold the edge of the bottom crust over the top dough and crimp with your fingers or a fork if you like. Prick the top crust all over with a fork and cut a few 1-inch (2.5cm) vents in the center to let steam escape. Brush the entire surface of the pie with the heavy cream and sprinkle with sugar.

4 Bake until the crust is deep golden brown and the filling is bubbling, 40 to 55 minutes. Let the pie cool on a rack until it's just warm to the touch, about 45 minutes before serving. Slab pie tastes best the day it's baked, but it can be kept at room temperature, loosely covered with plastic wrap, for up to 2 days.

Note: If you want to serve this on plates with forks, you can bump up the fruit amount to make it ooze molten fruit. But if you want people to be able to grab it like a Pop-Tart, stick with 6 cups (750g) of fruit.

FLAKY VESSELS FOR FRUIT

Piekies

FROM JENI BRITTON BAUER

Meet the piekie, a dessert with the casual snatchability of a cookie and the flaky, buttery brightness of a fruit pie. It's the invention of Jeni Britton Bauer, the founder of Jeni's Splendid Ice Creams, who serves hers with ice cream as a cheeky take on pie à la mode. But they're maybe even more head-turning when their bejeweled colors are just laid out on a big platter.

For the pie-cookie base, you roll out a pretty traditional pâte sucrée—the kind of dough used for sweet, shortbread-like tart crusts that holds its shape well as cutout cookies, too—though this dough has cream cheese to make it a bit flakier and more pie-like. Then, you simply dunk tiny slices of fruit into a sugar and cornstarch mix that thickens and sweetens the juices as they bubble out.

Fresh fruit is unpredictable, so it might take a few test cookies to figure out the right proportion of fruit and sugar to dough—too much and the juices will run freely onto the pan, too little and the piekie won't be as luscious as you might have hoped. Kids will have a real hootenanny putting these together; you will, too.

MAKES ABOUT 2 DOZEN PIEKIES

DOUGH

1½ cups (190g) all-purpose flour (see page 5)

½ cup (110g) unsalted butter, very cold and cut into ½-inch (1.3cm) cubes

⅓ cup (65g) sugar

2 ounces (55g) cream cheese, very cold

2 large egg yolks, lightly beaten

2 tablespoons heavy cream, very cold

TOPPING

1 cup (200g) sugar

1 tablespoon cornstarch

8 ounces (225g) strawberries, plums, peaches, nectarines, and/or apples, pitted and sliced very thin (about ⅛ inch/3mm) using a very sharp knife or mandoline, or cherries, pitted and diced

Ice cream, for serving (optional)

1 To make the dough, in a food processor, pulse the flour, butter, sugar, and cream cheese until the mixture looks like bread crumbs or almond meal. (You can also rub the butter and cream cheese into the flour and sugar with your hands, but work quickly so the butter doesn't melt.) Add the egg yolks and cream and pulse a few times to blend in (or finish mixing with your hands).

2 Divide the dough in half. Knead one half until it comes together in a ball, then flatten it into a disk that's about 2 inches (5cm) thick. Repeat with the second half. Cover each disk of dough in plastic wrap and refrigerate until firm, about 1 hour.

3 Heat the oven to 350°F (175°C), with racks in the upper and lower thirds. Line two large rimmed baking sheets with parchment paper or silicone baking mats.

4 On a lightly floured surface or between two lightly floured pieces of plastic wrap, roll out the dough until it's about ⅛ inch (3mm) thick. Using a 2½- to 3-inch (6.5 to 7.5cm) diameter cutter, cut the dough into circles (or other similar-size shapes) and place on the baking sheets.

5 To make the topping, stir together the sugar and cornstarch in a small bowl. Dip each slice of fruit into the sugar mixture, turning to generously coat. Decorate each piekie with 1 to 3 slices of fruit, covering about three-quarters of the surface of the dough, overlapping the fruit slightly as needed. The fruit will shrink while baking, so it's okay to have slices reach, or even extend slightly beyond the edges of the dough. Repeat with the remaining dough and fruit.

6 Bake until the piekies are golden, about 25 minutes, rotating the baking sheets from back to front and top to bottom halfway through baking. Let cool on the baking sheets for 2 minutes, then transfer to a rack and cool completely. Serve the same day, alone or with ice cream. Refrigerate any leftovers airtight for a breakfast treat.

Double Blueberry Tart

FROM MINDY FOX

It's really the blueberries that do the lion's share of the work in this tart. All you do is make a simple press-in crust and toss some flour and sugar with half the berries; they bubble down merrily, their natural pectin unleashed to meld into a jammy layer without any further prodding from you. More fresh berries roll onto the top, staying bouncy and juicy-tart.

The tart is a specialty of cookbook author Mindy Fox and her mom, Phyllis, who have fiddled with the ingredients over the years, adding whole wheat flour for a deeply flavored crust and caramelly turbinado sugar instead of white. They serve it with tart Greek yogurt instead of whipped cream or ice cream, to bring out even more of the berries' natural sweetness.

Since you're parading out all of blueberries' best sides—cooked and saucy; raw and alive—it's best to save this one for the height of blueberry season. You could get away with frozen or bland berries in the bottom layer, but on top, there's nothing for them to hide behind.

SERVES 8

CRUST
½ cup (110g) unsalted butter

¾ cup (95g) all-purpose flour (see page 5)

¼ cup (30g) whole wheat flour (see page 5)

2 tablespoons turbinado sugar

¼ teaspoon kosher salt

1 tablespoon white vinegar

FILLING
½ cup (100g) turbinado sugar

2 tablespoons all-purpose flour (see page 5)

½ teaspoon ground cinnamon

½ teaspoon freshly grated nutmeg

4¼ cups (640g) fresh blueberries

Confectioners' sugar, for dusting

Whole or 2% Greek yogurt, for serving

1 Heat the oven to 400°F (200°C), with a rack in the center.

2 To make the crust, cut the butter into cubes, then freeze until firm and very cold, about 10 minutes. Meanwhile, in a food processor, pulse the flours, sugar, and salt to blend. Add the vinegar and chilled butter and pulse just until the dough forms a ball. Scrape the dough onto a large sheet of plastic wrap and pat the dough into a 7-inch (18cm) disk. Invert the disk into the center of a 9-inch (23cm) springform pan (not nonstick) or 10-inch (25cm) fluted tart pan. Use the bottom of a juice glass to evenly press the dough into the pan, then use a combination of the glass and your fingers to press the dough about 1 inch (2.5cm) up the sides of the pan so that it's about ⅛ inch (3mm) thick.

3 To make the filling, stir together the sugar, flour, cinnamon, and nutmeg in a large bowl. Add 2½ cups (380g) of the blueberries and toss to combine. Spoon the blueberry mixture into the crust, then sprinkle any leftover sugar mixture in the bottom of the bowl evenly over the top of the berries.

4 Set the pan on a rimmed baking sheet and place in the oven. Bake until the crust is deeply golden brown, about 1 hour. The filling will bubble at about 50 minutes, but take it further for the fruit to fully cook and set—this will all take a bit less time if using the 10-inch (25cm) tart pan. There may be a bit of the sugar mixture still visible on top of the cooked berries, but don't worry about it. It won't be noticeable once the fresh berries and confectioners' sugar are on top.

5 Let the tart cool completely in the pan on a rack, about 2 hours, then carefully remove the sides of the pan. (For the fluted tart pan, see the tip in step 7 on page 200.) If you want to remove the bottom of the pan, slide an offset spatula or a butter knife under the entire crust to loosen it, then slide the tart onto a serving plate. Just before serving, top the tart with the remaining 1¾ cups (260g) of blueberries. Put a spoonful of confectioners' sugar into a fine-mesh sieve and dust over the tart. Serve the same day with Greek yogurt . Refrigerate any leftovers airtight.

Cranberry Sage Pie

FROM FOUR & TWENTY BLACKBIRDS

A pie that skews a little tart and savory is pretty thrilling anytime, but it's all the more so on Thanksgiving, as it winks at you from the sweet lineup of apple, pumpkin, and pecan.

The Elsen sisters from Four & Twenty Blackbirds bakery in Brooklyn like to push pies in directions they haven't gone before, splashing bitters into their fillings and showering salt across the top. Here they mulch up tart raw cranberries with the grounding presence of fresh sage, adding the pectin from a grated apple to help thicken the filling—an old trick used often by smart pie bakers, like you!

If you're feeling nervous about making a lattice, follow their lead. Just lay the strips down willy-nilly, or turn them into triangles or polka dots.

SERVES 6 TO 8

1 recipe No-Stress Pie Dough (page 204, prepped through step 4 for a double-crust pie)

¾ cup (90g) dried cranberries

½ cup (100g) sugar

½ cup (110g) packed light brown sugar

¼ cup (30g) arrowroot powder (or cornstarch)

1 tablespoon coarsely chopped fresh sage

½ teaspoon kosher salt

¼ teaspoon ground cinnamon

¼ teaspoon ground allspice

4 cups (400g) whole cranberries, fresh or frozen

1 small apple, such as Northern Spy or Golden Delicious

2 large eggs

1 tablespoon pure vanilla extract

Demerara or turbinado sugar, for topping

1 Bring a kettleful of water to a boil. In a heatproof bowl, pour enough boiling water over the dried cranberries to cover them by about 1 inch (2.5cm). Leave them to plump up.

2 Position the oven racks in the lowest and center positions. Place a rimmed baking sheet on the bottom rack and heat the oven to 425°F (220°C).

3 In a food processor, combine the sugars, arrowroot, sage, salt, cinnamon, and allspice and process until the sage is very finely chopped. Pour the spiced sugar mixture into a large bowl.

4 Without washing the food processor bowl, pulse 2 cups (200g) of the whole cranberries until coarsely chopped, then transfer them to the sugar mixture, along with the remaining 2 cups (200g) whole cranberries.

5 Peel the apple and shred it on the large holes of a box grater. Drain the plumped dried cranberries in a colander but don't press or squeeze them dry. Add the shredded apple and the plumped cranberries to the bowl with the rest of the filling and stir until well combined. Lightly beat 1 egg and add to the filling, followed by the vanilla. Stir again until well combined.

6 Pour the filling into the chilled pie shell. Cut several fat strips (about 1½ inch/4cm wide) from the chilled sheet of top crust, brush the edge of the bottom crust with water, and arrange the lattice strips randomly, like lights at a disco, on top, pressing at the edges to adhere the strips. Crimp the edges with your fingers or a fork if you like. Refrigerate the pie until the pastry firms up, 10 to 15 minutes.

7 Whisk together the remaining egg, 1 teaspoon water, and a pinch of salt in a small bowl to make an egg wash. Brush the pastry with the egg wash to coat; be careful not to drag any of the filling onto the pastry (it will burn). Sprinkle the top with the Demerara sugar.

8 Place the pie on the preheated rimmed baking sheet on the lowest rack in the oven. Bake until the pastry is firm and beginning to brown, 20 to 25 minutes. Turn the oven down to 375°F (190°C), transfer the pie and the baking sheet to the center rack, and continue to bake until the pastry is a deep golden brown and the juices are bubbling throughout, 35 to 45 minutes more.

9 Let the pie cool on a rack, 2 to 3 hours. Serve slightly warm or at room temperature the day it's made. Store any leftovers airtight in the refrigerator or for up to 2 days at room temperature.

Pumpkin Pie with Pecan Crunch

FROM *YANKEE* MAGAZINE

While there are close to a million pumpkin-pecan pie recipes already chugging around the internet, this is the only one that allows you to take a fully functional pumpkin pie and—very briefly—blast on a layer of pecan praline under the broiler.

Until I tasted this hybrid pie myself, I assumed it would be sweet-on-sweet and over the top. But this particular mash-up brings out the best in both. There's not much sugar in the pumpkin base, so the gooey praline topping brings out the pumpkin's savory, spiced side, and the slick pecan crackle up top gives clarity to the extreme smoothness of the custard below. With either layer alone, it would be easy to get bored and move on, but not here.

It might sound risky to subject a custard pie to such intense heat, but its time in the danger zone is very brief, and this actually allows you *more* control: sizzle it exactly as long as you like, rotating and checking when you want. Want to serve it still warm and bubbling? Do it. I like giving mine enough time to cool so that a thin crystalline shell can form.

SERVES 8

PUMPKIN PIE
1 blind-baked and cooled 9-inch (23cm) piecrust made from ½ portion No-Stress Pie Dough (see page 204)

1 (15-ounce/425g) can pumpkin purée

½ cup (120g) heavy cream

¼ cup (50g) sugar

3 large eggs plus 1 large egg yolk, lightly beaten

1 tablespoon dark rum or bourbon

½ teaspoon ground cinnamon

½ teaspoon ground ginger

½ teaspoon freshly grated nutmeg

Pinch of salt

PECAN CRUNCH
1 cup (115g) pecan halves, coarsely chopped

½ cup (100g) lightly packed light brown sugar

3 tablespoons unsalted butter, melted

2 tablespoons heavy cream

Whipped cream, for serving (optional)

1 To make the pumpkin pie, heat the oven to 350°F (175°C), with a rack in the center.

2 Stir together the pumpkin purée, cream, sugar, eggs, rum, cinnamon, ginger, nutmeg, and salt in a large bowl, then pour into the cooled piecrust and smooth the top.

3 Bake for 10 minutes, then turn the heat down to 325°F (165°C) and continue to bake until the filling sets, about 40 minutes more. A knife inserted 1½ inches (4cm) from the edge should come out clean. The center of the pie may still wobble gently, but shouldn't look liquidy. Let cool completely in the pan on a rack, about 2 hours.

4 To make the pecan crunch, at least an hour before serving, position a rack about 6 inches (15cm) below the broiler flame. Heat the broiler.

5 Stir together the pecans, brown sugar, butter, and cream in a small bowl. Spread the pecan crunch on top of the filling in an even layer, all the way to the edges. Protect the crust rim from burning by covering it with a ring of aluminum foil. Place the pie in the oven. Don't go anywhere! Broil the pie, turning frequently, until the topping is browned and bubbly, about 5 minutes. Watch closely and don't let the nuts turn black—though if any do, you can carefully scoop off the burned bits while the topping is still warm. Remove the foil ring and let the pie cool again on a rack. Serve at room temperature with whipped cream, if you like. Store any leftovers in the refrigerator airtight.

Almond Tart

FROM LINDSEY SHERE

For decades, Lindsey Shere's almond tart was Chez Panisse's most infamous dessert—"until too many customers apparently had a hard time eating it with a fork, so off the menu it went," as David Lebovitz tells it. "I lobbied—*hard*—to keep it there. It's the most delicious thing I've probably ever had."

Despite its reputation for being tricky to bake (and eat tidily with a fork), it's truly not hard to make—and it might be the most delicious thing *you've* ever had. There are a few ways you can go off track, but Shere gives you the tools to glide through the recipe easily, if you pay attention. Yes, your filling may bubble up over the edges in the oven, but she warns you to put a foil catchall underneath, just in case. The tart could stick fiercely to the bottom of the pan, but she recommends loosening it while it's still warm. (I've also included photos of the process on page 229, so you know what to look for at important stages.)

Even better, Shere's technique has several hidden benefits and shortcuts. You don't have to line and fill the crust with baking weights—straight from the freezer, it blind-bakes without collapsing or deforming. You don't even have to make a caramel—you simply bring the sugary mix to a boil and it all bubbles down into a chewy caramel in the oven on its own. Once baked, the tart is flawless, and almost indestructible.

> "It immediately became identified, for better or worse, as the house specialty of Chez Panisse." —Lindsey Shere

SERVES 12

TART SHELL
1 cup (140g) all-purpose flour

1 tablespoon sugar

¼ teaspoon fine sea salt

½ cup (110g) unsalted butter, slightly softened

1 tablespoon water

½ teaspoon pure vanilla extract

2 or 3 drops of almond extract

FILLING
¾ cup (175g) heavy cream

¾ cup (150g) sugar

1 teaspoon Grand Marnier

2 or 3 drops of almond extract

1 cup (90g) sliced almonds

1 To make the tart shell, stir together the flour, sugar, and salt in a medium bowl. Cut the butter into ½-inch (1.3cm) slices. Work the butter slices into the flour mixture with your hands or a pastry blender until the butter is the consistency of fine bread crumbs or almond meal and the mixture is beginning to hold together—the softer your butter is, the faster this will go.

2 Stir together the water, vanilla, and almond extract in a small bowl and then work it into the flour-butter mixture just until the pastry is blended and holds together when you press it. Gather it into a ball, cover it in plastic wrap, and refrigerate it for 30 minutes. You can also wrap the pastry in aluminum foil and freeze it for up to 1 month.

3 Choose a 9-inch (23cm) tart pan with a removable bottom that isn't black (or if that's all you have, just watch it closely in the oven to make sure it doesn't burn). Press the pastry into the bottom and sides of the pan, making sure that it's an even thickness. If at any point the dough gets too sticky and unmanageable, refrigerate it for a few minutes until it's firm enough to press without sticking to your fingers. Reserve any leftover pastry for patching. Wrap the pastry shell in aluminum foil and freeze for at least 30 minutes or overnight. You don't need to fill the shell with weights before blind-baking—this pastry doesn't shrink much.

CONTINUED

4 When you're ready to bake the tart, heat the oven to 375°F (190°C). Line a large rimmed baking sheet with aluminum foil (dull side up). Bake the shell on the baking sheet until it's golden brown all over, 20 to 30 minutes. Be sure the tart is fully baked because the pastry will not bake much more once it is filled. (Note: I haven't seen this happen, but per David Lebovitz, if the sides collapse in the oven, you can take it out halfway through baking and carefully push the half-baked dough back up the sides.) Let the pastry shell cool on the lined pan on a rack while you make the filling and turn the oven up to 400°F (200°C).

5 To make the filling, stir together the cream, sugar, Grand Marnier, and almond extract in a large saucepan (it should have enough room for the mixture to triple in volume, just in case it bubbles up quickly). Cook over medium heat, stirring occasionally, until it comes to a rolling boil. Remove from the heat, stir in the almonds, and let the mixture stand for about 15 minutes.

6 Meanwhile, patch any cracks in the tart shell if necessary. Smooth a small piece of reserved soft dough gently over any crack that looks like it goes all the way through the shell. (Note: If you forgot to save some dough or didn't have enough, David Lebovitz recommends mixing together a thick slurry of flour and water and smoothing that in, instead. It works!) Be careful not to break through the crisp top of the baked crust as you patch. Fill the shell with the still-warm filling, making sure that the almonds float evenly in the filling. If they are piled on top of the liquid, the finished tart will have a cornflake-like texture instead of a smooth, glossy surface.

7 With the tart still on the lined baking sheet in case the filling bubbles over, bake the tart until the top is a creamy brown caramel color, 30 to 35 minutes; it will continue to brown a little more when you take it out of the oven. Let the tart cool in the pan on a rack, loosening the sides of the pan slightly every minute or two with an offset spatula or butter knife until set, 5 to 10 minutes. Remove the tart from the ring (see tip in step 7 on page 200) and return it to the rack to cool completely.

8 If you want to remove the tart from the bottom of its pan, carefully slide an offset spatula or butter knife between the pastry shell and pan while the tart is still warm, 15 to 20 minutes after it comes out of the oven. Then lift the tart off the bottom of the pan with a wide spatula and return it to the rack to finish cooling.

9 Serve at room temperature in thin wedges and remind your guests to eat the tart with their hands like a cookie. Leftovers keep quite well—store airtight at room temperature.

GENIUS TIP: DON'T MISE EVERY LAST LITTLE THING

Most cooking and baking endeavors will go more smoothly if you follow the classic principle of *mise en place*, aka measuring and prepping everything on the ingredient list before you just dive in. But some ingredients shouldn't be left exposed to air for too long—egg yolks will take on a tough skin, citrus zests will fade and wither, and vanilla extract and other alcoholic substances will evaporate, leaving only a dry residue in no time. Either cover these volatile ingredients tightly with plastic wrap, or don't bust them out till the last minute.

Obsessive Ricotta Cheesecake

FROM GINA DEPALMA

When Gina DePalma, the late, brilliant pastry chef at Babbo in New York City, finally settled on her ideal ricotta cheesecake for her cookbook *Dolce Italiano* in 2007, its utter smoothness came from American cream cheese, which might surprise purists of the Italian variety of cheesecake (it surprised her). But, as she wrote on her blog, "If you lived in Italy as I did, you'd know that Italians are big fans of the ole' Philly."

But she wasn't done obsessing yet. By 2013, she'd scrapped the crust entirely to speed up the process, only buttering and dusting the pan with bread crumbs and sugar. She'd also discovered that matzo meal— not cornstarch, flour, or rice flour—was the most undetectable binder to soak up lingering moisture from the ricotta. If you're making this outside of Passover and can't find matzo meal anywhere, don't worry, you can go back to the original tablespoon of cornstarch. Oh, and I brought back her original crust for those of us who feel a cheesecake isn't complete without one, but feel free to take the quicker route, depending on how obsessed you feel today.

SERVES 8 TO 10

CRUST
Fine dry bread crumbs or salt-free matzo meal, for dusting the pan

¾ cup (70g) sliced blanched almonds, toasted

¼ cup (30g) all-purpose flour (see page 5)

3 tablespoons sugar

Pinch of kosher salt

1 large egg yolk

2 tablespoons unsalted butter, melted and cooled

½ teaspoon pure vanilla extract

FILLING
2 (15-ounce/425g) containers whole-milk ricotta cheese

2 (8-ounce/225g) packages cream cheese, at room temperature and cut into cubes

1 cup (200g) sugar

2 large eggs

2 tablespoons salt-free matzo meal

2½ teaspoons finely grated lemon zest

1 tablespoon freshly squeezed lemon juice

2 teaspoons pure vanilla extract

⅛ teaspoon kosher salt

Confectioners' sugar, for dusting (optional)

1 To make the crust, heat the oven to 350°F (175°C), with a rack in the lower third. Lightly butter a 9-inch (23cm) springform pan and dust it with bread crumbs or matzo meal, tapping out the excess.

2 In a food processor, pulse the almonds, flour, sugar, and salt until the nuts are finely chopped. Lightly whisk together the egg yolk, melted butter, and vanilla in a small bowl. Pour the wet ingredients into the nut mixture and pulse several times until moistened and well combined. If you pinch the mixture between your fingers, it should hold together easily. Press the mixture onto the bottom and about 1 inch (2.5cm) up the sides of the springform pan. Refrigerate the pan until the crust is firm, 15 to 20 minutes.

3 Meanwhile, put the ricotta in a large fine-mesh strainer set over a bowl and let any excess liquid drain for 30 minutes. After the crust has chilled, bake until it is golden brown, about 10 minutes. Let the crust cool completely in the pan on a rack.

4 To make the filling, transfer the drained ricotta to a food processor and purée until smooth. Add the cream cheese and purée again until smooth. Add the sugar, eggs, matzo meal, lemon zest and juice, vanilla, and salt and purée, scraping down the sides as needed, until smooth, about 30 seconds. Scrape the batter into the cooled crust.

5 Set the pan on a rimmed baking sheet and bake the cheesecake until golden brown and just set, about 1 hour. It should jiggle like Jell-O when you shake it gently; if you insert a toothpick, it should show damp crumbs, not batter. Transfer to a rack and let cool in the pan for about 1 hour (the cake will fall slightly). Refrigerate uncovered until cool, about 3 hours, then cover and refrigerate for at least 4 hours more or overnight. The cheesecake is best served fully chilled the following day.

6 To serve, wrap a warm towel around the pan to release the cake. Remove the sides of the pan. Use a wide, sturdy spatula to carefully slide the cheesecake off the bottom of the pan and onto a serving dish. Dust with confectioners' sugar and cut into wedges. Refrigerate any leftovers airtight.

Egg Tarts

FROM YANK SING WITH RACHEL KHONG & GEORGE MENDES WITH GENEVIEVE KO

Tracing the path that the egg tart has taken around the world is dizzying: there seems to be an almost primal attachment to it that we humans share, from Portugal's charred *pastéis de nata* to Macau, from crumbly English custard tarts to Hong Kong's *dahn taht* to mainland China and beyond. Everywhere it lands, it roots and changes little enough that you'll recognize them all as kin.

Maybe it's fitting or maybe it's heresy: this recipe is a mash-up of my two favorite egg tarts I've tried at home. The supersmooth, cinnamon-scented filling comes from *My Portugal* by George Mendes and Genevieve Ko and is friendly to singeing and caramelizing on top. And the flaky crust was collected by Rachel Khong for *Lucky Peach*'s *All About Eggs* from Yank Sing, a revered third-generation dim sum restaurant in San Francisco that's been serving a version of these tarts since it opened in 1958. Over the years, Yank Sing has updated the recipe as customer tastes have changed, making the pastry flakier, and ditching shortening for butter (though the terms "oil dough" and "water dough" remain). Making the dough at home is more fun than tricky—a more playful, less precise, though slightly stickier path to homemade puff pastry. And unless you're in San Francisco (or Lisbon or Macau), this recipe is the only way you get to taste them at their warm, miraculous best.

MAKES 12 LITTLE TARTS

PUFF PASTRY
¾ cup (170g) butter, very cold and cut into ½-inch (1.3cm) cubes

1½ cups (190g) all-purpose flour (see page 5)

½ teaspoon kosher salt

1 large egg

2 tablespoons water

EGG CUSTARD
½ cup (100g) sugar

½ cinnamon stick

⅓ cup (80g) water

½ cup plus 3 tablespoons (170g) whole milk

¼ cup (30g) all-purpose flour (see page 5)

3 large egg yolks

Pinch of kosher salt

1 To make the puff pastry, using your hands or a pastry blender, work the butter, ¾ cup (95g) of the flour, and ¼ teaspoon of the salt together just until it will hold together in clumps (there will still be small lumps of butter showing), to form an "oil dough." Knead the dough into a ball, cover it in plastic wrap, and refrigerate until very cold, at least 20 minutes.

2 Meanwhile, use a rubber spatula to stir together the egg, water, and the remaining ¼ teaspoon salt in a small bowl. Put the remaining ¾ cup (95g) of flour in a separate bowl and add the egg mixture, stirring together to form a "water dough." Cover the bowl tightly with plastic wrap and refrigerate for 20 minutes.

3 Generously dust a work surface with flour. Spoon an extra mound of flour to the side of your workspace so that you can easily grab more as needed. Remove the water dough from the refrigerator. Scrape the dough onto the floured surface and sprinkle the top of the dough and a rolling pin with more flour. Roll out the dough into an 11-inch (28cm) square, adding more flour as needed to keep the dough from sticking to the surface or the rolling pin.

4 Remove the oil dough from the refrigerator and crumble it on top of the water dough in the center, leaving a 3-inch (7.5cm) border of the water dough uncovered around the edges. (The border should be large enough that it can fold over to cover the oil dough entirely—see the upper right of the photo on page 235). Fold the sides of the water dough over the oil dough to meet in the middle, covering it completely.

5 Roll out the dough again into an 11-inch (28cm) square and mentally mark it into thirds. Fold each outer third over the center third, like folding a letter, then roll out the folded rectangle into an 11-inch (28cm) square again. Repeat the folding and rolling process two more times.

CONTINUED

6 After the third time, roll out the dough again and, this time, mentally mark it into quarters. Fold each outer quarter in so that the outer edges meet in the center, and then roll out the rectangle until it's ½ inch (1.3cm) thick. Cover the dough in plastic wrap and refrigerate for at least 20 minutes.

7 On a lightly floured work surface, roll out the dough until it's ⅛ inch (3mm) thick. Using a 3½-inch (9cm) round cutter, cut the dough into 12 rounds.

8 Lightly butter the inside of 12 fluted tart molds or a muffin pan and press the pastry disks into the molds. Refrigerate while you make the egg custard.

9 To make the egg custard, combine the sugar, cinnamon, and water in a medium saucepan and bring to a boil over high heat. Boil for 1 minute, then remove the pan from the heat and set aside.

10 To form a nest to stabilize your mixing bowl as you whisk, roll a damp kitchen towel into a long tube shape, then set on the counter and curl into a circle to form a nest. Set a large bowl into the nest snugly, then whisk 3 tablespoons (45g) of the milk with the flour in the large bowl.

11 Heat the remaining ½ cup (125g) of the milk over medium-low heat until scalded (bubbles will begin to form around the edges). Pour the scalded milk in a slow, steady stream into the large bowl with the milk-flour mixture, whisking continuously. The milk–flour mixture will be very thick at first, so it's okay to do this in a few stages. Discard the cinnamon stick, then pour the syrup into the scalded milk mixture in a steady stream, whisking continuously. Pour the mixture back into the medium saucepan and cook over low heat, whisking constantly, until thickened, about 2 minutes.

12 Add the egg yolks and salt to the mixture and whisk well to combine. Strain the mixture through a fine-mesh strainer set over a large measuring cup or other container with a pouring spout.

13 Heat the oven to 350°F (175°), with a rack in the center. If using tart molds, evenly space them on a rimmed baking sheet. Pour the egg custard into the pastry-lined muffin pan or tart molds until each tart well is three-quarters full. (The filling will puff during baking, then settle as it cools.)

14 Bake until the crust is puffed and golden and the filling is set, 30 to 45 minutes. The filling should jiggle, not slosh around, when you tap the pan. Let cool in the pans on a rack for 5 to 10 minutes, then carefully tap the molds or muffin pan to remove the tarts and let them cool completely on the rack. Serve the same day, warm or at room temperature. Refrigerate any leftovers in an airtight container.

Chocolate Caramel Tart

FROM CLAUDIA FLEMING

This is perhaps the most imitated dessert in this book and, like Claudia Fleming's ginger cake on page 138, it was one of the most forcefully recommended recipes on my genius dessert hunt.

For one thing, just look at it. Hidden below that salt-strewn sheet of dark chocolate ganache is a pool of soft caramel. "Like a highly sophisticated Rolo candy, the caramel in these tarts oozes when you cut into them," Fleming writes in 2001's *The Last Course*, a cult cookbook among bakers.

But beyond these clear visceral joys, the tart's popularity also heralded a new trend—the more aggressive salting of desserts that spread everywhere in the early 2000s. Now, it's entirely commonplace to see flaky salt sprinkled on a cookie or announced as a primary flavor in ice cream, but when Food52 cofounder Amanda Hesser wrote about the salt on this tart in the *New York Times* in 2000, it was news, rippling outward. A year later, in *The Last Course*, Fleming still had to coach us, "If you're unsure about whether or not to add the salt, why not make it a fun experiment to try with your guests?"

At Gramercy Tavern restaurant in New York City (and at her own wedding), Fleming served these in miniature tartlet form. If you make the recipe in one big tart pan, Fleming cautioned that the caramel would escape as soon as you cut the first slice. Good to be prepared, but also good to remember that's exactly the point.

MAKES ONE 10-INCH (25CM) TART (12 TO 16 SERVINGS) OR TWO DOZEN 2-INCH (5CM) TARTLETS

CRUST
½ cup (110g) unsalted butter, softened

½ cup plus 1 tablespoon (70g) confectioners' sugar

1 large egg yolk

¾ teaspoon pure vanilla extract

1¼ cups (155g) all-purpose flour (see page 5)

¼ cup (20g) Dutch-processed cocoa powder (see page 5)

CARAMEL
2 cups (400g) sugar

½ cup (120g) water

¼ cup (80g) light corn syrup

½ cup (110g) unsalted butter, cut into tablespoons

½ cup (120g) heavy cream

2 tablespoons crème fraîche

GANACHE
½ cup (120g) heavy cream

3½ ounces (100g) best-quality bittersweet chocolate, finely chopped

Pinch of flaky sea salt (such as fleur de sel or Maldon), for serving

1 To make the crust, in the bowl of a stand mixer fitted with the paddle attachment, cream the butter and confectioners' sugar on medium-low speed until well combined and smooth, about 1 minute. Add the egg yolk and vanilla and beat until smooth. Turn off the mixer, sift in the flour and cocoa powder, and beat on low speed until just combined. Press the dough evenly into the bottom and sides of a 10-inch (25cm) tart pan (or into mini muffin pans or twenty-four 2-inch/5cm tart pans) so that it's about ¼ inch (6mm) thick. Prick the bottom all over with a fork. Cover in plastic wrap and refrigerate until firm, at least 1 hour or up to 3 days.

2 Meanwhile, heat the oven to 325°F (165°C), with a rack in the center. Line the chilled dough with aluminum foil and fill with pie weights or sugar (see page 42 for more details about roasted sugar). (If making the tartlets, lining them and filling them with sugar is unnecessary—simply bake until the pastry looks dry and set, about 15 minutes.) Set the pan on a rimmed baking sheet. Bake until the sides of the tart are firm and set, about 15 minutes. Carefully lift

CONTINUED

Chocolate Caramel Tart

out the foil (and pie weights or sugar) and bake until the pastry looks dry and set, 5 to 10 minutes more. Let cool completely on a rack. (The tart shell[s] can be made 8 hours ahead and covered loosely with plastic wrap, once cool.)

3 To make the caramel, in a large saucepan with a light-colored interior, combine the sugar, water, and corn syrup and cook over medium-high heat, swirling the pan occasionally, until you have a dark amber caramel, about 10 minutes. Turn off the heat and carefully whisk in the butter, cream, and crème fraîche—it will steam and bubble up, so stand back—until smooth. (Store the caramel in an airtight container and refrigerate for up to 5 days, if you like.) Pour the caramel into the cooled tart shell while still warm (or reheat the caramel in the microwave or over low heat until it is pourable) and let cool at room temperature until the caramel firms up, at least 45 minutes.

4 To make the ganache, pour the cream into a medium saucepan and bring to a simmer over medium heat. Place the chocolate in a heatproof bowl. Pour the hot cream over the chocolate, let stand for 2 minutes, and whisk until the chocolate is completely melted and smooth. Pour the warm ganache over the tart in a thin layer. Let cool at room temperature until the ganache sets, at least 2 hours.

5 If your tart pan has a removable bottom, to unmold, center the tart pan on top of a large can or sturdy glass so that it balances midair as the rim of the tart pan falls to the counter. Leave the bottom of the pan under the tart for support, or be bold and remove it like so: run a large, thin spatula between the crust and the pan, using the spatula to ease the tart onto a serving plate. (For the tartlets, carefully tap them out of their molds onto a serving plate.)

6 Just before serving, sprinkle the top of the tart with flaky sea salt. Serve in messy slices, oozing with caramel. Store any leftovers in an airtight container at room temperature, unless you'd like to eat them cold.

French Lemon Cream Tart

FROM PIERRE HERMÉ

Lemon curd tends to follow a fairly standard procedure: heat together eggs, sugar, lemon juice, and butter, then cool into a spoonable, flexible substance to be used in all sorts of jam-like ways. But when legendary French pastry chef Pierre Hermé decided to take the butter out of the process and then whip it back in without giving it a chance to melt, the butter emulsified and expanded, capturing big gulps of air. He'd created something buoyant in texture, like a smooth aioli or French buttercream rather than a pourable curd. It was entirely new and, to most who taste it, great leaps and bounds better.

This tart is adapted from the one that Hermé's longtime collaborator and friend Dorie Greenspan translated and shared in her book *Baking* in 2006, calling it The Most Extraordinary French Lemon Cream Tart. But the lemon cream can, and should, travel through your desserts. Unlike curd, it's firm enough to stand up well on its own, which means you can still swirl it over a pavlova or fold it into Eton mess (page 76), but you can also layer it into cakes and pies and between cookies, or serve it in tiny bowls, as the most electrifying lemon pudding.

SERVES 8 TO 10

1 cup (200g) sugar

Finely grated zest of 3 lemons (about 2 tablespoons)

4 large eggs

¾ cup (180g) freshly squeezed lemon juice (from 4 or 5 lemons)

1¼ cups plus 1 tablespoon (295g) unsalted butter, at room temperature and cut into tablespoons

1 fully baked 9-inch (23cm) tart shell (such as the Double-Blueberry Tart crust on page 220 or the Almond Tart crust on page 227)

Fresh blueberries, for garnish (optional)

1 Gather a whisk, a thermometer (preferably instant-read), a fine-mesh strainer, and a blender (preferably) or food processor. Fill a large saucepan with 2 inches (5cm) of water and bring it to a boil over high heat, then lower to a simmer.

2 In a large metal bowl, rub the sugar and lemon zest together with your fingers until the sugar is well moistened, a bit clumpy, and very aromatic. Whisk in the eggs, followed by the lemon juice.

3 Set the bowl over the saucepan (be sure the bottom isn't touching the water) and cook the mixture, whisking constantly as soon as the mixture feels tepid to the touch (this will happen quickly). Cook the cream until it reaches 180°F (80°C). The mixture will start out light and foamy, then the bubbles will get bigger, and then, as it's getting close to 180°F (80°C), it will start to thicken and the whisk will leave tracks, which means it's almost ready. Don't stop whisking and don't stop checking the temperature—this can take as long as 10 minutes but may happen more quickly, depending on the heat.

4 As soon as the mixture reaches 180°F (80°C), remove it from the heat and pour it through a fine-mesh strainer set over a blender (or food processor), stirring with a rubber spatula to coax as much of the curd through the strainer as possible. Let the curd cool at room temperature, stirring occasionally, until it is 140°F (60°C).

5 Set the blender to high and, with the machine running, drop in about 5 pieces of butter at a time. Scrape down the sides of the blender as needed. After the butter is all blended in, continue to blend for 3 minutes more to whip in even more air. If your blender gets a bit too hot, run it only a minute at a time, giving the machine a short rest in between.

6 Scrape the cream into a container and smooth a piece of plastic wrap over its surface to form an airtight seal. Refrigerate the cream for at least 4 hours. (You can store it in the refrigerator for 4 days or in the freezer for up to 2 months.)

7 When you are ready to fill the tart, whisk the cream to loosen it. Scrape it into the tart shell, smooth the top, and refrigerate if not serving shortly. Serve the tart cold the day it's made.

Mostly Fruit

Four-Ingredient Strawberry Shortcakes

FROM PJ HAMEL OF KING ARTHUR FLOUR

This is the most pared-down, immediate strawberry shortcake you can bake. PJ Hamel, the developer of this recipe who's been at King Arthur Flour for more than 25 years, initially made the shortcakes with two ingredients (self-rising flour and cream), and then went wild tacking on the strawberries and whipped cream.

How do such light, fluffy shortcakes come from so few ingredients? For one thing, self-rising flour has a proportional amount of baking powder and salt already in it, which makes it rise virtually on its own—the baking powder in the mix gets bubbling with nothing more than the introduction of a liquid and heat. But self-rising flour is also made with softer wheat than all-purpose. This makes it lower in protein and especially nice for quick breads like shortcakes, where you're looking for a lot of lightness and very little gluten development. Thanks to the forgiving nature of heavy cream, these are also very hard to overbake. And psst, if you use a scale for the shortcakes, the ratio of flour to cream by weight is 1:1, making the recipe all but impossible to forget.

MAKES 7 SHORTCAKES, PLUS 1 FOR SACRIFICIAL TASTE-TESTING

2 cups (300g) fresh, ripe strawberries

2 to 4 tablespoons sugar, plus more to taste

1½ cups (175g) self-rising flour (see page 5)

2 cups (470g) heavy cream

1 tablespoon pure vanilla extract, plus more to taste (optional)

1 Rinse, hull, and halve or quarter the strawberries, depending on their size. Toss them in a medium bowl with 2 tablespoons of the sugar or more to taste, depending on the berries' sweetness. Set aside to macerate while you bake the shortcakes.

2 Heat the oven to 450°F (230°C), with a rack in the upper third. Line a large rimmed baking sheet with parchment paper.

3 Whisk together the flour and, optionally, the remaining 2 tablespoons of sugar in a large bowl. Pour in ¾ cup (175g) of the cream and the vanilla. With a rubber spatula, stir just enough to make a stiff dough. Using a cookie scoop or a spoon, scoop the dough onto the baking sheet in 8 balls, about 2 tablespoons each in size. Brush the tops with cream and sprinkle with sugar.

4 Bake until the shortcakes are a very light golden brown, about 10 minutes. Remove from the oven and break one open—your sacrificial snack!—it should be baked all the way through. If it isn't, return to the oven to bake for a few minutes more. Transfer the shortcakes to a rack to cool briefly while you make the whipped cream.

5 Whip the remaining 1 cup (235g) or so of cream to soft peaks, sweetening it a little with sugar and adding a splash more vanilla if you like. Split the shortcakes in half crosswise and spoon macerated strawberries and whipped cream on each cake bottom. Cap with the cake top.

GENIUS TIP: WHY WE BRUSH BISCUITS WITH CREAM (OR OTHER THINGS)

Brushing the tops of shortcakes and biscuits with cream isn't just an optional flourish for more flavor and color. It actually helps them rise in the oven by keeping the surface moist and steamy, allowing it to expand—a quicker-to-dry top would impede the rise. PJ Hamel also discovered that this means you can brush the tops with any liquid you like—cream, milk, melted butter, or even water—to get the same pouf in the oven.

Meme's Blackberry Batter Cobbler

FROM VIRGINIA WILLIS

This juicy, cakey cobbler from *Bon Appétit, Y'all* author Virginia Willis's grandma, who she calls Meme, is as speedy as any batter cobbler should be, and you can make it in any kitchen that has an oven, a skillet, and a couple of bowls. It also features the satisfying shortcut of melting the butter directly in the skillet as the oven heats up, while you stir together the rest of the batter (go Meme!).

But the real genius is in what you *don't* do. After crushing the blackberries a bit to free their juices, you pour them directly into the middle of the batter and then leave them be. The oven will do the rest, so that after baking, you end up with a jammy berry puddle radiating outward, first to a ring of puffed cake, then crisp, buttery edges. Although Meme made it with blackberries, you can set this method loose on whatever ripe fruit you want.

SERVES 8

½ cup (110g) unsalted butter

4 cups (600g) fresh blackberries

1 cup (125g) all-purpose flour (see page 5)

2 teaspoons baking powder

Pinch of fine sea salt

1 cup (200g) sugar, plus more as needed

1 cup (245g) whole milk

1 teaspoon pure vanilla extract

Whipped cream, crème fraîche, or ice cream, for serving

1 Heat the oven to 350°F (175°C), with a rack in the center. Put the butter in a 10-inch (25cm) cast-iron skillet or other ovenproof baking dish (this will be your serving dish), then stick the skillet in the oven until the butter melts, 5 to 7 minutes.

2 Meanwhile, put the blackberries in a large bowl. Using a potato masher, mash the blackberries gently to release their juices. If the blackberries are tart, sprinkle with a little sugar to taste.

3 Whisk together the flour, baking powder, and salt in a separate large bowl. Add the 1 cup sugar, the milk, and the vanilla and stir with a rubber spatula until well combined. Remove the skillet from the oven and pour the melted butter into the batter, then stir just to combine. Pour the batter into the hot skillet, then pour the blackberries and their juices just into the center of the batter—resist the impulse to stir!

4 Transfer the skillet back to the oven and bake the cobbler until the top is golden brown and a toothpick stuck in the batter comes out clean or with just crumbs clinging, about 1 hour. Serve warm or at room temperature with whipped cream, crème fraîche, or ice cream. Store any leftovers airtight at room temperature, or to extend their life, in the refrigerator.

Peach Cobbler with Hot Sugar Crust

FROM RENEE ERICKSON & SUSAN KAPLAN

When beloved Seattle chef Renee Erickson took over Boat Street Café from Susan Kaplan in 2003, she inherited this quirky peach cobbler recipe along with it. The café closed in 2015, but its spirit lives on through a half dozen other sunny Erickson restaurants, and in recipes like this one. The peaches aren't peeled or even thickened with flour or starch, because the fruit is the point—juicy and textured however it may be. It's brightened with lemon juice and zest and nothing else, a counterweight to the sweet batter and sugary top.

Only after smoothing on a layer of batter and dusting the top with sugar do you encounter the uncomfortable step of sloshing hot water over the top of your lovely cobbler. You won't want to do it, but if you poke around on enough blogs or in community cookbooks, you'll find similar recipes—though the water is usually poured over a mix of cornstarch and sugar. The topping here is pared down to just sugar, which melts and then fuses together in the oven as the water steams away. A dainty crust forms, blanketing the cake and saucy peaches like a sheet of Bubble Wrap, begging to be popped.

SERVES 8

10 large, ripe peaches (about 4½ pounds/2kg), pitted but not peeled, cut into 1-inch (2.5cm) chunks

1 large lemon

½ cup (110g) unsalted butter, softened

2 cups (400g) sugar

1½ cups (190g) all-purpose flour (see page 5)

2 teaspoons baking powder

1 teaspoon kosher salt

¾ cup (185g) whole milk

½ cup (120g) hot water

Heavy cream, for serving

1 Heat the oven to 350°F (175°C), with a rack in the center. Line a large rimmed baking sheet with aluminum foil.

2 Arrange the peaches in a single layer in a 9 by 13-inch (23 by 33cm) or similar-size baking pan or gratin dish. Using a zester or Microplane, zest about 2 teaspoons of lemon zest evenly over the fruit. Cut the lemon in half and squeeze about ¼ cup (60g) of lemon juice over the top.

3 In a stand mixer fitted with the paddle attachment, cream the butter and 1½ cups (300g) of the sugar on medium speed until creamy but sandy, about 1 minute. Add the flour, baking powder, and salt and beat on medium speed until all the flour is incorporated and the mixture is evenly crumbly, about 30 seconds more. Scrape down the sides of the bowl. With the mixer on low speed, slowly pour in the milk. Increase the speed to medium and beat until the batter is light and fluffy, about 2 minutes.

4 Scoop the batter in about 6 large blobs over the peaches. With an offset spatula or the back of a big spoon, carefully spread the batter evenly over the fruit so it's no more than about ½ inch (1.3cm) thick in any one place.

5 Sprinkle the remaining ½ cup (100g) sugar over the batter. Drizzle the hot water evenly over the sugar, using it to melt the sugar topping.

6 Set the pan on the foil-lined baking sheet and bake the cobbler until the top is golden brown and cracked, 70 to 80 minutes. A toothpick stuck in the topping should come out clean or with just crumbs clinging—be sure to check in a few places.

7 Let the cobbler cool for about 30 minutes to firm up. Serve warm, scooping it into big bowls and pouring a little heavy cream over the top. Refrigerate any leftovers airtight.

GENIUS TIP: EMBRACE POURING CREAM AND PUDDLING CREAM

In addition to pouring cold cream over many of her desserts, Renee Erickson serves some—like her bread pudding—in a warmed, boozy puddle of sweetened condensed milk. It's a soothing cushion for anything you don't care to keep crisp underneath, and little could make you feel more swaddled.

Apricot-Raspberry Crisp with Almonds

FROM JIM DODGE VIA RUSS PARSONS

The secret to making a crisp that lives up to its name—the crumbly bits actually staying crisp and golden on top instead of slipping beneath the tide of bubbling fruit—is a simple matter of girth.

As Russ Parsons, former food editor at the *Los Angeles Times*, learned from cookbook author and pastry chef Jim Dodge, the clumps of dough need to be substantial enough to perch on top of the fruit and bake in the dry heat of the oven, without getting pulled down into the juice. Here, following Dodge's technique, Parsons balls up a crumbly dough and plucks off pieces about the size of a hazelnut, though bigger is just fine, too. This method can be used on any fruit, with all sorts of mix-ins.

"When I'm feeling too fearful to make a piecrust, which is fairly often, I turn to crisps." —Russ Parsons

SERVES 8 TO 10

2½ pounds (1.1kg) pitted apricots, cut into 1-inch (2.5cm) wedges (about 8 cups)

1 cup (125g) fresh raspberries

⅓ cup (115g) honey

2 tablespoons freshly squeezed orange juice

⅓ cup (65g) sugar, or to taste

2 tablespoons cornstarch

1½ cups (190g) all-purpose flour (see page 5)

1½ cups (300g) lightly packed light brown sugar

Pinch of salt

¾ cup (170g) butter, very cold and cut into ½-inch (1.3cm) cubes

1 cup (90g) toasted sliced almonds

Vanilla ice cream, for serving (optional)

1 Heat the oven to 375°F (190°C), with a rack in the center. Butter a 9 by 13-inch (23 by 33cm) baking pan or similar-size gratin dish.

2 Combine the apricots, raspberries, honey, and orange juice in a large bowl and stir gently. Taste an apricot for sweetness and stir in a bit of sugar to taste. Add the cornstarch and stir gently to mix well.

3 In a food processor, pulse the flour, light brown sugar, and salt to combine and break up any clumps of brown sugar. Scatter the butter over the dry ingredients and pulse again, just enough times for a crumb mixture to form—it should hold together when pinched with your fingers. Scrape the crumbs into a bowl and stir in the sliced almonds.

4 Scrape the apricot mixture into the baking pan and spread in an even layer. Gather up handfuls of the crumb mixture and press them into rough balls—they won't hold together well, but that's okay. Break off chunks about the size of a hazelnut and scatter the chunks evenly over the fruit (a mix of sizes is okay, as long as they're mostly hazelnut-size).

5 Bake the crisp until the topping is golden brown and the filling is bubbling at the edges, 40 to 45 minutes, rotating the pan halfway for even browning. Let the crisp cool slightly on a rack before serving warm, alone or with vanilla ice cream. Refrigerate any leftovers airtight.

Poached Nectarines in Rosé

FROM DIANA HENRY

While the first poached fruit that pops to mind is most likely a classic wine-soaked pear, heavy with fall spices, poaching fruit is a special boon in summer. It makes a speedy dessert that doesn't ask you to turn on the oven and lets good, ripe fruit do the talking.

This one is from cookbook author Diana Henry, who has an especially delicate touch with fruit and aromatics. For her cookbook *Simple*, she developed this five-ingredient study in pinks, with juicy, ombré-skinned nectarines and fresh raspberries relaxing in an electric rosé syrup.

Though most poached fruit recipes call for diluting the flavorful wine syrup with cups of water to fully submerge the fruit, Henry proves this isn't necessary if you turn the fruit a few times, and it only adds needless time in bubbling down the syrup afterward. The fruit softens quickly enough that it doesn't have a chance to get terribly drunk on wine and still tastes very much like itself.

SERVES 6

6 ripe white nectarines or white peaches, halved and pitted but not peeled

2½ cups (570g) rosé wine

1 cup (200g) sugar, or to taste

2 (1½-inch/4cm) strips lemon zest, cut with a vegetable peeler

Juice of ½ small lemon (about 1 tablespoon)

2 cups (250g) fresh raspberries

1 Find a saucepan or stockpot that's wide enough to hold all the halved nectarines in a single layer. The fit can be quite snug; just don't let them pile on top of each other (use two smaller pots if needed). Take out the nectarines if you've been using them for sizing, put the saucepan over medium-high heat, and pour in the wine, sugar, lemon zest, and juice. Bring to a boil, stirring until the sugar dissolves. Have a glass of the remaining rosé while you stir.

2 When the sugar is completely dissolved, turn the heat to medium-low and ease in the nectarines with a slotted spoon or tongs. Very gently simmer the nectarines, uncovered, carefully turning them over every couple of minutes, until tender throughout, 8 to 12 minutes. Check for tenderness by piercing the nectarines with the tip of a paring knife (don't worry, it won't show much). You want the knife to slide in easily but with a slight resistance, as the nectarines will continue to soften a bit after they're removed from the liquid. Carefully lift out each nectarine half as it's ready and place it on a rimmed baking sheet to cool slightly.

3 When all the nectarines have been removed from the rosé, turn the heat to medium and simmer until reduced and slightly syrupy, about 10 minutes (it should measure 1 to 1½ cups/240 to 355ml, but it's more important to go with what tastes best to you). The flavors will intensify the longer you simmer the syrup; be sure to taste a sip occasionally and don't reduce it to the point that it tastes like cough syrup. Remove from the heat and let the syrup cool to room temperature; if you're in a hurry, transfer it to a bowl nested in an ice water bath and stir occasionally. The syrup will thicken more as it cools.

4 Place the poached nectarines in a serving dish and pour over the rosé syrup. Cover and refrigerate for at least 15 minutes or up to 24 hours.

5 To serve, spoon the nectarines and raspberries into small dishes and spoon a bit of syrup over the top. Store any leftovers airtight in the refrigerator.

Baked Caramel Pears

FROM LINDSEY SHERE

With a handful of ingredients and about 30 minutes, you can have a pure, joyful dessert that looks festive as all get-out, but that you can casually throw together as others clear the table or between rounds of after-dinner charades.

The recipe comes from Lindsey Shere—pastry chef at Chez Panisse for 27 years and the author of *Chez Panisse Desserts*. Its genius is in harnessing a small amount of butter and sugar to do their good work twice. First, by basting the pears in the oven, coaxing them along as they sweeten and singe. In their second act, the butter and sugar pour off into the bottom of the pan, where they form a sticky toffee fond that you then use as the base of a fruity caramel on the stovetop.

This recipe is much more like cooking than baking. Even though it calls for making caramel, the act is entirely imprecise—and forgiving. I've halved the cream for a thinner, sweeter caramel. I've also taken the caramel as far as I could, until the sugars crystallized and the butter broke and seeped out. If this happens to you, just keep cooking, and drip a little water into the pan while boiling and scraping and stirring, and it comes right back together.

Shere recommends Comice pears because they're tender but don't turn to mush, and they're sweet but with an important acidity to balance the rich caramel. The trouble is, Comice aren't always easy to find, unless you (a) live in Berkeley or (b) have recently received a Harry & David gift pack. I recommend Bartlett and D'Anjou instead (less so Forelle and definitely not Bosc).

SERVES 6

3 large, ripe Comice, Bartlett, D'Anjou, or Warren pears

3 tablespoons unsalted butter

3 tablespoons sugar

½ cup (120g) heavy cream

Pinch of fine sea salt, plus more flaky sea salt, for topping (optional)

1 to 2 tablespoons chopped pecans or almonds, lightly toasted (optional)

1 Heat the oven to 375°F (190°C), with a rack in the center. Halve, core, and peel the pears (or leave them unpeeled if you prefer—note that a melon baller is a perfect coring tool). Choose a flameproof pan like an enameled iron gratin dish or large ovenproof skillet that will fit the pears in a single layer and arrange the pears in it, rounded side down.

2 Cut the butter into bits and scatter them over the pear halves. Sprinkle evenly with the sugar and slide the dish into the oven. Roast until the pears are just tender when pierced in their thickest part with a sharp knife, 20 to 30 minutes, basting occasionally with the juices.

3 Gently remove the pears from the dish with tongs or two large spoons, tipping to allow all the juice and any undissolved sugar to drain back in.

4 Set the dish over high heat and cook, stirring constantly, until the mixture turns a golden caramel color. It will look very thick and bubbly, because of the butter and pear juice. Carefully pour in the cream (it will steam and bubble up, so stand back) and bring to a boil, scraping and stirring frequently, adding a pinch of fine sea salt if you like. Cook until the sauce is smooth and a rich, dark brown, which will only take a minute or two.

5 Place a warm pear half on each plate and spoon some of the caramel over it. Sprinkle with the nuts and serve with flaky salt on the side, if you like. Store any leftovers in an airtight container in the refrigerator.

Fried Stuffed Dates (*Khajoor Ka Meetha*)

FROM MADHUR JAFFREY

You've probably seen the natural sweetness of dates put to work in baked goods or the classic Palm Springs date shake, or served along with a cup of tea as a simple afternoon pick-me-up. Their status as dessert is well established, written by their very nature.

But dates really come alive when you subject them to a bit of fat in a hot pan. Their skin tightens and blisters, while the middle goes soft and toffee-like. Legendary author and actress Madhur Jaffrey included a basic version of this recipe in her debut cookbook, *An Invitation to Indian Cookery*, in 1973. Though this is still about the simplest dessert you can make, Jaffrey now fancies up the dates a bit, melting them around a core of finely chopped pistachios and walnuts. Soft whipped cream calms and cools them, not unlike the relationship between vanilla ice cream and hot caramel.

MAKES 16 STUFFED DATES

16 medium dates, pitted or unpitted

About 3 tablespoons finely chopped raw pistachios and/or walnuts

3 tablespoons ghee (or start with 5 tablespoons butter and spoon out the white foam to make clarified butter)

1 cup (235g) heavy cream, whipped to very soft peaks

1 If the dates haven't been pitted already, make a slit down one long side of each one with a paring knife, open them up slightly, and pull out the pits. Stuff each hollow with about ½ teaspoon of the nuts and press them closed. If the pits have already been pulled out from the top, push the nuts in from the top and bottom of the date. Cover the stuffed dates with plastic wrap and set aside at room temperature until ready to serve. This can be done well in advance, but the frying should be done at the last minute.

2 Heat the ghee in a medium nonstick frying pan over medium heat. When hot, add the dates and stir them around for 20 seconds or so. You want the skin to blister a bit, and the middle of each one to warm through. Using a slotted spoon, quickly transfer the dates to a dish and serve immediately. Serve the whipped cream in a bowl on the side to spoon on top of the dates.

GENIUS TIP: SALVAGING OVERWHIPPED CREAM

Whipped cream can go from soft-peaked and luscious to grainy in just a few strokes of the whisk. But it's remarkably easy to loosen and restore the cream's smoothness, just by dribbling in a bit more cold heavy cream and gently folding it in. However, if you've gone so far as to start to make butter, there's no turning back, and you should probably just finish the job.

Slow-Roasted Strawberries

FROM MICHELLE POLZINE

If you've ever tried to casually roast or sauté strawberries, you might have seen how they can turn to mush before their sweetness really comes into focus. This is because they're 92 percent water (the same as a watermelon), with little structure to hold them all together. It's no wonder they're prone to collapse.

The answer is so simple: you just need to give them time. Strawberries' delicacy makes them especially good candidates for very, very slow roasting, as pastry chef Michelle Polzine does at 20th Century Cafe in San Francisco. All that excess water gets the chance to escape slowly without steaming its neighbors disruptively, and the berries' sweetness concentrates to a wild, exponential degree. You only shake them occasionally but don't stir, so their little bodies shrink but stay intact, floating in deep red syrup. Polzine roasts whole flats of strawberries at once, then uses them everywhere—on top of custards and ice creams, in strudel with rhubarb, in a crostata on their own. They're particularly handy mixed into ice cream (page 179) or frozen yogurt (page 176)—because of their high sugar and low water content, they stay soft, not icy. As Polzine explains, "The natural invert sugar (sugar + fruit acid + heat = invert sugar) helps make the ice cream texture very smooth!" They also preserve well, can be frozen, and keep for months in the refrigerator. Cooked strawberries: former sad sacks. Now, what can't they do?

MAKES ABOUT 1½ CUPS (450G)

6 cups (900g) fresh, ripe strawberries

½ cup to ½ cup plus 2 tablespoons (100g to 125g) sugar, depending on the strawberries' sweetness

1 Heat the oven to 250°F (120°C). Rinse and hull the berries. Leave any tiny ones whole and quarter or halve the rest so they all cook at about the same rate.

2 In a nonreactive baking pan that will hold the strawberries closely packed in a single layer, gently toss the strawberries with the sugar, then spread in an even layer.

3 Roast slowly in the oven, uncovered, for 3 to 6 hours, shaking occasionally but not stirring. If they start to look dry on top, gently flip them over with a wide spatula.

4 They are done when their juices have reduced to a syrup, but not darkened into caramel, and the berries are very jammy but not dry. Store in an airtight container in the refrigerator.

Yogurt Whipped Cream
From Saveur

Not only does whisking in yogurt make for a lighter whipped cream, but the flavor is also better and tangier—a lively and effective foil to sugar. Add up to twice as much yogurt as heavy cream and it will still resemble whipped cream, but taste increasingly like yogurt. You can fold in the yogurt after whipping, but I actually prefer to dump it all in together and start whisking—that way I can stop when it's exactly the texture I like without having to recalibrate at the end. Better still, with the milk fat slashed by swapping in the lighter yogurt, it's also nearly impossible to overwhip the cream into butter. It probably won't go past soft, loose peaks. This ratio is only a guideline—play with it as you like.

How to make it: In a stand mixer fitted with the whisk attachment, beat **1 cup (235g) cold heavy cream** and **½ cup (115g) plain yogurt, Greek or otherwise**, full-fat or otherwise, on medium-high speed until soft peaks form. Alternatively, you can use a handheld mixer or whisk by hand. Add more yogurt or cream to taste and whisk again to soft peaks. Makes about 3 cups (710ml) of whipped cream.

FRUIT DRESSED UP

Pumpkin Butter

FROM PAUL VIRANT

While most pumpkin butter recipes come together on the stovetop or in a slow cooker, for the best, most concentrated flavor, chef Paul Virant roasts his—twice. The first go is to simply cook the halved squash through to make it tender and scoopable. Kindly, he doesn't make you hunt down any particular kind of pumpkin—you can use any hard squashes you find, even the wonky-shaped ones you don't know how to peel.

The second spin in the oven is to caramelize the scooped-out pulp along with brown sugar and spices. Lots of the pumpkin's surface is exposed to hot air and steam is allowed to escape, so the mix intensifies and thickens quickly. And while other pumpkin butters are butter in name only, this one roasts with bits of real butter stirred in to help with the sizzly, sweet transformation.

Virant likes to work the pumpkin butter into ice cream custard bases and pumpkin bars. I also recommend slipping it into the middle layers of a trifle, with hunks of Claudia Fleming's dark, gingery stout cake (page 138), whipped cream, maple syrup, and toasted hazelnuts, like you see here.

MAKES ABOUT 6 CUPS (1.4L) PUMPKIN BUTTER

5 pounds (2.3kg) pumpkin or winter squash (about 2 or 3), halved but not peeled or seeded

Neutral oil (such as grapeseed), for brushing

1 ¾ cups (340g) lightly packed light brown sugar

½ cup (110g) unsalted butter, cut into cubes

1 teaspoon kosher salt

1 teaspoon ground cinnamon

½ teaspoon freshly grated nutmeg

½ teaspoon ground ginger

¼ teaspoon ground cloves

1 Heat the oven to 400°F (200°C), with a rack in the center. Brush the cut sides of the pumpkin with oil. Place the halves, cut side down, on a rimmed baking sheet and roast until the pumpkin is tender when pierced with a paring knife, about 45 minutes. (This varies quite a bit depending on the type of squash—a delicata may cook in 35 minutes while a butternut or kabocha can take 1 hour, so if you're mixing types, remove them as they're done.) Let cool on the baking sheet.

2 When the pumpkin is cool enough to handle, using a large spoon, scoop the seeds out, then scrape the flesh into a bowl and compost the skins. (You can also clean off the seeds and toast them with olive oil and salt for a snack.)

3 Turn the oven down to 350°F (175°C). In a large bowl, stir together 6 cups (1.4kg) of the roasted pumpkin pulp (saving any extra to eat another time), the sugar, butter, salt, cinnamon, nutmeg, ginger, and cloves. Scrape the mixture into a 9 by 13-inch (23 by 33cm) baking pan. Roast, stirring every 15 minutes with a rubber spatula, until the pumpkin is thick, darker in color, and slightly caramelized, about 1½ hours.

4 Stir it well at the end—it should be smooth and spreadable. If you like a perfectly smooth pumpkin butter, blend it in a food processor. If it's thicker than you want, thin it with a little water.

5 Once the pumpkin butter is cool, store in an airtight container in the refrigerator or freezer. Note that because the butter is low in acidity, it's not safe for water-bath canning.

A HANDY FORMULA TO MEMORIZE:
FRUIT + CREAM + SUGAR + HEAT

In my hunt for desserts for this book, the same idea came up so many times that I like to imagine it springing up, organically and unprovoked, in kitchens all over: simply put fruit, along with cream and sugar, in one big vessel or smaller custard cups, and apply heat.

Sometimes the cream is whipped, sometimes it's simply sour cream or crème fraîche, either layered on top or folded through. It's spiked with liqueur or citrus zest or spices, or not. It's broiled or baked or torched, and can be served warm, or chilled briefly for the brûléed top to regain its crunch. Every time, it amounts to juicy, ripe fruit swimming in cream and should be repeated often.

	Joy of Cooking's FRUIT BRÛLÉ	River Café's FIGS BAKED WITH CRÈME FRAÎCHE	Andy Husbands's HOT BLACKBERRIES & CREAM	Roy Finamore's BAKED NECTARINES WITH CREAM	Jeremy Lee's RASPBERRY BRÛLÉE
FRUIT	seedless green grapes	figs	blackberries	nectarines	raspberries
+	+	+	+	+	+
CREAM	sour cream	crème fraîche	sour cream	whipped cream	whipped cream
+	+	+	+	+	+
SUGAR	brown sugar	honey	brown sugar	sugar	Demerara
+	+	+	+	+	+
HEAT	broiler, over a pan of ice	425°F (220°C) oven	broiler	350°F (175°C) oven	torch
+	+	+	+	+	+
OPTIONAL DOODADS	vanilla	grappa	lime zest + cinnamon	brandy or amaretto	extra spoons

THANK-YOUS

To Amanda Hesser & Merrill Stubbs, my dear bosses, mentors, and friends, for guiding the good ship Food52 (and me) since 2009, and never turning down a test cookie.

To the Ten Speed team: Aaron Wehner, Hannah Rahill, Julie Bennett, Kelly Snowden, Emma Campion, Margaux Keres, Lisa Ferkel, and Serena Sigona, for being a pleasure to work with for many years now, and letting me keep the story about Maida Heatter's elephant omelet.

To my sweet Mike Dunkley, who I married with cobbler and ice cream floats, and who helped me eat the leftovers and talk out every last little thing. To my brother Billy Miglore, my sharpest, most honest proofreader and partner in used cookbook scavenging.

To my mom Susan Miglore, for teaching me how to measure at the meniscus and my dad Allen Miglore, who loves all cookies indiscriminately. To my grandmother Grace Cowan, who kept oatmeal cream pies in the fridge, and to the rest of the Cowan clan. To my grandparents Mike and Thann Miglore, who told me that I could be the dessert princess, because Grandma was already the dessert queen, and to the rest of the Miglore family. To my family-in-law Art, Tuny, Dan, Erin, and Riley Dunkley, aka the pie-cobbler-crisp fan club.

To our longtime photographer and dulce de leche consultant James Ransom, for making this book the moodiest and richest compendium of splatters and crumbs this world will ever see. To our art director Alexis Anthony, for building all of the achingly beautiful scenes for me to smear whipped cream on. To James's photo crew, Sarah Wight and Mark Weinberg, and our own Amanda Widis and Eddie Barrera, for stepping up when it mattered most in the studio.

To Erin Jeanne McDowell, a real live Sugar Plum Fairy, for leading the baking styling team of Allison Bruns Buford, Sarah Jampel, and Yossy Arefi, for swooping frostings and building bonus Eton Messes (turn the page!) just for fun, and sharing all her tips when cakes and cookies misbehaved. To our test kitchen director Josh Cohen for patiently shepherding every recipe retest (and re-retest) and a good half-ton of sugar through the kitchen, leading a team of crack cooks including Shani Frymer, Chris Roberts, Molly Corrigan, Caroline Lange, Erica Graff, Scott Cavagnaro, Taylor Murray, and Amelia Rampe.

To Makinze Gore, for assisting me in the kitchen every Saturday (and magically remembering what kind of molasses we used last time) for the better part of a year, always with a calm smile, even when we were putting away dishes until the wee hours. To Ali Slagle, for organizing me and holding my hand backstage, and Sarah Jampel, for years of baking advice and cheerleading—and to both, for holding the record for most genius tips. To Kenzi Wilbur, Marian Bull, Brette Warshaw, and Joanna Sciarrino, for editing the column all these years, no matter what time it came in. To Lyna Vuong, our Julia Child Foundation Fellow, for literally building this book by transcribing recipes and organizing our recipes for shoots better than I knew how. To CB Owens, for applying his laser eyes at the last hour, as he's done for every Food52 book since *Genius Recipes*. To Tim McSweeney, for helping bring the chart on my favorite pages (262 and 263) to life. And to all of my recipe testing heroes: Stephanie Bourgeois and other brave members of the Food52 team, Lauren Shockey, María del Mar Cuadra, Anna Gass, Dawne Shonfield, and the Food52 Baking Club on Facebook, whose velocity in volunteering brought me to tears.

To Nick Malgieri, Charlotte Druckman, Anita Shepherd, Lori Galvin, Raquel Pelzel, Marian Burros, Rose Levy Beranbaum, Emily Luchetti, Anita Jaisinghani, Sherry Yard, Mindy Fox, and Matt Sartwell, who were especially giving with their time and wisdom.

And most of all, to the geniuses in these pages and the hundreds of Food52 community members, home bakers, cookbook authors, editors, writers, and pastry chefs who generously gave their time and advice to strengthen this book—I wish there were enough pages to thank each of you personally.

GENIUS TIPSTERS

Below are the people—some given names and some chosen Food52 avatars—whose tips I could pinpoint most directly in this book, but countless others enriched this collection with their emails, comments, calls, debates, Instagrams, tasting notes, jokes, and more. I promised to return the favor, so I hope you find new gems in this book.

Charlotte Druckman
Bobbi Lin
calendargirl
Anita Shepherd
Ali Slagle
Fairmount_market
Merrill Stubbs
WhiskyMead
Joanne Chang
Mindy Fox
Tina Ujlaki
Joan Heymont
Shuna Lydon
Brette & Sheri Warshaw
Gena Hamshaw
Luisa Weiss
Nick Malgieri & Nancy Nicholas
BakerRB
Jenny Rosenstrach
Alexandra Stafford
J. Kenji López-Alt
Max Falkowitz
Victor Hazan
asbrink
Diane Morgan
Rivka
Gabriella Gershenson
Lauren Shockey
Molly Yeh
karen

Nozlee Samadzadeh
Sarah Jampel
Amanda Hesser
Emily Connor
samanthaalison
Rachel Khong
Elana Carlson
Trucster
JJ Goode
mrslarkin
Ina-Janine
Peggy Dunagan
Emily Stephenson
hardlikearmour
Molly Stevens
drbabs
Marian Bull
Kate Heddings
Lori Galvin
Peter Miller
Antonia James
Emily Kaiser Thelin
Melissa Clark
Nora Singley
Russ Parsons
Nicole Krasinski
Megan Scott
Kate Leahy
Cheryl Redmond
Jessica Robison

INDEX